A BEAUTIFUL IDEA: HISTORY OF THE FREEDOM PRESS ANARCHISTS

The story of Britain's oldest anarchist publisher, by Rob Ray

Chapters:

This first edition published by Freedom Press, 2018

84b Whitechapel High St, London E1 7QX freedompress.org.uk

ISBN 978-1-904491-30-9

Printed in the UK by Imprint Digital

Introduction

A major problem with writing a history of Freedom Press, 132 years at the time of print, became apparent when researching its early days — in many ways it is the history of a movement. It's turned what I initially imagined to be a relatively short pamphlet into a full-sized book, and even so I am sure I've missed a great deal out both from Freedom's story and certainly from the anarchist movement's.

While it was only briefly the sole voice of anarchism in Britain, Freedom Press is the oldest, one of the earliest and most historically influential anarchist publishing houses in the English language. Its paper from the first days drew in internationally-renowned writers, big thinkers and political heavyweights.

A bewilderingly huge ensemble of people have drifted in and out of its circles over the decades, from quiet stalwarts whose contributions are mentioned in memoirs but difficult to draw with certainty, to the flaming comets whose short political lives left waves of disturbance and occasionally total devastation in their wake.

Sometimes *Freedom* was the core to which people retreated when everything else had been lost, or it could at times be the example people pointed at when explaining how not to do things.

Its totemic aspect for British anarchism has on several occasions seen Freedom Press itself become the source of dreadful upset, from hastening the collapse of the Socialist League in 1890 to accusations that Tom Keell had stolen it away in 1918 and Vernon Richards similarly in 1945. A poisonous feud between Vero and former *Freedom* writer Albert Meltzer managed to characterise nearly four decades of a (broadly) intellectual-liberal/class conflictualist argument within the wider movement.

In more recent times the Freedom Group has lost much of that ability to sit so heavy on the movement's affairs, but this is no bad thing. Its influence stemmed, often, from being one of the few well-known or even the only printed outlet for anarchist ideas and theory to get a showing. That situation was never ideal and has faded markedly since other publishing houses arose such as Cienfuegos Press, the eco-activism of *Earth First!* and *Do or Die!*, AK Press, PM Press and Active Distro — even some sympathetic academic treatments at places such as Zed, Verso and Pluto. Let alone the enormous historical archives now available online such as libcom.org and The Anarchist Library. The ability of one and all to self-publish via the internet, and the advent of print on demand has had a hugely encouraging effect of lessening *Freedom*'s heft.

The challenge for Freedom Press today is a different one, to provide a stable base for the movement in what is currently a low point for involvement in libertarian struggle, a political clearing house that can be heard above the cacophony of often fatuous noise produced by a billion rattling keyboards and hundreds of hours of audio-video content being uploaded every minute, and to preserve our histories for future generations.

This book is part of that effort, and takes a great deal of advantage of the explosion of accessibility our histories have seen, from Nick Heath's many biographical works to consulting the Kate Sharpley Library's research, and rare books now available online through to the work of the Bristol Radical History Group. Many thanks too go to the Anarchist Studies Network, which provided numerous useful pointers, and the Sparrows' Nest which digitised many early papers.

Individually Nick Heath, Stuart Christie, and David Goodway have offered much appreciated feedback on sections of the book, and where I have been too kind or too harsh regarding people they've known I will happily cede to their lived experience. Each has a tremendous pool of written memoirs and researched works which are and will continue to be vital to historians of the movement. Martyn Everett deserves special mention for patiently walking me through the second half of the 20th century.

As this is intended more as a general overview than an academic work, I cannot claim credit for much of the original research on its early period and would recommend consulting titles listed at the end of this book for more information. Two particularly relevant works dealing with the movement's early days are T*he Slow Burning Fuse* by John Quail and *The International Anarchist Movement in Victorian London* by Harmia Oliver, while Albert Meltzer's *The Anarchists in London 1935-55* helps fill in some of the immediate post-war period. Many thanks are also due to Sheila Rowbotham, who kindly allowed us to use her unique interview with Lilian Wolfe.

As we move closer towards the present several sections are reproduced from *Freedom / a Hundred Years*, produced in 1986 as part of Vernon Richards' centenary series of works, including memoirs from the time. Short biographies (see People, page 223) have also been plundered and while there is some repetition of information I have left them largely untouched. Bespoke comments have also kindly been provided for this work by *Freedom* alumni, with Donald Rooum, Dave Peers, Jayne Clementson, Martin

Peacock and Steve Sorba in particular offering many unique insights and recollections.

The deeper philosophical and academic analysis of *Freedom's* many writers is an important aspect of looking into its influence and impact, and I would recommend David Goodway's writing when looking at the post-war period, in particular *Anarchist Seeds Beneath the Snow* and *Talking Anarchy*, his long-form conversation with Colin Ward. Carissa Honeywell's *A British Anarchist Tradition* is also a standout.

Regarding the modern era (loosely defined as the two decades following Vernon Richards' final retirement), as the longest-surviving continuous collective member (15 years an Alley cat) I find myself in a difficult position.

It is easy, when in control of the prose, to lapse into partisan approaches in a book of this kind, as its subject matter often revolves around the heat generated by active politics undertaken by people fighting difficult and often losing battles. I have attempted to offer both sides of these arguments where they occur, and can only apologise for areas where I fall short.

For the final chapters however I have skated over or only briefly mentioned many such disputes, from confrontations between members to the impacts of different core groups upon the direction of Freedom Press. This is not for want of an opinion, but given most of those involved have their own take on matters it would be unfair to inflict my perspectives above theirs in an "official" history. I'll try to leave such judgments for someone else's 150th anniversary edition (fingers crossed), and contain personal sentiments within my blockbuster memoir *No Seriously We Really Did Have Massive Arguments About That, Count Yourself Lucky You Live in the Post-Revolutionary Utopia* (coming soon).

In my general approach I have attempted to hold true to the idea that the many people featured in this book are, ultimately, flawed human beings trying their best to keep the flame of anarchism alive rather than angels, monsters or concreted political positions. Kropotkin's turn toward war in 1914, the wincingly-bad condescension and sometimes outright bigotry on race and gender to be found across many of *Freedom's* yellowing pages are all pretty horrifying to a modern eye, and represent the bad that must, ultimately, be acknowledged along with the good. We cannot pretend that in the early 20th century, for example, *Freedom* did not regularly advertise the *American Journal of Eugenics* on its back page alongside Emma Goldman's *Mother Earth* and the brilliant insights of Errico Malatesta.

I expect however, simply because the core source of my reading is *Freedom*'s own pages and it's a Freedom Press title with all that implies, this will in places lead to bias. *Freedom* and its editors have been heavily criticised throughout its existence from within the movement on numerous grounds, often justifiably, and I'd strongly urge checking out work by the many other tendencies and groups which make up that mess of knotted string we call the anarchist movement. From *Black Flag* to *Class War*, the environmentalist fluffies and the battling anarcho-syndicalists, amongst the essays and pamphlets and books are brilliant critiques well worth reading.

A History of Freedom is published, near enough, on the 50th anniversary of the Press's purchase of 84b Angel Alley in Whitechapel, where we increasingly seem to have the aspect of a nail house — surrounded by London's elite but not, as yet, budging. Which in a funny sort of way encapsulates much of our enduring appeal. Tiny, endlessly fractious, rarely more than a moment away from some sort of crisis. But we're a stubborn bunch.

~ Rob Ray, 2018

1886-1895
Victorian anarchism

Launched in October 1886 as a monthly four-page paper, sold for a penny as a "journal of anarchist socialism" the tone of *Freedom* at the time reflected the makeup of its membership. Around 1,600 copies were sold of that issue in the first three weeks, rising to around 2,300-3,000 per month in the 1890s. Largely middle-class led and with aspirations of a socialist utopia in mind, its opening salvo railed against "the slavish trembling ignorance of mankind, their misty unreasoning terror of all that revealed itself as power". Other passages appealed direct against the callousness of "fashionable mansions" stood silent as a poverty-stricken woman sings in the bitter wind.

Much of its ambition would be recognisable to critics of the Silicon Valley tech-gurus we see around us in the early 21st century, with the paper launching tirades at how the "marvellous increase of knowledge left social feeling behind, and enabled the few who monopolised the newly-acquired power over nature to create an artificial civilisation." It lashed mightily against the then-fashionable policy of economic *laissez-faire*, recognisable today as an ancestor to modern neoliberalism:

1. When the proprietors molest the proletariat, *laissez-faire*
2. When the proletariat resist the proprietors, interfere to help the proprietors

Following the lead of its theoretical big name Peter Kropotkin, a famed Russian geographer, social scientist and political philosopher, the paper went full-tilt against capitalism, prisons, war and want, presenting "advanced" opinions and debates on everything from capital punishment to cooperativism, the use of strikes and the role of mutual aid in evolution.

Perhaps less easily-recognised however would be its corollary of the critiques — hope. The year of 1886 was part of a great flowering of European optimism for the future of a socialist humanity, untainted by the horrors of mechanised warfare and industrial slaughter that World War I would bring.

The paper's opening address spoke confidently of "living on the eve of great events" amid a growing impulse to freedom in France,

England, the Netherlands, Switzerland and Bohemia (now part of Czech Republic but then within the Austro-Hungarian empire). Essays expounded on the possibilities for social revolution and considered the best ways to fashion a utopia on Earth. How it would happen, where would be first to take the plunge, what projects were already in play that might point the way towards the new society. And there were good reasons for such optimism.

A boom in revolutionary acts

The late 19th century had seen a huge march of class struggle worldwide, with its greatest moment (and failure) being the Paris Commune of 1871, where for two months the masses of the city declared and tried to implement a true socialist society before being brutally put down by the French army. Anarchism itself had only been named as a coherent modern political philosophy by Pierre-Joseph Proudhon for the first time in 1840, and saw its first major ideological clashes with statist socialism in the First International of 1864–1876, as Mikhail Bakunin debated with Karl Marx for the future of that movement. As the International split, a conference at St Imier in Switzerland marked the birth of the anarchist movement in earnest.

In Spain and Portugal, what would become the greatest expression of popular anarchism ever achieved with the CNT union was beginning its long climb, as anarchists travelled there to argue the case for libertarian socialism. Germany's Chancellor Bismarck meanwhile had been pushed to ban social democracy in 1878 following failed radical attempts to kill the Kaiser. And Russia was in uproar, rebellious circles beginning to thrive underground in the aftermath of the successful assassination of Tsar Alexander II despite vicious repression.

Propaganda of the deed, championed by radicals such as Bakunin, Johann Most and Sergey Nechaev, was sweeping Europe, Latin America and the US with bombs set off and senior politicians killed in an effort to catalyse the social revolution through spectacular individual acts of revolt.

In 1886 alone one of the great epochal moments of that period took place just five months before *Freedom* was founded — the Chicago Haymarket Affair. At a rally calling for an eight-hour workday a bomb had been set off, leading to a police crackdown and the opportunistic arrest of eight known anarchist agitators. August Spies, Samuel Fielden, Adolph Fischer, Albert Parsons,

Michael Schwab, George Engel, Louis Lingg and Oscar Neebe were put on trial with a hang 'em judge and handpicked jury on trumped-up charges.

The trial was so heavily biased against the defendants it became an international cause celebre, and when the verdicts came down, convicting them for their beliefs rather than for the bombing, it was to a global audience. Engel, Fischer, Parsons, and Spies were hanged, Lingg committed suicide and the rest were jailed. At his execution, Spies famously said: "There will be a time when our silence will be more powerful than the voices you strangle today."

After their deaths newly-installed mayor John A Roche ordered a ban on banners, flags, arms or music at the funerals — but 16,000 people marched behind the coffins nonetheless. Vast crowds lined the route. It was a day like no other in US history, a detonation of working class pride and solidarity that would echo around the world.

And even in Britain, that dour imperial island, interest in the libertarian ideal began to pick up.

Peter Kropotkin, joint founder of *Freedom* and writer some of its most celebrated early essays, had been distinctly unimpressed by his first visit to England in 1881, where he attempted to help hold an international conference but had found ...

> no atmosphere to breathe in ... John Burns, Henry Hyde Champion, Keir Hardie, and the other labour leaders were not yet heard of, the Fabians did not exist; William Morris had not yet declared himself a socialist; and the trade unions, limited in London to a few privileged trades only, were hostile to socialism.
>
> The only active and outspoken representatives of the socialist movement were Henry and Matilda Hyndman, with a very few workers grouped around them.*

Kropotkin was not quite right in ascribing the beginnings of the new radical wave entirely to the post-1881 period. Particularly outside London a radical spring of sorts can be found in the wake of the 1867 Reform Act, through an expansion of workingmen's venues such as the Commonwealth Club and Patriotic Club, socialist preachers and farmworker unions in the 1870s, the First International itself

---

* Hyndeman, a former Tory and business tycoon, founded Britain's Social Democratic Federation.

etc. Indeed future *Freedom* supporters Henry Glasse* and Ambrose Barker could be found agitating at progressive-minded meetings in 1880 and the first known anarchist in Britain, Ambrose Caston Cuddon, had died aged 89 just two years before Kropotkin's arrival.

Frank Kitz, a veteran of the movement who provided a link to the old Chartists, would note in his memoir that in the 1870s, as part of the Manhood Suffrage league:

> From the West we extended our work into the East End. Mile End Waste was our outdoor rallying-point, and indoors — let not the temperance reader be shocked — the club-rooms of various public houses, where under the guise of debating societies or similar harmless-sounding titles we pursued our propagandist work. The Radical clubs had still a leaven amongst them of Chartists and Republicans, and their platforms were at our disposal.

But it is certainly true that the mid-1880s marked the first time in which overtly anarchist ideas made much serious headway in Britain outside of small newly-arrived communities of European emigres. The political philosophy had thus far only made much impact on English consciousness through the death of the Russian Tsar, and eyes were more fixed on the febrile situation in Ireland. It was thus migrants who would bring much of the fire to English socialism.

Exiled en masse from political crackdowns in other countries, many fled to London, the "last free city" in Europe. They created the first anarchist clubs, with Germans, French and Italians in central London and Eastern European Jews in the East End, making up a backbone of perhaps 2,000 radicals throughout the capital speaking a wide variety of languages. German emigres were in fact so prominent in this early period that even English speakers on anarchism were frequently referred to as "damn Germans", according to Kitz. Police were unimpressed by such efforts and regularly harassed public speakers, repeatedly arresting Kitz's comrade Charles Mowbray. When this happened jail was usually preferred to a fine, as it caused more inconvenience to the State.

The Bavarian activist Johann Most had arrived in 1878 and set up a paper, *Freiheit*, which by 1880 was publishing anarchist essays until he was jailed in 1881 for incitement (the first ever English-

---

* Glasse fought as a guerilla in Spain's third Carlist war and backed most major anarchist-leaning papers off and on, even after moving to South Africa in 1881.

language anarchist paper, a translation of *Freiheit*, was sold in front of the Central Criminal Court where Most went on trial).* His case sparked the creation of the first international anarchist club at Stephen's Mews, Rathbone Place in Fitzrovia, London in 1882 as spectacular events in nearby France were beginning to make an impact on public consciousness. Foreign language papers such as *Le Revolte* were being sold around the chaotic markets of Covent Garden, though the most influential anarchist essays came from the US paper *Liberty*. Even the first anarchist school was French, set up in Fitzroy Square by former Paris Communard fighter Louise Michelle for the children of political refugees.

The key moment in the forming of a British movement from this disparate collection of radicals however was probably a gathering of socialists around the Democratic Federation (later the Social Democratic Federation, which eventually became part of the Communist Party of Great Britain), putting together William Morris and Andreas Scheu in 1883, leading to the formation of the anti-parliamentary Socialist League two years later. With Morris's financial and reputational support as a globally renowned textiles designer, the League proved a springboard for libertarian socialist thinking, immediately founding the influential *Commonweal*, a monthly paper which was joined by Henry Seymour's independently-produced *Anarchist* that same year.

It is here that the group which would give rise to *Freedom* appears. Seymour's contacts in newly-formed progressive organisation the Fabian Society, particularly its more radical wing, helped give his paper a readership of perhaps 1,000 and led to the formation of the Circle of English Anarchists in May 1885. While Seymour himself was a mutualist,** both the group and publication are better considered as broadly libertarian-socialist in aspect, including contributors such as George Bernard Shaw — a progressive but by no means anarchist. It did include shoemaker James Harrigan, formerly of the First International and one of the first known English anarchist public speakers, but the most notable regular writer for our purposes was Charlotte Wilson (see People, page 287).

---

* This is not to be confused with the first anarchist pamphlet, that honour goes to Ambrose Cuddon's *A Contribution Towards the Elucidation of the Science of Society*, produced in October 1853 by perhaps the first known overtly anarchist group, the London Confederation of Radical Reformers.

** A society where workers and co-ops operate within a free market where interest, rent, profit, landlordism and capitalism has been eliminated.

Born in 1854, the daughter of a wealthy doctor, Charlotte Mary was one of just 14 of the earliest students at what became Newnham College in Cambridge. The phenomenon of women being admitted was so new that she would be prohibited from graduating (women were not eligible until 1923) but she did the equivalent of English, Logic, Psychology and Political Economy. Leaving the university "deeply dissatisfied with orthodox economics" she was heavily influenced by the philosophy of Herbert Spencer and, after marrying stockbroker Arthur Wilson, became an active member of the Fabian Society in 1884, joining as the only woman on its first executive committee, and was among its most radical members, well-liked and persuasive.

Charlotte Wilson

Her interest in anarchism had been piqued slightly earlier however, as she read reports in 1883 of a French trial of 60 anarchist members of the then-outlawed International Working Men's Association which included, among others, Peter Kropotkin. She wrote of the by then globally-reported case: "When the noble words of Kropotkin's defence ran through the length and breadth of France, they found an echo in the hearts of all honest seekers after the truth."

Wilson's workrate when roused was impressive. Alongside her activities with the Fabians and anarchist circles, she involved herself in the Society of Friends of Russian Freedom from 1885, intervened in Pearson's Men and Women's Club and gave many lectures. Widely-read and corresponding with leading anarchist figures, she held "advanced" Fabian discussion meetings at her Hampstead home inviting luminaries such as Sidney Webb, George Bernard Shaw and Annie Besant to read and discuss the works of Marx and Proudhon. Shaw would later remark that when she joined "a sort of influenza of anarchism soon spread through the Fabian Society".

In the course of her activism, and introduced by Max Nettlau (later a major figure in the movement and *Freedom's* history, see People, page 268)) she also began a correspondence with Kropotkin's wife, Sofia Ananiev, while he languished in prison, and it is likely during this period when the plan was hatched to found a second outright anarchist paper, as Wilson's anarchist-communist outlook was increasingly clashing with Seymour's mutualism.

When Kropotkin was released in France in January 1886, Wilson was responsible for inviting him to come to Britain to join them and historian John Quail notes that, when explaining his decision to move, Kropotkin said he was called to "found" a new anarchist-communist publication, rather than join one. He settled in England two months later,* and would go on to declare himself overjoyed at the decision, writing in *Memoirs of a Revolutionist*:

> In 1886 the socialist movement in London was in full swing. Large bodies of workers had openly joined in all the principal towns, as well as a number of middle class people, chiefly young, who helped it in different ways ... I was asked to lecture over the country, partly on prisons, but mainly on anarchist socialism and I visited in this way nearly every large town of England and Scotland.
>
> Whether it was in the worker's small parlour, or in the reception rooms of the wealthy, the most animated discussions went on about socialism and anarchism till a late hour of the night — with hope in the workingman's home, with apprehension in the mansion, but everywhere with the same earnestness.

People who would go on to become core *Freedom* activists such as George Cores and William Wess were at this time already active in the Hackney Socialist League, alongside Kitz, Welsh agitator Sam Mainwaring and John Turner (see People, page 284), an Essex smallholder's son active in trade union organising.

Wilson was heavily involved in this debate as a leading member of the Fabians, writing an account of anarchism's theories in the fourth Fabian tract, *What Socialism Is*, which was published in June of that year, and in September she led the anarchist faction against Annie Besant at the meeting which formally committed the Fabians to parliamentary socialism by a two-to-one vote, at Anderton's Hotel in London. She would resign from its executive a few months later.

But Wilson's ambitions were far from thwarted by her failure to bring over the Fabians, and *Freedom* began publication in October 1886, using the premises of the Freethought Publishing Company with the permission of Besant and printed at the Socialist League offices with the blessing of William Morris.

---

* He met Seymour at around this time and, according to the *Anarchist* editor, Kropotkin "induced me to stifle myself and my individualist tendencies and be incorporated into a 'cojoint editorship' for future issues.

Early days

Despite strong early links to the League, *Freedom* was projected not as the organ of a particular group but rather as an independent voice in the wider movement. At first it was described as "a Journal of Anarchist Socialism," but in June 1889 it became a "Journal of Anarchist Communism," quickly supplanting the *Anarchist*'s more mutualist effort as the Circle fell apart and Seymour became embroiled in a spy scandal which killed his reputation — and paper — in 1887. *Freedom* was thus, in its earliest incarnation, responsible only to its own members and backers. Those initial figures included Wilson, Francesco Merlino, Nikola Tchaikovsky, John Burns Gibson, Frank and Lena Hyde, Nannie Dryhurst, Edward Carpenter and Emma Brooke.

Its membership was also fast-shifting, with Agnes Henry and William Wess being recruited in short order while Gibson, a police surgeon, vanished as of 1887. Its list of writers was even wider, and included the occasional high-powered voice from outside the movement, such as playwright George Bernard Shaw and Sydney Olivier (later a minister in the first Labour government under Ramsay MacDonald).

While noted as a founding member, and the theorist who gave *Freedom* its initial gravitas, Kropotkin himself was in poor health following his imprisonment and also heavily committed to other publications when he moved to Britain, including *La Revolte*, meaning he did not write as much in the late '80s, though eventually settled into a routine of producing one article per month through to 1914. Indeed he complained to William Morris in April 1886 that he could not contribute to *Commonweal* as he was so busy that "even with the best will I could do nothing".

The most active part of the workload to establish *Freedom* therefore fell on Wilson's shoulders, both in terms of managing the publishing and financing its existence. During production, she would submit all proposed articles to the entire group, including numerous essays of her own. When Kropotkin's articles did come in they were a nightmare to edit, as not only was his written prose prone to errors,* he habitually went back over his hastily-written notes inserting scribbled clarifications and expansions.

---

* Kropotkin is often characterised as having a poor grasp of English, but this is largely a myth — he was fluent if not complex in his use of the language and noted as an effective public speaker both in Britain and the US.

Tchaikovsky's writing also frequently needed "considerable alterations", according to Wilson.

What Kropotkin (and to a lesser extent Merlino) did provide however was star power. He was globally famous, charismatic and near-idolised by almost everyone in the movement, though prone, according to fellow theorist Errico Malatesta, to inflexibility in promoting his ideas. His essays were the instantly recognisable explorations of a revolutionary polymath. Tchaikovsky too was well-regarded as an outstandingly able anarchist-communist, and approvingly cited by Wilson: "He devotes himself to the cause of the workers in England and retains his individual sympathy for every seeker of truth or [sufferer from] injustice." The propaganda column of the new paper was run by Nannie Dryhurst, effectively Wilson's deputy, a highly active writer and speaker who supported the paper until the end of the century and drew her hatred of the state from her Irish roots — she was also a strong early supporter of Sinn Fein. Dryhurst was an accomplished translator, which was hugely important in enabling *Freedom* to become a conduit for international anarchist writing. Distribution meanwhile was supported by Frank and Lena Hyde from their upmarket home on Kentish Town Road.

Although the new Freedom Group concentrated on the periodical, from 1889 it also produced other publications as Freedom Press — first pamphlets and then booklets and books. Mostly these were works by foreign writers (Kropotkin above all, but also Errico Malatesta, Jean Grave, Gustav Landauer, Max Nettlau, Emma Goldman, Alexander Berkman and many others) but British essayists also featured such as Herbert Spencer and William Morris.

From the start there were regular discussions and occasional public meetings. Alfred Marsh (see People, page 264) later to become editor of the paper upon Wilson's retirement, estimated that around 80,000 copies of 49 different titles were produced from 1886-1900. Kropotkin's *Conquest of Bread, Fields Factories and Workshops, Mutual Aid* and *Modern Science and Anarchy* were all written and first published in this 1890s-1912 period.

For most of the first decade *Freedom* was edited, published and largely financed by Wilson and it became the main English language anarchist paper in the country, alongside the *Commonweal*. With Wilson and her contacts at the helm it was a paper reflecting a membership of some means, with Wilson summing up much of her motivation saying: "We spend the best years of our lives in struggling to free ourselves from prejudice which our youth was passed in acquiring." She described its basic format at the time as "a small double sheet, containing a leader on some current topic, notes on passing events, one or two short theoretical or literary articles, a poem sometimes, and a monthly chronicle of 'The Struggle For Freedom' in the world. In this form the paper appeared monthly for two years and a quarter."

It thus stood with a somewhat carefully supportive air towards the rest of the movement, tempered also by Kropotkin's hostility towards propaganda of the deed. This helped insulate the paper from the consequences of various dramatic acts which took place over the course of the next few years, but also led to it to be viewed with some suspicion by working-class anarchist militants such as Charles Mowbray and Frank Kitz. *Commonweal* editor David Nicoll (himself the inheritor of substantial funds, unwisely spent), accused the group of indulging in "middle-class faddism", which for some may have been an accurate characterisation but was not entirely fair, especially on Wilson who would dedicate ten years to *Freedom* and much of the rest of her life, in one way or another, to the pursuit of socialism.

The fledgling paper was given an initial boost, according to Wilson, by the ongoing fallout from Chicago as the Haymarket Affair became a global phenomenon. The collective took an active role in promoting solidarity in London, setting up "indignation meetings" alongside the Socialist League and Social Democratic Federation. Frank Kitz recalled:

> I cannot compute the thousands of copies which were issued in several editions of the *Chicago Martyrs*. The sale was phenomenal, and cheaper editions were published ... Through all the intervening years the memory of our Chicago comrades has been kept green by annual celebrations convened by the Socialist League and later by the Freedom Group. Sometimes the police have deprived us of the use of halls for these meetings, but that has not prevented the gatherings being held. As the years have rolled by we have witnessed the growth and spread of anarchism, and the attempt to silence it on the scaffold has been frustrated.

Wilson spoke at one such meeting at South Place Institute in London on October 14th 1887, giving a step-by-step explanation of

---

* This was not always the case, in Kropotkin's younger years he had been in favour of the tactic but became far more careful once in England.

the events and the trial to great cheers from the crowd as she said the five sentenced to death were being prosecuted as "prominent advocates of the cause of the toilers". Stepniak, Kropotkin, George Standing and Shaw also spoke, though the latter were for free speech only, reflecting mostly that Wilson could call on powerful friends. A later visit from firebrand Lucy Parsons, widow of Haymarket martyr Albert, also drew support from working people, though her fighting talk also alienated some "lukewarm" sympathisers, Wilson felt.

A second boost took place on November 13th, when a protest was held against unemployment and coercion in Ireland, which turned into a bloodbath following an attack by police and army thugs. The brutal repression saw 400 people arrested, 75 injured and three killed, including a protester who was bayonetted. The event, which had been attended by both Wilson and Morris, became known as Bloody Sunday, and was followed by more violence a week later. Marking the two outrages became an annual event.

A startling throwaway note in Alred Marsh's *A Brief History of Freedom*, published at the turn of the century, even suggests that an anarchist conference part-organised by the group in March 1891 was when May 1st was picked for the first time to rally in memory of the Chicago Martyrs, on the grounds it was already a holiday "claimed by the workers" — a now global tradition which has continued in Britain to this day.

However this campaigning solidarity put *Freedom* into immediate hot water with both the Freethought Publishing Company's founder Charles Bradlaugh, whose strongly anti-anarchist views led him to expel the paper from this premises, and Annie Besant who booted them out of the Socialist League offices in favour of her own publication *The Link*. This reflected a bitter ongoing struggle within the League between Statist-inclined members such as as Edward Aveling and Eleanor Marx, and the anarchists. Though too late for Freedom's benefit, this would be comprehensively won by the latter, led by Max Nettlau, Thomas Cantwell (see People, page 231), David Nicoll and Henry B Samuels (of whom more later). Indeed it was the success of the Freedom Group in promoting anarchism to members of the League which was in part blamed for its increasingly fractious atmosphere.

The expulsion lead to a period of upheaval, with *Freedom* moving a half dozen times in the course of the next few years. The group were initially taken in by *The Socialist* editor Thomas Bolas at Cursitor Street in February 1888, and briefly printed by Leaflet Press before production was taken over by Thomas Binning, a former Socialist Leaguer who was now running his own printer in Union Road. *Freedom* kept these premises until 1891 when, after Binning went bankrupt and having acquired new type, it moved to the New Fellowship Press in Newington Road, Stoke Newington, close to Henry Seymour's old address. Morris, still trying to foster some semblance of co-operation within the League, also lent them use of the group's hall in Farringdon, where Freedom Group speakers held a number of further talks.

Regardless of the forced moves, interest around Chicago and the meetings it fuelled brought in new members and readers, also leading to an increase in pages from four to eight. Among the fresh faces were Alfred Marsh, Edith Nesbit, Marx Edgeworth Lazarus, accountancy pioneer John Manger Fells, O Bertoni, Dyer Lum and Tom Pearson — valued as a rare working-class member of the group. Speeches primarily by Wilson were also offered to other gatherings, such as a large Paris Commune commemoration in Store Street, on labour and its rewards at Farringdon Street etc.

Keeping up this pace was difficult however and in June, Wilson told a friend she was experiencing family anxieties, largely around the illness of her mother. She cancelled her appearances at a number of meetings in late 1888, including the one at which Lucy Parsons spoke. In January 1889 she dropped out from the paper for several months naming former SDF member James Blackwell as co-editor, who had also been recruited the previous year.

Blackwell, an anarchist-communist who had clashed in print with William Morris in the late 1880s as the Socialist League declined, cleared out much of the international news focus and relaunched the paper in March in favour of serialising longer articles, particularly by Errico Malatesta — recently returned from Latin America and based in an Islington attic — along with Jean Grave. Kropotkin's *The Wage System* was also part of this series, published in 1890. Blackwell expanded the paper with a supplement sheet reporting on propaganda work taking place in England before stepping back as editor in 1891.

In April 1890 the group ran weekly talks and meetings, held in the Autonomie Club and a larger gathering took place in November at South Place to commemorate the Chicago deaths, with Wilson returning in August to participate at a meeting on "the evils of authority". She did however remain mostly out of the picture through 1890, during which time the Socialist League finally split for good, leaving the anarchists fully in charge of the *Commonweal* — albeit with a major cash shortfall as William Morris was among those who left.

This rupture and the arguments surrounding it are best understood as symptoms of a far wider ideological clash going on throughout the period, as socialists worked through the implications and arguments around Statism and libertarian critiques in the pre-USSR era. *Freedom* was reporting on outbreaks of animosity within the movement such as Marxist clashes with anarchists at the International Labour Conferences of 1889 and 1891, with repeated attempts to expel the latter finally being successful in 1893.

Though exhausted from dealing with her mother's illness, Wilson returned in 1891 as sole editor. William (Woolf) Wess meanwhile, whose role had previously mainly involved typesetting, took over management of the Freedom office in 1891 — he would go on to continue an association with the paper in one form or another into the 1930s. A multilingual Jewish emigre from Lithuania, Wess was a key figure in organising the Jewish unions in London. When Freedom's new landlord tried to seize the New Fellowship assets in 1892, it was Wess who secretly transported its office once again, to the house of sympathiser Hermann Stenzleit.

Freedom Group members made some effort to publicise the wider movement's comings and goings in this period and regularly frequented the capital's anarchist clubs with one report from March 1891 describing an event at the Club Autonomie:

A glance round the large room, with its pleasant little tea tables, each brightened by the music of friendly talk, showed Germans and Frenchmen from the Autonomie in conversation with Englishmen from the provinces, Jewish comrades from Berners Street, laughing and talking with members of the Italian group, the editor of the *Arbeter Fraint* in amicable discussion with one of the *Freedom* staff, friends from the Hammersmith Socialist Society, the London Socialist league, all cordially mingling with anarchist-communists from every group in London.

Autonomy Club interior, *Daily Graphic* 1894

This rosy view conflicted somewhat with that of Scotland Yard undercover Patrick McIntyre, who characterised the club as a shabby, long narrow room with a canteen and three or four other small rooms off it, complaining that:

Autonomy Club, *Daily Graphic* and *Illustrated London news*

Malcontents of all nations fraternised and denounced their various governments to their hearts' content, mixing with their denunciations the largest possible quantities of lager beer and miscellaneous liqueurs.

I have met at this rendezvous the Russian Nihilists, the German Social Democrats, the Italian Irredentist, the French Communist and, on rare occasions, one or two of the sons of Hibernia. Most predominant amongst the crowd was the mouchard or agent provocateur. Had you been able to take away from the club those gentlemen who were thriving on the foolishness of other people, you would have reduced the number of habitues of the club by a third. I know, of my own knowledge, that a large minority of those frequenting the place were in the service and pay of continental governments.

The differences in tone give an idea of how the movement was simultaneously a place of debate, bonhomie and seething undercurrents, utopian dreamers rubbing shoulders with insurrectionists and the agents of a dozen fearful nationstates. Where champagne socialists and furious class strugglists tried to find room to say their piece.

The Walsall plot

Unattributed recollections in the December 1900 issue of *Freedom*, possibly by Alfred Marsh, note how the upheavals of 1892 affected the movement, especially the Walsall bombing plot, the first major incident of its kind to take place on British soil:

> With 1892 began an era of repression on the one hand and revolt on the other throughout the civilised world. In England, first came the Walsall Police Plot; exposed, month by month, as it dragged out its shameful details before the courts by *Freedom*, which also opened a defence fund for the prisoners. Next followed the prosecution of the *Commonweal* for taking the same line in less measured English.
>
> Meanwhile unemployed riots in Germany and the Ravachol affair in France [where an anarchist was guillotined for attempting to blow up a senior judge] were followed by great strikes in Australia, in the English shipping, weaving and coal trades, the Carnegie riots and violent police persecutions in America ... endless imprisonments and several barbarous executions in Italy and Spain — an era of violence and wholesale injustice.
>
> In England in the same period we had the Francois and Meunier extraditions, the Cantwell and Young /Cantwell and Quinn prosecutions and attacks on free speech, notably in Hyde Park and at Manchester. During this troubolous two years, *Freedom* stood firmly on the side of the rebels and against the suppression of rebellion in word and deed, even when the rebels used weapons which no humane person can approve in cold blood.
>
> On the other hand *Freedom* did not either advocate or applaud outrage; its own policy advocated a continuous and energetic endeavour on the part of the workers, organised in trades unions, co-operative societies and other voluntary associations, to obtain by direct action, such as refusing to work as wage slaves, the control of the means of production; so that the producers and distributors may become their own employers, with the right to dispose of what they make.

Freedom was careful in its treatments of bomb plots, resolutely condemning propaganda of the deed as a concept but regularly backing arrestees as victims of State repression. Its philosophy through this period instead called for mass action by the workers, aiming to push people beyond reformist demands for government welfare and arguing that only the destruction of private property as a social form could solve unemployment and the poverty resulting from it. In 'The Root of the Unemployment Problem' (1893) for example the paper notes:

> We know only one remedy, and it is one no government can apply. That remedy is to destroy the monopoly of private property. When the workers themselves seize upon the land and other necessary means of working; when they insist on the use of these; and when they are defined those who do the work shall dispose of the produce, then the unemployed problem can be solved: till then, never.

As time wore on this led to a great deal of twisting about. Following the infamous Siege of Sidney Street, in which two Latvian revolutionaries engaged in a lethal gunfight with police over a jewellery store robbery, *Freedom* argued that "it is the desperate work of the Tsar's victims". This fit with the core anarchist doctrine of repression begetting violence while stopping short of celebrating the robbers — but required some clumsy rhetorical footwork on the part of the paper.

The Walsall plot did however have a serious impact on the movement at large, affecting not just the people initially arrested on charges of attempting to manufacture a bomb (no active explosives were found, though blueprints were present) but of anyone considered to be part of the "widespread conspiracy".

A mass meeting was called on March 25th following the four initial detentions of Joe Deakin, Fred Charles, Victor Cails and Jean Battloa, at which the police were accused of conducting a "sham dynamite plot" for the purposes of arresting anarchists. The revolutionaries weren't far wrong in the assessment. Later research into police files has shown that an agent provocateur, August Coulon, instigated the bombings at the behest of Special Branch.

At the time however it was a major coup for the force, opening the door for raids across the city which eventually saw *Commonweal* publisher Charles Mowbray and editor David Nicoll detained for incitement (Nicholl had already fingered Coulon as an agent by this point) while the Walsall four got between five and ten years each in prison. *Freedom* remained untouched, largely because Wilson had retained a lawyer who advised against printing Nicoll when he sent her the article for republishing.

Where the bomb arrests had frozen the movement however, the seizing of Mowbray and Nicoll along with the assets of *Commonweal* had quite the opposite effect, spurring a major free speech campaign which saw a May Day protest for the eight-hour day numbering around 18,000 people and large meetings in most major cities ahead of their trial. Mowbray was acquitted and Nicoll sent down for 18 months in Chelmsford prison as a result, rather than facing exemplary terms of up to ten years.

The loss of Nicoll from the League was to have a lasting impact on both the fortunes of *Commonweal,* already struggling financially after the 1890 exit of William Morris, and on *Freedom* itself as the anarchists attempted to keep things going.

In February 1893 *Freedom's* access to premises was still in flux, initially moving to Agnes Henry's house in St Augustine's Road, Camden Town, where Wess also moved with the type. But her basement was plagued with damp, impairing Wess' health, and the type was shifted to Charlotte Wilson's house on Hampstead Heath in March 1894, with publication done first in St John Street and then in Old Street, both in Clerkenwell.

The editorial offices remained in St Augustine's Road until January 1895, when Charlotte Wilson, suffering from poor health, finally retired from running the paper for good. *Freedom* was stopped for three months before a new showrunner was found, violinist Alfred Marsh stepping forward as editor while John Turner took the role of publisher. Though Wilson had officially retired, she continued to aid *Freedom* financially until 1901.

Events were already in train however that would gift *Freedom* a home for the next 30 years as a sad result of the implosion of the rest of the anarchist press. When it re-opened in April, it would be with an increasingly huge say in the affairs of the wider movement.

Clockwise from top, Keel in the production room at Ossulston Street, Alfred Marsh, and the back yard

1895-1927
Ossulston Street

1894-95 was a watershed moment both for the *Commonweal*, as it slowly went under, and for *Freedom*, which would be shored up by that process.

Here it's worth a brief detour to talk about a third publication, *The Torch*, which while it didn't loom large in the history of the broader movement, did in the end provide both Freedom's long-term premises and its printer at the turn of the century, as well as an entertaining half-history, half-fiction piece by its main editors, denouncing the entire movement as an unmitigated shambles. In his *A Short History of Freedom*, Donald Rooum writes:

> The nieces and nephew of the artist Dante Gabriel Rossetti had been printing their own paper, *The Torch*, a journal of anarchist communism at 127 Ossulston Street, near Kings Cross, since 1885. In 1898 they decided to cease publication and arranged for the Freedom Group to take over the premises. The Rossettis' printing equipment was bought and donated to *Freedom* by two sympathisers. Freedom Press stayed in Ossulston Street for the next 30 years.

The nieces and nephew were Olivia, Helen and Arthur Rossetti, cousins to Ford Maddox Ford, whose stories are said to have helped inspire Joseph Conrad's famous farce *The Secret Agent*. While teenagers (they were 16, 11, and 14 respectively) they had founded *The Torch* in their father William's basement at 3 St Edmund's Terrace, London in 1891, which led to the extraordinary spectacle of the home of the Secretary of the Inland Revenue — William's job — being under constant surveillance by "English detectives, French police spies and Russian agents provocateurs" as Ford put it.

In 1892 the teenage trio acquired a derelict printing press formerly belonging to Joseph Lane (who had resigned from the Socialist League three years before), taken from the loft of the old *Commonweal* offices at Clerkenwell Road, and by 1893 were corresponding with well-known members of the British anarchist movement, including Thomas Cantwell and Henry Samuels of *Commonweal*, Dr Fauset Macdonald (a middle-class militant who had entered the movement that year and associated with *Freedom*, see People, page 255), as well as international figures such as Kropotkin and Malatesta.

However after the death of their mother William expelled them from the basement and the Press was removed, first to Goodge Street and then to 127 Ossulston Street, a slum housing site, in December 1894. The building, rented out from a Mr Quantrell, consisted according to Olivia of a damp, poorly-lit basement shop with a ladder leading to a larger, lighter room. They would operate out of this space until the paper was closed in 1896.

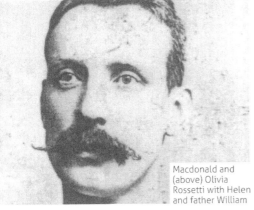

Macdonald and (above) Olivia Rossetti with Helen and father William

Late in 1894 Fauset Macdonald had become official publisher of the *Torch*, having already pitched in to help finance *Commonweal* along with Max Nettlau, creating connections with a wide variety of anarchists including those of a more insurrectionary bent. This would prove disastrous for both papers in short order.

Having already inveigled himself into the *Freedom* and *Torch* groups, Fauset made himself a key figure in the final ousting of *Commonweal*'s jailed editor David Nicoll, on the grounds that the man had lost his mind in prison. Nicoll tried to return to the fold in 1895, hoping to regain the editorship, only to find Fauset's good friends Thomas Cantwell and Henry Samuels in charge. Claiming the official support of the Freedom Group, Fauset and Tom Cantwell made it clear Nicoll would not be allowed back. Nicoll would write of the affair:

Mr Samuels had the advantage of the official support of the *Freedom* people. There were two delegates present — Agnes Henry and Dr Macdonald. Miss Henry was neutral,

Dr Macdonald supported Samuels with enthusiasm (...)
Seeing how everything had been "arranged" I threw up the
editorship.

Nicoll would, sadly, bear a truly debilitating grudge in the wake
of that coup, and by 1897 had been all but drummed out of the
'official' movement, written off as a paranoiac and censured by the
Freedom Group. He would take particular exception to Samuels
and Macdonald, who he accused of being police provocateurs in
the wake of the Greenwich bombing (see below).

George Cores, a former Socialist Leaguer who briefly helped edit
Commonweal between Nicoll's and Samuels' editorships, was one
of the few who continued contact with Nicoll as he sunk into the
mire until his death in 1919, and felt he had been ill-treated by the
likes of Max Nettlau, Macdonald and Samuels especially through
their interference. Writing in his memoirs, he noted:

> In the concluding years of his life I often met him and I
> am gratified with the firm conviction that he regarded me
> as a true friend and comrade till his death, though he was
> suspicious of so many about him.
>
> The restoration of the editorship would have saved him
> from very much mental, moral and physical suffering. He was
> truly a martyr. The wretched, petty, greedy vanity of a man
> was a greater blow to Nicoll than anything the enemy could
> do, and made the concluding phase of his life a tragedy. No
> man ever lived who was more idealist, more concerned with
> the freedom and welfare of humanity than David J Nicoll.

Nicoll certainly became paranoid following the *Commonweal* coup
if he wasn't before, but Samuels really was a nasty piece of work,
disruptive and aggressive and dogged by persistent rumours that
he was in cahoots with police spies — though coherent evidence
never materialised. Under his management *Commonweal* became
exceptionally bloodthirsty, and in November a gathering requested
by Samuels was banned on the grounds "its attendees applaud
and justify the wholesale massacre of innocent persons."

Cores would later write disparagingly that Samuels: "Was simply
an advocate of violence — by others. He ruined the paper and
his editorship came to an end when his brother-in-law Martial
Bourdin, a young Frenchman, accidentally killed himself through
a bomb which he was carrying, exploding in Greenwich Park, in
the vicinity of Greenwich Observatory."

The Greenwich bomb and *Commonweal's* demise

In the aftermath of the botched bombing in February 1894, raids were carried out across London, most notably at the Club Autonomie. The police had long been itching for a chance to close the place down and a threat to Greenwich Observatory, which infuriated the public, provided the perfect excuse. Arrests took place across the city and amid the crackdown even the funeral of Bourdain was attacked by a mob, led by the police.

Beyond ruining Samuels' reputation, and Fauset's as the doctor from whom some of the bomb materials were allegedly sourced by Samuels, the infamous Greenwich attack would also force closure of *Commonweal*. Arrests had temporarily eliminated most of the support base of the paper, which was then taken on by basketmaker Thomas Cantwell, an irascible personality badly affected by a stretch of six-months' hard labour handed down in 1893, who had a habit of starting fights.

A deeply unflattering description of the scene directly after the raids is offered by the Rossettis in their fictionalised collective memoir, *A Girl Among the Anarchists*.* In their novel, the "Bomb" (*Commonweal*) newspaper found itself in dire straits after the arrest of key comrades, and was left in the hands of "Short" — a thinly disguised rendition of Cantwell. She describes a scene the day after the arrests:

> The comrades had not seen fit so far to muster round the paper. To say there was none, however, is an injustice, for there on the sofa, still huddled in the red flag, lay Short, apparently little affected by what had taken place since I last saw him. He had been aroused from his slumbers by the yelping of his dog, whose tail had been trodden on by one of the detectives, and he had raised himself on his elbow, and was looking round, uttering curses volubly. He nodded slightly on seeing us enter, but did not change his position. There he lay, quite heroic in his immovable sloth; of all the many fighters he alone remained staunch at his post; and that because he was positively too lazy to move away from it.

Under Cantwell's direction *Commonweal* finally fell apart. Fauset and his money skipped the country, moving to Australia (where he

---

* Olivia is commonly picked as the main author, David Goodway spoke to younger sister Helen however and she said it was a joint effort.

would, bizarrely, go on to become a fan of eugenics and help set up the supremacist White Australia movement), which crippled the paper financially, while Cantwell had few real allies left to call on.

The paper had finally closed by 1895, with three of its alumni, Joseph Pressburg, John Turner (as publisher) and Cantwell himself subsequently being recruited to *Freedom* by Alfred Marsh, reinforcing it in the wake of Charlotte Wilson's retirement, which had by 1896 been matched by that of compositor William Wess, who stepped back to pursue a professional career.

Greenwich bomb sketch, 1896

Last paper standing

Commonweal wasn't the only paper killed off by Greenwich, which largely heralded the end of London's period as an international anarchist hub. Amid growing public anger and state pressure, not only did many English anarchists step back from their roles, including Wilson and Agnes Henry (who had fostered a child), but many key European radicals also left, such as Merlino and Malatesta, who both decamped to Italy that year. In short order, the *Torch* ceased publication as well. Fauset's disappearing act had left it without a publisher, while all three of its youthful founders left, through work requirements, illness or disillusionment.

This was key for the future of *Freedom*, as upon hearing they intended to sell up, former *Commonweal* backer Max Nettlau approached Olivia in March 1896 and offered to buy the lot, including the (already elderly) print machine of Johann Most's *Freiheit*, for "the benefit of the movement." That printer would go on to do another 30 years of service, off and on, before being moved to the Whiteway Colony (see The Wilderness, page 53).

Alongside his friend Bernhard Kampffmeyer he paid £20 for the equipment and guaranteed much of the rent of the premises. Nettlau's move over to *Freedom* would prove vital in a number of ways, not least in gaining him as a regular writer up to and after

World War I. Cantwell moved over the *Freedom* and *Commonweal* type assets to the building in April 1896, though its official address only changed in December 1897. By that time every other notable anarchist paper had been closed down, leaving just *Freedom*.

A description of the setup at Ossulston through that period is provided by Harry Kelly, an American member of the Freedom Group from 1898-1904:

> Notwithstanding that *Freedom* advocates the most modem of social theories, there is an old world atmosphere about the office and an artistic charm to the people who conduct the paper. A small two-storey building situated in a backyard, in one of the poorest neighborhoods of London, houses it ... The building had two rooms, one upstairs for the composing room, and one downstairs, the press room. The old press was of what we call here the 'Oscillator' type, and its vintage at that time was some 75 or 80 years. Here each month gathered Marsh, the musician; Turner, the trade union organiser; Tcherkesoff, the literary man; Nettlau, the philologist; Tchaikovsky, Miss Davies, Mary Krimont, and myself ... (Cantwell and I were the only simon-pure workingmen in the group).
>
> The press had neither power nor automatic sheet delivery, so it required three of us to operate it. Two or three of the men alternated in turning the crank, I fed the press, and Miss Davies, wearing always black gloves, hat and veil, took the sheets off as they were printed. With her face with its fresh color and her grey hair she looked the picture of an old master
> ...
> We often regaled ourselves with kippers and tea after getting off a forme of four pages, and the others had at least two hours' rest while the writer made the second forme ready ...
>
> Sometimes when the men grew tired or short of wind, a navvy was stopped in the street and hired to turn the crank, and we soothed our consciences by paying him ninepence an hour instead of the dockers' 'tanner' (sixpence). Mary's job was to prepare tea for us. It was under such conditions as these that the paper was printed, and it was there that many of Kropotkin's best theoretical articles on anarchism appeared.

This status as sole survivor, and its new intake of Socialist Leaguers, gave the paper a reputation boost and it brought a great deal of support from the US particularly, with major figures such as Emma Goldman and Voltairine de Cleyre visiting the Freedom Group in 1895 and 1896 (Goldman's meeting with Kropotkin at the time is credited with her conversion to anarchist-communism). Its political weight was highlighted in 1896, when a key gathering of the International Socialist Workers and Trade Union Congress (the Second International) was held in London, chaired by Henry Hyndman. Described by historian George Haupt as "the most agitated, the most tumultuous, and the most chaotic of all the congresses of the Second International", it saw 768 delegates from across Europe attend, but was dominated by English (475) and French (129) members and reflected the fully disagreeable atmosphere which had developed between the statists and anarchists.

Across three days multiple factions scrapped over everything from policy and procedure to whether delegates had been brought in as ringers. At the conference were no less than four *Freedom* alumni and fellow-travellers, with temporary editor Joseph Pressburg, William Wess, Frank Kitz and Max Nettlau on the committee representing machinists, compositors, garment dyers and carmen respectively. *Freedom* itself was refused formal entry, and on the second day of the conference a mob of angry anarchists, barred from the hall, picketed outside while Pressburg railed against the bad faith of the Marxists from within. It marked another low point for the attempt to unify socialism, and led to the expulsion of the anarchist faction once again.

Nettlau, writing in his later histories of the movement, believed that English anarchism took root in the 1889-1891 period, profiting from the pioneer work done by agitators drawn from the original Socialist League such as Joseph Lane, Sam Mainwaring, George Cores, Fred Charles and John Turner, saying that with their introduction to the more Fabian-inclined Freedom Group 'the difference was like that between a plant on dry ground and one on fertile soil.'

That is not to say this was a universal view. *Freedom* itself reported, in rather hurt tones, on an 1897 conference discussing the possibilities for a new weekly paper where:

Freedom was described as a philosophical, middle-class organ, not intelligible to the working classes, not up to date in late information and in O'Shea's eyes less revolutionary than *Comic Cuts* ... It was edited and managed by an inaccessible group of arrogant persons worse than the Pope and his seventy cardinals and written by fossilised old quilldrivers.

Within the revised collective however there were immediate problems, with Cantwell cutting a problematic figure until a Belgian, F Henneghien, replaced him in September 1898. Cantwell's unreliability and inability to bring anything out on time was noted by Cores, who wrote that he "had, as acting editor, a peculiar habit of censoring all contributions, making everything which appeared conform to the gospel according to Cantwell. This did not suit the comrades." Cantwell at one stage went as far as to point a gun at Italian supporter Pietro Gori and often tried to bully editor Alfred Marsh, who would write in an 1897 letter to Nettlau that "you cannot imagine what a time I had. Two-and-a-half years with Cantwell is enough to kill anyone" (Cantwell had left *Freedom* in November, at least temporarily).

Cantwell came back as *Freedom* compositor after Henneghien left in 1900, but had a stroke in 1902 and was found by Tcherkesoff on Christmas day, lying with his head in the ashes of the fireplace, all but dead. He made a partial recovery, however was never able to work again and died in 1906, Nettlau writing an obituary that took note of his faults, but lauded his endless loyalty to the cause.

It was at this rather low point (Harry Kelly complained in 1904 that the group was down to six members) that one of *Freedom's* longest-serving compositors and editors would step in, Thomas Keell (see People, page 247).

The 36-year-old had been apprenticed as a letterpress printer, and had become a trade unionist through the London Society of Compositors before being drawn into anarchism in the late 1890s and *Freedom's* circles in June 1898 via Kelly. Asked to take over by Alfred Marsh, Keell began by clearing out the mess at Ossulston Street and bringing orders up to date, quickly being made became responsible for the whole of the business side of the enterprise, as well as compositing.

A direct recollection of the time is offered by Karl Walter, writing in *Freedom* shortly after its 1961 redesign [see page 120] as it inspired him to think about the first time he visited its offices in the early 1900s:

> I am wandering up Ossulston Street, St Pancras, marked rather than lighted by one or two remote gas lamps, the unbroken blank wall on my right studded with couples standing against it careless of the flickers of white betraying their pleasures, the customary penny having been paid to the policeman on the beat — a mur tolere, a bit of London as crude as any described by Boswell.

That afternoon I had been introduced to a Prince Kropotkin at the old-time salon of a friendly friend, Lady Low, identifying him presently as the author of two books I had recently read that set him above all princes. What led to my visit to Ossulston Street was an amazing conversation I heard in which this anarchist hero of my dreams talked in amicable agreement with Sir Hugh Low, whom I rather scorned as governor of various tropical colonies—and about those very "natives" over whom I imagined the latter had cracked a cruel whip for many years.

I was modest enough to keep my mouth shut and my ears open, so I learned that Sir Hugh's attitude to "natives" was not in the least of that kind; he was asking Kropotkin about the best way for Malayan peasants to organise in order to secure for themselves the profits of rubber planting, which Sir Hugh had promoted by a first shipment of rubber saplings from Brazil.

Kropotkin outlined some form of cooperative organisation which might be suitable; I was able to add a word about cooperative production societies in Italy; on which Kropotkin said he thought that *Freedom* might like an article on the Italian societies, and saved me the embarrassment of confessing my ignorance of the publication by turning to Sir Hugh

Street frontage, No. 127

and explaining that it was a paper run by some friends of his; he gave me their names and the Ossulston Street address, advised me to go and see Tom Keell there, adding with a twinkle for Sir Hugh, "the finest type of English native".

I went in search of them that evening, excited by the prospect of meeting my first English anarchists and writing an article for their press. The Freedom Press, I gathered, must be in some building behind the slummy long row of sordid dwellings facing the mur tolere. I looked for an opening, a gateway, a passage to the anarchist counterpart of Printing House Square. I peered in vain at the numbers on the doors; the gas lamps were far apart; I guiltily struck a match, fearing righteous protest from the wall brigade, and read a low number. A uniformed figure emerged from the gloom. I had never been questioned by the law before; I didn't dare tell a lie; with the greatest misgiving I said I was looking for No. 127.

"Freedom print shop you're after, is it?"

I repeated the number less bravely, chilled by a thought that I might be giving away an anarchist secret, a feeling excused by my years and the climate of opinion in those days before bombs were nationalised. For all I knew, No. 127 might be an armoury. But the officer knew all about No. 127 and took me there, guided me away from the front entrance to a passage which indeed led to a printing house if not to a square.

A hand press, a case of type, a kitchen chair, two high stools, a dull gas lamp at which a small bearded man was reading a slip proof. When I told him Kropotkin had sent me he stuck his beard out with half a smile but eyes kindly twinkling, I thought it best to confess at once that I had never seen a copy of *Freedom* — which seemed to please him or at least relieve him for he was able to give me a file of back numbers to read while he got on with his work.

...

Think for a moment what London was like in those days, what England was like, what the world was like. The world — contained in Europe, for most writers and nearly all social purposes; England — a country of pacifists where warmongers were the cranks, the asylum of political rebels, refuge of the persecuted, a country that believed itself to be free, just being roused to the truth of its own injustice and cruelty at home and abroad.

London — a great intellectual centre, the salon still existing, drawing-rooms dedicated to intelligent converse, the clearing-house of information about progressive thought and action throughout the world, people who remembered Darwin still living, and Mazzini, and other noble refugees. That brief Edwardian period, in so many ways the blindest and most futile of our history, was an editor's paradise. You couldn't go wrong. There was comparatively little competition; much went unobserved, uncommented. What you picked out as important, you thereby made important."

Somers Town

Freedom now, for the first time in a decade, had its own premises. But much as Rossetti had intimated, the Ossulston Street offices were far from the salubrious surroundings that had been inhabited by its affluent founder members.

The road was a poor one and a major thoroughfare on the edge of Somers Town, showing up on Charles Booth's famous 1890s maps of poverty. The Midlands Rail Goods Depot and Potato Market was on the site of what is now the British Library, while 127 Ossulston was a little way north, on a site between Phoenix Street and Aldenham. In Booth's colour scheme the street shows up as mix of purple and blue (darker shades here), suggesting poor and impoverished housing.

Black was what marked serious poverty — the infamous rookeries would fall into that category, and the Somers Town slums are still sometimes portrayed as such in novels. Nearby Clarendon (now Werrington) Street was one of these and described by Booth in 1898 as "a narrow thoroughfare of bad repute — the worst spot in the immediate neighbourhood and a good many prostitutes and amateurish thieves are living here. The local name for the street is 'Little Hell'."

Initially the area had been a cheap haven for artisans fleeing the French Revolution, described in 1878 by *Old and New London*:

> This district, rents being cheap, was largely colonised by foreign artisans, mostly from France, who were driven on our shores by the events of the Reign of Terror and the first French Revolution. Indeed, it became nearly as great a home of industry as Clerkenwell and Soho ... the exiles of the poorer class found their way to St Pancras, and settled down around Somers Town, where they opened a Catholic chapel, at first in Charlton Street, Clarendon Square, and subsequently in the square itself.

The population soared from the 1830s onwards, leading to high density slums with transitory and multinational demographics, with transport links which made it a useful spot for incoming radicals. *Freedom's* former Judd Street premises can be found just the other side of Euston Road, while other premises further south that *Freedom* had published from included 28 Grays Inn Road, 57 Chancery Lane and 7 Lamb's Conduit Street. In 1921 the census found density in Somers Town averaged three people to a room.

This gives some idea of the situation for the paper around that time, which had for so long been produced with the aid of well-to-do radicals of all stripes. With the stepping back of Wilson much of the glitz had disappeared, leaving just the hard work of distributing propaganda to the masses.

The Great Unrest

The late 1900s and 1910s were a relatively vibrant time for syndicalism in Britain from the South Wales Cambrian Combine miners dispute onwards, with the anarchist-leaning union strategy playing a surprisingly large role in the Great Unrest of 1910-1914, a period of major strikes and riots across Britain as capitalists struggled to maintain order in the face of spiralling inequality and falling living standards. This influence was partly drawn from a global rise in syndicalism taking place at that time and the efforts in Britain of groups such as the Industrial Syndicalist Education League, led by Tom Mann and Guy Bowman and backed by the East End's Jewish tailoring workers.

By 1909 the League had 14 branches, and syndicalist ideas were widespread among transport and mine workers. Its input was notable in events such as the 1911 seamen's strike and 1912 Liverpool transport walkouts. In 1912 coal miners in South Wales especially had strong syndicalist tendencies, possibly based in part on work done years prior by anarchist agitator Sam Mainwaring, bolstered by a successful visit from famed IWW militant Big Bill Haywood in 1910. Activists such as George Barrett and Frank Kitz were organising major conferences.

At *Freedom*, with Marsh as editor and Keell keeping the business stable the pair had, in the wake of the failed Russian revolution of that year and in the light of increasing worker militancy, begun to focus on reporting industrial activities and pushing for direct action. In 1907 *Freedom* was joined by an agitational paper, *The Voice of Labour*. Contributors at the time included Guy Aldred (in his own name and also as 'Ajax junior'), Karl Walter, Harry Kelly, S Carlyle Potter and Jimmy Dick.

The programme of this second paper was initially drafted by Kropotkin, with John Turner's name again on the masthead as publisher and Marsh as effective editor. Keell was asked to composite *Voice of Labour* on top of his *Freedom* duties, and gave up his work for the *Spectator* as a result.

The 1907 run of *Voice of Labour* was however full of contradictions, linked to Turner's habit of lauding direct action activity instigated by the union leaderships and willingness to compromise with parliamentary process. Turner, who had for a time been very active as a grassroots union organiser was in the process of becoming widely disliked within the radical movement thanks to his increasing sympathy for reformism. The official publisher of *Freedom* had become a well-heeled fulltimer for the Shopworkers

Assistants Union and as a result his union politics were all over the place. As John Quail relates in *Slow Burning Fuse*:

> Though the *Voice* was written in a much more punchy style than *Freedom* and though the coverage of labour disputes in Britain and abroad was full and relevant, there were developing contradictions in the paper. The direct action talked of by John Turner was action instigated and directed by the official structures of the unions. His propaganda was fundamentally directed towards trades unionists and was designed to encourage them to fight directly for gains in wages and conditions rather than allowing Parliament to mediate these demands.
>
> Even here he was prepared to compromise. For example, his union was committed to abolishing the "living-in" system, where employees not only lost a job if they were sacked, but also lost a roof over their heads. This commitment was being followed through with some success by industrial action but at the same time the Shop Assistants Union-sponsored MP was pressing for legislation to make the living-in system non-compulsory. John Turner's comment was only that industrial action might well succeed before the Bill was made law. Thus Turner stood for militant official trades unionism, though he was prepared to countenance parliamentary action if it had any prospects of success. What he did not understand and in his position probably could not understand, was the rising tide of anti-officialism in the unions.

This position also contributed to a difficult split between *Freedom* and Guy Aldred, a talented agitator originally brought to anarchism by Errico Malatesta, who Turner then recruited to the *Voice*. Aldred, after a brief period as mainstay writer, quickly turned into a vocal critic. He had begun losing faith in the role of Turner over the contents of the *Voice* almost immediately but following a visit to Liverpool, where several vocal critics of *Freedom* lived, he fell out with both publications, eventually denouncing Turner as a "Labour fakir" during a huge row — to which Keell took exception.

The spiralling argument and heavy workload killed *Voice of Labour* a few months later, though it is worth noting that Keell himself was increasingly no fan of Turner, who he resented for lording it around the office as publisher without doing any work. Turner would cease being the publisher of *Freedom* that same year. Quail, arguing that *Freedom* was basically dysfunctional at this point, quotes Guy Aldred's unfinished autobiography *No Traitor's Gait* in explaining how affairs ran at the time:

> The Freedom Group, at this time, as a group never functioned. I never saw its members and they certainly never held regular meetings. Nor did the group seek converts. It operated as a close corporation or not at all. Its policy was decided by Keell who was incapable of really intelligent decision inspired by imagination; and Marsh whose attitude was dilettante.

Aldred, a major figure in the movement into the 1930s who married birth control pioneer Rose Witcop, was perhaps allowing general annoyance to get the better of him in this assessment. It is not true that the Freedom Group was entirely closed for example, as even the increasingly difficult Turner is regularly mentioned in the paper as speaking across the country, and *Freedom* continued to advertise events such as the charming-sounding (if revealingly titled) Anarchist Communist Picnic and Conference.

Following the row with Turner, Aldred had been embittered further in 1909 following his arrest and detention for sedition related to his publishing of *The Indian Sociologist*, espousing home rule for the country. In *No Traitor's Gait!* he alleges: "The anarchists attacked me in *Freedom* and suggested that I was either a police agent or a tool of police agents".

Guy Aldred and Rose Witcop

Freedom actually offered a front page report on Aldred's trial defending him in October, and began a fundraiser for his wife which lasted until January, but does not appear to have made any public allegations against him over the following few months — it's possible one appeared later.

Marsh in any case was anything but a dilettante, doggedly keeping Freedom going through thick and thin for more than 20 years despite illness and using money inherited from his father's death to subsidise production of many of the Freedom group's pamphlets. And if Keell lacked vision, and possibly harboured controlling tendencies, he certainly couldn't be faulted for dedication.

However it is true to say that in the 1905-11 period *Freedom*, while it did report on events such as the mass riots and barricade building of Liverpool dockers of 1911, failed to reach the heart of Great Unrest. The League was off running its own paper, *The Industrial Syndicalist*, and while some recovery related to the rise of industrial unionism did occur as old comrades got involved again and interest picked up more generally, sales didn't initially match the haydays of the 1890s. Keell was forced to report a drop from around 3,000 at the end of the 19th century to 1,500 in 1907 at the Amsterdam International Congress, the first gathering of its kind since the anarchists' expulsion from the Second International.*

The line taken by Errico Malatesta that year in particular on *Freedom's* front pages waxed long on the limitations of the general strike. His insistence on the need for revolution to come from an organised anarchist movement and his observation that "certainly syndicalism ... can emancipate a part of the workers, but not all. It is only too obvious that the syndicates make a serious division of the workers and often without doing any harm to the capitalists," was incisive, but did not fit with the broad trend of thinking in the workers' movements. Kropotkin too had little encouraging to say of events, playing them down in *Syndicalism and Anarchism* (July-Aug 1912), and arguing that while mass syndicalism was the only way to bring about the revolution it needed "the other element" or it would not succeed. For Quail, this period marked a decisive missed opportunity for *Freedom* under Marsh and Keell:

> While *Freedom* and Freedom Press pamphlets could provide some theoretical armament, the growth of the anarchist movement was dependent on local organisation ... if *Freedom* was the centre it was a hollow one. If the militant anarchists were part of the wider movement, *Freedom* was apart from it. It was not a question of the movement controlling the paper — for better or worse the traditional anarchist mode of publishing newspapers has been by an autonomous group more or less sensitive to criticisms from the rest of the movement. There was a group of two involved in publishing *Freedom* with a passive group of contributors who took little part in editorial activity.

---

* Keell and Karl Walter were the English delegates. Walter, a journalist and bank clerk by trade, turned towards fascism while living in Italy in the 1930s before returning to anarchism in the '60s and contributing to *Freedom* alongside his grandson, Nicolas, until his death in 1968.

Despite this, by 1910, when Marsh was step back significantly due to ill health, the building was seemingly ticking over in reasonable order, dominated by Keell in its offices. In his essay 'A Visit To London' written the same year for *Mother Earth*, Ben Reitman notes:

> On my arrival, I called at the office of *Freedom*, the leading English anarchist paper, that has been proclaiming the message of liberty to the world for nearly 28 years. Dozens of publications have come to life and died, but *Freedom* has weathered all difficulties. The man who has charge of *Freedom* and publishes all the anarchistic pamphlets is Tom Keell, a jovial, hardworking, and devoted soul, whose entire life is consecrated to his cause.
>
> He gave me a truly comradely reception and bade me make myself at home in the office. Nor did his cordiality diminish during my entire stay. Gloomy or cheerful, Tom always greeted me with kind words and a cup of tea. And when I incurred the curiosity of Scotland Yard, members of which were eager to locate my place of "conspiracy," it was Tom Keell who beat them off my track and took me to his home.

Keell himself felt through this period that the main issue was a lack of editorial support for the paper due to a more general malaise in the wider London movement, and despite the reappearance of *Voice of Labour* (from 1914-1916), which saw new faces involve themselves including Lilian Wolfe (see People, page 291), George Barrett and editor Fred Dunn, he was eventually forced to take on *Freedom's* editorial duties as well as business ones.

It is impossible from this distance to definitively say what kind of man Keell truly was or what was to blame for the pre-war malaise in *Freedom* personnel and engagement. Quite likely a variety of factors were at play, from a scarce organised anarchist scene deciding their priorities lay with the site of greatest struggle (i.e. not *Freedom*), to Keell being the sort of personality who, generous-minded though he clearly was, possibly struggled to engage with and bring in new people to help — and of course the normal personality clashes that happen within small, heavily political groups.

Keell certainly made enemies, but as a former *Freedom* editor myself while it was still fortnightly, I would note that this is a risk with every rejected letter and every critical article published under that masthead. Freedom Press, independent though it ultimately may be, has a sense for many of being part of the moral property and living history of all British anarchism. That weight of expectation was reputedly part of what kept at least one fantastic organiser, George Barrett, from getting more involved.*

Nevertheless, readership of *Freedom* did in the end become quite healthy as the 1910s wore on, with the imprisonment of Malatesta increasing interest in his writings alongside a boost provided by a blockbuster series of articles from William Owen (see People, page 272), writing from Mexico on the 1911-1914 revolution. Circulation hit around 3,000 once more.

This uptick, which also saw the first anarchist national conference for years take place in 1912 in Leeds, would not last long. Keell took on yet another full-time role in 1913, becoming "acting editor" when Marsh became too ill to work — and would in short order become embroiled at the heart of a major movement split over engagement with the first world war.

Top row, Tom Keell, John Turner and George Barrett. Main pic, An anarchist holiday camp in Harlech, 1915. Left to right, Lilian Wolfe, George Wilkinson, Bert Wells, Ciss Wilkinson, Mary Darley and 'Joan'

---

* Barrett was asked, and initially agreed, to edit *Freedom* as a weekly title, but having thought it over declined saying the "tradition" of the paper was too strong.

World War and Freedom's nadir

Freedom had, from its earliest days, been strongly anti-nationalist and heavily critical of imperialist conflicts — it courted significant unpopularity by denouncing the Second Boer War in 1899 as an imperial scam, to the point where open-air meetings had been disrupted by gangs of nationalist thugs. In an 1896 article, 'War' the paper was explicit in arguing that State conflicts have repeatedly been used to distract the fighting spirit of the workers from the class struggle and the growing revolutionary ferment. Further, it published many articles along the lines proposed by Elisée Reclus, including a translated piece by the renowned French writer in 1898 suggesting that in order for war to stop, it would be necessary to prioritise the resolution of the social question — abolishing the need to fight over private property. As of 1911, in 'An Open Letter to a Soldier' the paper was urging desertion in the ranks of armies everywhere.

So when war broke out in 1914 the lead article *Freedom* carried in September was a predictable one, and in theory not at all problematic. 'Blood and Iron' cast curses on both houses, Allies and Central Powers, thundering to workers:

> The same powers that deprived you of the fruits of your labour, and compelled you by hunger and starvation to create riches for a minority of privileged thieves and idlers — the same powers will now take away the lives of your sons and brothers, and force you with their guns to die for their interests.

It was rendered controversial in short order however by Kropotkin's sudden announcement that Germany must be defeated at all costs. This must have been something of a surprise to Keell, as on the back page of that very September issue was a new pamphlet written by Kropotkin, *Wars and Capitalism*, which was unequivocal in suggesting the masses must not be distracted from social revolution by the belligerent maneuvering of States, colonialists, financiers and business tycoons.

Jotting down his memories of the time, Keell described meeting Kropotkin "in a noisy Lyons cafe in Oxford Street" where the old soldier was drawing up military movement maps, supported by a (very ill) Marsh. Keell refused point blank to run Kropotkin's pro-war essay, and instead a bodged article on communal kitchens appeared.

He could not keep the Russian's new leanings quiet for long though, and in a letter to Swedish professor Gustaf Steffen, published by the paper in October, *Freedom*'s core theorist plumped publicly for the Allies, writing: "The territories of both France and Belgium MUST be freed of the invaders. The German invasion must be repulsed — no matter how difficult this may be. All efforts must be that way." Rejecting the possibility of using labour stoppages to deter the onset of the conflict, he argued that the anti-militarist's duty must therefore be to support the invaded nation, or risk through inaction supporting the invader. In particular, he voiced his fears that a victorious Germany would impose a hardline "Bismarkian imperialism" which would cause irreparable damage to workers' power. He noted:

> The last 43 years were a confirmation of what Bakunin wrote in 1871, namely, that if French influence disappeared from Europe, Europe would be thrown back in her development for half a century. And now it is self-evident that if the present invasion of Belgium and France is not beaten back by the common effort of all national of Europe, we shall have another half-century or more of general reaction.

Writing later, historian Max Nettlau would argue it was inevitable, in an era where nationalism was scorched onto the psyches of all, that even among the anarchist movement many would take sides on the Allies vs Central Powers question. Kropotkin's love for French enlightenment and fear of Germanic aggression pushed him into precisely that mode.

As editor Keell was left in a difficult position. Anti-war in his own views, he initially went to some pains to provide impartiality and carried Kropotkin's articles verbatim, along with criticism from many other writers, but would ultimately place himself squarely against the "secular saints" who were advocating getting behind the Allies.

One of the most significant essays published under Keell's editorship was to arrive that November from Errico Malatesta. 'Anarchists Have Forgotten Their Principles' was a powerful reiteration of the case against support for State militarism and a scorching, prescient riposte to Kropotkin's position:

> I have no greater confidence in the bloody Tsar, nor in the English diplomats who oppress India, who betrayed Persia, who crushed the Boer republics; nor in the French Bourgeoisie, who massacred the natives of Morocco; nor in those of Belgium, who have allowed the Congo atrocities

and largely profited by them — and I only recall some of their misdeeds, taken at random, not to mention what all governments and capitalist classes do against the workers and the rebels in their own countries ...

Besides, in my opinion, it is most probable there will be no definite victory on either side. After a long war, an enormous loss of life and wealth, both sides being exhausted, some kind of peace will be patched up, leaving all questions open, this preparing for a new war more murderous than the present.

Keell was denounced as "unworthy" of his editorial role by Kropotkin for his troubles and effectively asked to resign. He was backed primarily by the *Voice of Labour* collective, including George Barrett, Fred Dunn, Mabel Hope, Elizabeth Archer, Tom Sweetlove, W Fanner, and Lilian Wolfe, but would not be exonerated of accusations that he was disgracing his office until the next national anarchist gathering on April 4th-5th 1915 at Hazel Grove, Stockport. There he would face off against George Cores, speaking on behalf of Tcherkesoff, Turner and others to denounce what they regarded as a unilateral bid for total control over the paper.*

The delegates however, including influential Irish Liverpudlian Mat Kavanagh, took Keell's side, approving his actions in keeping the paper on an anti-war path.

Following this Kropotkin and others in the pro-Allies camp, notably Jean Grave, became thoroughly hostile to Keell's *Freedom*, and they would go on to write the *Manifesto of the Sixteen* in 1916. The manifesto, eventually signed by a little over 100 anarchists including a number of leading international figures, but denounced across the rest of the movement, notes:

> To speak of peace while the party [Germany] who, for 45 years, have made Europe a vast, entrenched camp, is able to dictate its conditions, would be the most disastrous error that we could commit. To resist and to bring down its plans, is to prepare the way for the German population which remains sane and to give it the means to rid itself of that party. Let our German comrades understand that this is the only outcome advantageous to both sides and we are ready to collaborate with them.

---

* Cores had previously been put up for the job of joint *Freedom* editor in 1911, but this had been refused by Keell, sparking something of a feud

They would again be rebuked by Malatesta, marking a permanent rift between him and Kropotkin, never healed, marking "one of the most painful, tragic moments" of his life.

And with that, Kropotkin largely left the stage of *Freedom's* story, though Freedom Press would continue to republish his old works for years to come (and still does at time of print). Isolated from the living movement, the father of anarchist-communism nevertheless retained many friends and would go on to live in France before returning to Russia at Lenin's invitation towards the end of his life.

The split was to prove a fatal blow to the Keell-era *Freedom*, though it tottered along on for a decade more with a declining sphere of support. Amid what was already a precipitous downturn in the movement's fortunes, Turner and Cores went along with Kropotkin and formed the nucleus of a sort of Freedom Group in exile. Max Nettlau, a somewhat tepid supporter of the Austrians, had meanwhile moved to Vienna. Writing in his memoirs many years later, Cores would explain how he and his group saw what had happened:

> Keell took full possession of *Freedom* and all the literature. He declared to me that he considered himself to be a trustee for the movement, and that *Freedom* was to be carried on as an anti-war journal. Everyone else in the Freedom Group he regarded as a 'war party' — at least so he professed, I suppose he did. He called to his support the *Voice of Labour group*, it's most prominent members being William Dunn, a postal sort, and miss Mabel Hope, a telephone operator. In this way *Freedom* lost everything.

Initially however *Freedom's* anti-war sentiment found an audience, with circulation again growing and the editors becoming involved in forming the Anti-Conscription League. The radical objectors swiftly became the target of State repression as a result, with raids against individuals and four separate raids of the *Freedom* office taking place throughout 1915. The wider movement was heavily repressed throughout the rest of the war period and beyond, with radicals largely identifying themselves for the State as up to 6,000 became conscientious objectors. Many anarchists were jailed, including eventually both Keell and Wolfe,* as told by the *Freedom* centenary history:

---

* This wasn't the only time Wolfe took jail time for her activism, she was also put away for handing out leaflets on birth control.

After the passing of the Military Service Act in January 1916 both *Freedom* and the *Voice of Labour* soon ran into trouble, first for an article 'Defying the Act' by 'one of those outlawed on the Scottish Hills' [Fred Dunn, who had been called up, arrested and subsequently escaped from a military prison], which was published in the April issue of the *Voice* and subsequently as a leaflet [10,000 copies were printed]. This was enclosed with a letter from Lilian Wolfe to Malatesta which was intercepted by the police. The consequent raid on the *Freedom* office then brought to light another article just set up for *Freedom*, headed 'The Irish Rebellion' and worthy of a second charge.

On June 24th 1916 Tom Keell and Lilian Wolfe were tried at Clerkenwell Police Court under the Defence of the Realm Act. The charge arising from the second article was dismissed, but for the first article Keell was sentenced to a fine of £100 or three months imprisonment, and Wolfe to £25 or two months. Both refused to pay and were imprisoned. The whole affair at least proved *Freedom's* office to be quite a tempting place for the police, for it was raided three more times in the course of the next year.

By the time of the arrests Keell and Wolfe had become companions and the then 40-year-old Lilian was pregnant, so she was kept in the hospital at Holloway Prison. Worried about the possible effects on the child, she paid her fine two weeks before she was due for release. After the birth of Tom Junior she withdrew from frontline agitation and engaged mainly in support work.

The raids intimidated professional print firms, and in the absence of Keell and Wolfe the job of finding alternative methods of keeping the paper going fell to temporary editor Percy Meachem. Very much the hero of the hour, Meachem brought out the mothballed oscillator printer originally used for the *Commonweal*, *Torch* etc and once again brought it back to working order. In a letter to Max Nettlau he notes:

With emery cloth, oil can and spanner I spent from 8am on Monday morning till 6pm on Saturday — one week — I spent doing nothing but turn the handle in half-hour to one-hour shifts to make the machine run smoothly. After one week it did and we were able to defy the attempts of the authorities so that *Freedom* and *The Voice of Labour* were printed whilst Keell was in prison. F Sellars, A Mancer and myself.

No-one helped us those 14 dreary weeks, daily expecting arrest, to bring out *Freedom*. Sellars laid on the paper, I turned the wheel for one-hour spells which Mancer took off. Mancer gave me ten minutes' rest. In this manner the papers were brought out.

On July 27th 1916, we printed 4,000 sheets on one side. Cut in half these would have made 8,000 4-page Freedom papers. Of these over 7,000 were ordered but alas A Mancer had a nervous breakdown on the Friday and could not turn up till on the Saturday am. At 9am we were raided and it was a finish as far as we were concerned. Four months — 18 months — two-year sentences for refusing to become soldiers (the hired assassins of the propertied class) was the fate both of Comrade Sellars and myself. Mancer's case was tragic. We found he had been taking drugs to bony himself up — alas too much did he take — with the result — a nervous collapse. He put on khaki but the lamp still flickered. He deserted from time to time — walking to London seeking the help of comrades to hide from the military.

During the second raid officers took vital parts of the printer as well and further production looked impossible until help was offered from an unexpected quarter — the Independent Labour Party, which provided its own facilities. Once Wolfe and Keell returned they managed to keep *Freedom* going via the ILP, Utopia Press and their own grit. Even more amazingly they actively expanded the press's offerings, publishing a small monthly paper called *Satire* from December 1916 to April 1918 (when it was suppressed by a raid which stole all related documents and money). Edited by a deaf-mute contributor since before the war called Leonard Motler, it is notable for publishing perhaps the first serious anarchist critiques of the Russian Revolution in English, noting in December 1917:

> The Russian Revolution is running agley [askew]. These little things happen when the people permit new rulers to pose as their saviours, instead of saving themselves by running the country on their own.

Satire was about as devil-may-care as it could be in its approach, given the circumstances, getting the Press raided twice more on November 20th 1917 and February 14th 1918, along with the printers in April 1918 — this last saw it shut down entirely.

As time went on most of the remaining group dissolved, many fleeing to the US and from 1918 the British anarchist movement found itself in continual crisis. Radicals were for the most part overjoyed with the victory of Lenin over Russian feudalism and rushed to support the Bolsheviks who were fighting to hold off the (Westminster-backed) Whites. There was plenty to be done in undermining Winston Churchill's expeditionary force as it attempted to re-install the aristocratic system.*

Women radicals meanwhile threw themselves into the suffragette movement, and pacifists into the peace movement. Most foreign activists left or were deported (almost all the Germans left or were removed via prisoner swaps), depriving the anarchists of their most able supporters. The large part of the Russian-speaking community left to aid the new revolutionary government, the French comrades largely integrated into everyday life in Britain, and the community of Jewish radicals collapsed after the departure of key figures Rudolf Rocker and Molly Witkop, who had been transferred to the Netherlands.

As time went on it was mainly Keell alone who did all the production work in this hollowed-out environment, with Wolfe organising distribution, occasionally helped by first Meachem and then by William Charles Owen, who came to live with Keell and Wolfe for two years. Nettlau did eventually also return to writing for the paper after the war ended, but in contrast to his prior ability to help with *Freedom*'s funding, post-war inflation had wiped out his savings leaving him, at points, reliant on food parcels sent by friends, including Keell.

W C Owen

Freedom's final days of decline left it unable to make much of a mark on the most important event of that decade for the working class, the General Strike of May 1926. The paper, now largely monthly but beset by such financial difficulties that it was unable to produce an April issue at all, came out as normal for its May and June issues, almost entirely untouched by a now disinterested government, and reads in a singularly dry (if optimistic) fashion, with its main analysis of the situation written by William Owen

---

* Particularly notable in this cohort was Tom Mann, who moved from anti-Parliamentary syndicalism to be one of the founder members of what became the Communist Party of Great Britain.

and 'Senex' — the pen name of Mark Schmidt, a well-read Jewish militant who would go on to help found *Vanguard* in the US before turning towards Leninism. Taking up the centenary book:

> In the decade after the war *Freedom's* existence was a long struggle for survival, one appeal for help following the other. Except for a few comrades abroad, and W C Owen and Lilian Wolfe, nobody actually came to help. The price of *Freedom* was increased in May 1918 from 1d to 2d; but the income in the mid-1920s was not more than that in 1914, when the printing costs were only about a third of those in 1925.
>
> In December 1926 Keell officially retired as compositor to live off the superannuation income provided for by the Society of Compositors, and when in 1927 the London County Council gave notice to quit 127 Ossulston Street, as the whole quarter was to be pulled down, he issued a last desperate appeal, again to no avail. Finally, with the agreement of Lilian Wolfe and Owen, he decided to close down *Freedom*.

On this last part however Cores again offers a slightly different slant, noting that:

> The movement declined after the war and Tom Keell ended the publication of *Freedom* saying that he "laid down his own as editor for the last time". But there was an outstanding debt of £100 and the Freedom Group was reconstituted, John Turner, William Wess, with one or two other old Freedom comrades joining them, and the £100 was eventually cleared off.

With Ossulston Street's demolition in 1928 as part of a slum clearance program and Keell's ostensible retirement, Cores and Turner wanted to restart the paper in 1929. According to Cores, Keell rejected this idea out of hand, taking both the ancient printer and *Freedom's* stores of pamphlets with him when he moved to Whiteway Colony* in the Cotswolds with Lilian.

---

* Founded by a Quaker journalist on Tolstoyan principles in 1898, Whiteway, near Stroud, was even at the time a controversial spot, having been declared a "failed experiment" by Mahatma Ghandi as early as 1909, but it retained friendly links with the anarchist movement for many years. It still exists and retains some traditions from its founding, though is no longer any sort of radical hub

Keell himself on the other hand raged that the likes of Cores and Turner had continually demanded the paper be kept going while not raising a finger to help, leaving him with little choice.

Both sides were clearly embittered at this point. Keell was, evidently, wrong that there was no appetite for hard work from his critics, as the production of a rival *Freedom (New Series)* from 1929 would prove (see below). But support for both that and his own project certainly was lacking from the wider movement, which had been decimated not only by the war but by the turn of so many towards the seeming success of Bolshevism as well. At this point, the scene seems to have been one of fractiousness and exhaustion and it's quite easy to see both Keell's bitterness and that of Cores, Turner and the rest as an understandable response amid the vast disappointment and trauma of the time. Their once gloriously optimistic movement had been all but wiped out by war, the capitalists were triumphant and, within the socialist left, Leninism was ascendant.

Clockwise from above: community members building a house at the Whiteway Colony in 1925, Marie Louise Berneri speaks at a Glasgow rally in 1945, Lilian Wolfe selling *War Commentary*, the Bristol bookshop and a pre-war sketch of Red Lion Passage

1928-1945
The wilderness and World War II

Keell's *Freedom* did not entirely disappear despite his retirement. From 1928 there was an irregular *Freedom Bulletin*, which continued to be published until 1932 by Keell and Wolfe from Whiteway, 15 issues being produced in all by the Workers' Friend printing set-up, Emmanuel Michaels and B Derzanski being responsible. Around 1,100 copies were produced of each issue, 800 being distributed, until the *Bulletin*'s principle financial backer Elisabeth Archer, a Californian, dropped out due to the Depression. The old printer, which had produced a vast chunk of the literature of British anarchists for nearly 60 years, would end its days being used as a learning aid for children of the colony.

Lilian was largely the breadwinner through this time as they raised their son, who had been born in 1916 shortly after her prison stint, and she kept what remained of that *Freedom* going by running health food stores (see People, page 291).

At the same time however a rival *Freedom (New Series)* was also produced by the opponents of Keell, principally under John Turner as publisher and treasurer with support from George Cores, Ambrose Barker, Len Harvey and Oscar Swede from 1930-34. They initially launched their monthly journal in May 1929.

The group was able to restart talks at the Food Reform Restaurant in Furnival Street, Holborn, but financially their project was a disaster. The onset of the Depression in October 1929, while not so horrifically damaging as it was in the US, hit Europe hard and for Turner's *Freedom*, meant an income of just £2.5.0 a month (approx £381 today, using commodity labour value) when production costs were £6 (£1,016). The Turner group was not made up of people with such deep pockets, and by 1931 the accounts had run dry, leading Turner to call time until Cores managed to recruit a new printer, Tube worker John Humphrey, to keep *Freedom (NS)* going via voluntary labour. Turner dropped out shortly afterwards, and died in 1934.

Supported by Fred Stroud, Cores managed to produce an eight-page monthly of 1,000 copies going until August 1936. That group could be found meeting at 144 High Holborn for several years, and held open-air talks at Hyde Park, but were poorly resourced and largely isolated from the wider anarchist movement in part due to their generally pro-Kropotkin perspective. They could pull in no major speakers and indeed were almost entirely ignored by Emma Goldman when she visited London. They put out the paper regardless, along with leaflets attacking Italian fascism, circulated to Australia, Canada, France, India and the US, drawing on the anti-fascist work of the remaining Italian comrades in London. Cores noted:

> We received extremely little outside support, probably owing to the fact that we were only poor working people, with no "distinguished" or well-to-do persons among us.
> The best friend to our indoor meetings was Frank Ambrose Ridley of the Independent Labour Party, who I am pleased to say, lectured to our most successful meeting. He was always willing to help us. I felt so grateful to him that I could not speak in opposition, though I was opposed to many of his opinions. Professor Herbert Read did come once, and lectured to our final meeting in high Holborn, which was very successful too.*

The situation between the last few holdouts of the original *Freedom* collective, on both sides, was so dire that, writing in 1938, Goldman would remark in a letter to Helmut Rudiger: "The London Freedom Group has been sleeping and quarreling for years," a sentiment heartily concurred with from 1935 by a new recruit, then still at school — Albert Meltzer, who found the group's activities to "lack relevance".

The 15-year-old East Londoner, upon joining the Freedom Group of Cores, found himself surrounded by older people who were in no fit state to begin the mammoth task of rebuilding British anarchism from the ground up. Writing in his memoir *I Couldn't Paint Golden Angels* he describes the scene:

> The pool in which the anarchists had swum had now been drained: the First World War had isolated the whole socialist movement from the working class, except in the heavy industrial areas where class struggle went on regardless of the war. Many had chosen conscientious objection, then a

---

* Read, already a celebrated cultural writer and critic, would continue to support Freedom Press in its various incarnations into the 1950s, providing a key link to the intellectual set and Bohemian London.

hard option, but this, however admirable, left them isolated from the mass in the Army, though if they joined the Army they often silently disappeared and it was thought they were lost in the general casualty list.

Years later an old militant who had been in the anarchist and shop stewards movements, Kate Sharpley, revealed to me that every one of the Deptford anarchist males disappeared that way.

She lost her boyfriend, brother and father in the War, the former (an anarchist) almost certainly by "disappearance" rather than casualty, and she had thrown their medals when presented in Queen Mary's face.

Though possibly the anarchists did not lose as great a number to other parties as is sometimes supposed, they rarely recruited anyone in Britain either in the 1920s and early '30s; waxing and waning according to birth and death like a doomed Indian tribe. Everyone in the old London Freedom Group (give or take a few, usually second generation libertarians) was up to 50 years old, or a lot over that. I was a rare exception.

His contemporary Tom Brown (see People, page 226), a Tynesider who had moved to London to work on planes, saw similarly that:

In summer 1936, all that remained of anarchism was the old Freedom Group of London and the Jewish *Worker's Friend* Group. Freedom was a very old organisation and all its members were elderly, too, having spent most of their lives in the cause of anarchism; some had known William Morris and been in Trafalgar Square on Bloody Sunday. These good people worked with handset type and a treadle machine to publish their paper, *Freedom*, monthly.

Brown was a good example of a radical *Freedom* had been unable to reach in the glory days of syndicalism — his experience of the tail end of the Great Unrest saw nothing of Malatesta's or Kropotkin's writing and he would not learn of the paper's existence until long after the Great War had ended.

As the last flames of the original *Freedom* groups sputtered towards their end in the late 1930s then it would, ironically, be the rise of fascism in Spain and the revolution it spawned that fanned a revival in English anarchism, bringing together a group that would eventually revive the Press.

Spain's last stand

When the Spanish Revolution began in 1936, it was in an atmosphere where, across Europe and in Latin America, anarchist and anarcho-syndicalist groups had been decimated by the rise of autocratic governments.

Following the Great War, the apparent success of the Russian Revolution had been damaging for anarchism, seemingly providing evidence that the theories of Marx and Lenin were correct. However in 1922, following a final breakdown in relations between syndicalist groups and the Russia-backed Profintern international of red trade unions, there was still a major mass movement to point to in mainland Europe. Unions such as USI in Italy, FAUD in Germany, CGT in Portugal and most of all the gigantic CNT in Spain brought together millions within the overtly anarcho-syndicalist International Working Men's Association.

Leading CNT fighter Buenaventura Durruti

By 1936 all that was over. Every major anarchist organisation bar the CNT had been crushed by the forces of Benito Mussolini, Adolf Hitler and Gomes da Costa, jailing, torturing and disappearing countless militants as they went, leaving just Spain to raise the red and black flag.

So when General Mola (later succeeded by Franco) followed in those dictators' infamous footsteps and revolted against the Spanish Republican government, the very last hope for a popular libertarian socialist revolution was at threat. The CNT responded with spectacular force, capturing Barcelona and almost single-handedly denying the reactionaries an easy victory, leading to a three-year war of attrition in which social revolution would go hand-in-hand with brutal violence, Republican infighting and eventual betrayal by the Stalin-backed statists.

Britain's government would, to its endless shame, refuse to help the Republican cause to "prevent escalation of conflict across Europe" — though in reality its most senior figures were quite open about preferring Franco, even going so far as to sabotage their own official "non-intervention" position by passing on intelligence information and using dirty tricks to protect his major ports. After World War II it would compound this disgusting behaviour by lending Franco resources as he bloodily repressed dissent, on the grounds his dictatorship provided a bulwark against the USSR.

The Freedom Group in London, despite being almost the only entity in the city that anarchists could plausibly rally to, was unable to cope with the task of building support for the CNT. An attempt was made by Ralph Barr, an activist in Hammersmith with the Communist Party-dominated National Unemployed Workers Movement (which had sprung up after the Great War), to push through internal reforms, which led several older members to quit, such as George Cores, while the remainder either moved over to the shortlived, Glasgow-based *Fighting Call* (Oct 1936-Feb 1937) or like Leah Feldman (see People, page 238) signed up with the drive for Spanish solidarity, ending that generation of *Freedom*. The official closure of *Freedom Bulletin* in 1937 meant that those final issues, sponsored in their entirety by the British office of the CNT-FAI, were to bookend the only sustained period in which no *Freedom* was to come out at all, and the title which had stood since 1886 would stay dormant for another eight years.

At the same time however a better plan was afoot, once again drawing on the international community for its initial drive, in this case the Italians. The key figures in the founding of *Spain and the World* were Maria Luisa Berneri (see People, page 223), her partner Vero Recchioni, Berneri's well-known father Camillo and Francesco Galasso, who between them raised enthusiasm and funds for a well-produced, forthright new paper. Its role was intended as an antidote to other left-leaning publications, particularly the *New Statesman* and *News Chronicle* which had been touting heavily for Soviet policy in Spain at the time, which was already heavily antagonistic to the aims of the anarchist revolutionaries there.

They were joined in this endeavour by Tom Keell and Lilian Wolfe, who shuttered the *Bulletin* to add their efforts and leant enormous encouragement to the new group. A direct continuity from the original *Freedom* was thus, relatively plausibly, claimed through the participation of members from both sides of the 1927 split. Keell certainly regarded *Spain and the World* as a successor to the original *Freedom* up to his death in 1938, lending his address and authority to use Freedom Press Distribution for pamphlet sales, while Wolfe in particular would continue on from the old Freedom Group to the new, remaining a core collective member for decades to come.

Clockwise from left, the King Bomba, Emidio Recchioni, Maria Luisa and Gionvanna Berneri, and Camillo Berneri

The Italian anarchists

The group of Italians who initially backed *Spain and the World* was well connected, highly mobile and multilingual, with both the Recchioni and Berneri families having produced well-known and well-travelled anarchist militants through two generations. The Berneris in particular were known across Europe thanks to the activities of Camillo and his wife Giovanna, who had been forced to flee from Italy to France in 1926 having taken part in the failed resistance against the fascist dictator Benito Mussolini.

Camillo, then in his early 30s, had gained a reputation as a dangerous intellectual while writing for *Umanita Nova*, the organ of the Anarchist Union of Italy (now the USI) and was immediately hounded by the French police. Betrayed by an undercover, he was expelled from the country in 1929, forcing him to temporarily leave Giovanna to raise their two daughters Maria Luisa* and Gilliana alone as he travelled to every western European country, being kicked out of each in turn, eventually being allowed to resettle in France as he had nowhere else to go.

As the Berneri sisters grew up they were thus surrounded by Italian political exiles and lived a precarious existence on the edge of Paris, where Giovanna ran a grocery shop which became a hub of contacts for the movement. 'Marie Luis' was drawn into these circles and briefly became involved with a French paper, *Revision*.

Vero Recchioni meanwhile was the London-raised son of Emidio, a business owner and associate of Malatesta who had fled to England after participating in a plot against the life of former Italian Prime Minister Francesco Crispi. Setting up a delicatessen at 37 Old Compton Street, Soho, cheekily named 'King Bomba', Emidio became a well-known face on the radical circuit, with his shop being regularly frequented by prominent socialists such as Emma Goldman, Sylvia Pankhurst and later, George Orwell. His cash was behind many of the initiatives of the time, including providing a stipend that supported Max Nettlau after his bankruptcy. Emidio maintained close ties with the old country, to the point where he was allegedly involved with raising an assassination fund and financing two plots to kill Mussolini, most notably that of Angelo Sbardellotto (who was arrested on the Italian border in 1932, tortured for a confession and killed by firing squad). Donald Rooum remembers being told by Vero that Emidio never used to tell his family about these exploits, and indeed once took his son to Paris for "sightseeing", only for Vero to end up stuck in the hotel while Emidio went off to plot with his co-conspirators.

---

* Confusingly, her name was slightly changed twice in her lifetime, once from Italian to French, and then to English.

By the mid-1930s anarchists within the Italian community in London were under heavy pressure, with fascist money and propaganda raising its leaders to dominance. Emidio in particular had opened King Bomba's doors to the anti-fascists and was heavily targeted for reprisals as a result via vandalism and denunciations which led to a near-total boycott of his business. An article in *The Gloucester Citizen* of Tuesday July 4th 1933 recounts that following a *Daily Telegraph* piece published about the Sbardellotto affair:

> The moment the article appeared, Mr Recchioni began to receive "black looks" from everyone. Things were scrawled on the shutters of his shop, there were insulting remarks, people passing him the street turned their heads away, and when he went to a cinema people turned and said "what cheek for a man like that to come in here". Business people wrote asking that his accounts should closed, money was sent back from charities to which he had subscribed, and finally the Italian Chamber of Commerce here wrote him for an explanation. Indignant at the treatment he had received Mr Recchioni resigned from the Chamber, but that did not prevent them from solemnly expelling him from membership.

He sued the *Telegraph* for libel and, due to a lack of evidence on the paper's part, won £1,177, a huge sum which largely saved his business and allowed him to continue funding anti-fascist activities. The secret services had a great deal of information on Emidio from Sbardellotto's confession, but refused to either extradite him or jail him themselves — whether this was reticence was linked to his known personal friendship with Prime Minister Ramsay MacDonald or not is unknown. He died in 1934 leaving a substantial legacy, and is buried in Kensal Green Cemetery.

Vero was, as he grew up, increasingly heavily involved in these conflicts and in the year his father passed was becoming active in the campaign against Mussolini. It was during this period that he travelled to France to meet with

Camillo Berneri and fell in love with Marie Luis — though he was quickly arrested due to his propaganda work against the Italian dictator and deported back to Britain in 1935.

When he returned to London he anglicised his name to Vernon Richards and, alongside Marie Luis in Paris, briefly published *Free Italy/Italia Libera*. Backed by his father's cash and a handful of resourced allies still remaining in London (notably doctor Francesco Galasso, cafe owner Vittorio Taborelli and tailor Decio Anzani) he, Marie Luis and Camillo were in a prime position to organise for *Spain and the World*.

Marie Luis Berneri did not move to London in the period when *Spain and the World* was being set up in December 1936 — she did however begin writing for the paper immediately, as MLB. Camillo meanwhile headed for Catalonia, where he would set up *Guerra di Classe* in Barcelona and began writing prolifically about the war, the revolution and the new anarchist society. A number of pieces published by *Spain and the World* were his work. Others were translated direct from powerful Spanish anarchist paper *Solidaridad Obrera*, giving *Spain and the World* a uniquely strong link to the conflict's goings-on.* Tom Keell, though still based in Whiteway, immediately volunteered as publisher for the new paper, helping to refound Freedom Press Distributors with the intent of selling some of the enormous hoard of classic pamphlets he and Lilian Wolfe retained. Whiteway was listed as the official publishing address for the first issue, printed by VWH Press (TU) in Farringdon.

The official London offices were at 207 Goswell Road, just a few doors down from where Guy Aldred had once held anarchist meetings in his mother's basement, and this was also used as an address for donations of aid to the Spanish fighters. It was not however used as a contact point for volunteers to fight, as the CNT had said they did not need to be looking after green recruits who couldn't shoot, speak Spanish or navigate the Catalan countryside, much preferring guns and ammo.

---

* Freedom would later return the favour, printing *Solidaridad Obrera* in exile during the 1940s.

It was therefore Vero who did most of the work of running the new paper, with a handful of writers and some help from the old guard (especially the tireless Lilian Wolfe as administrator, commuting from Whiteway), which also helped produce speakers at solidarity events. The four-page publication came out fortnightly, priced at tuppence and included writing from Max Nettlau, Pierre Ramus, Harry Kelly and Emma Goldman. Their biggest English name was Herbert Read, a celebrated writer and art critic who would continue to contribute to *Spain and the World* and its successor titles into the 1950s. The popular travel writer and novelist Ethel Mannin was also supportive during and after the war, having been disillusioned about the USSR during a visit to Russia in 1936. From 1937 the group benefited from writing by Augustus John, best known as a leading British portrait artist of the early 20th century, painting luminaries such as Thomas Hardy, W B Yeats and Lawrence of Arabia.

Augustus John

Meltzer also mentions another artist, Mark Gertler, a passionate Jewish portrait painter, who he says worked with the anarchists on Spanish solidarity, and was rendered so distraught by the Republican defeat that he killed himself in 1939.

Vero continued to receive help and advice from Camillo Berneri until that celebrated figure was murdered during the May Days of 1937, when the PSUS (Communist Party) officers, likely on direct orders from Stalin, dragged him to their headquarters where he was shot in the back. Writing on the front page of the May 15th edition of the paper, Vero noted:

At the age of 40, when his life was most intense, when his lifelong ideal was being realised, death has claimed him at its victim. But our comrade is not dead. His work, his abnegation, must live in our minds and must be a source of inspiration to us to continue in our struggle for what is just and noble. Camillo Berneri's sacrifice, Durruti's and Ascaso's sacrifices, the sacrifice of the hundreds of thousands of Workers fighting in Spain, must be the signal for the awakening of a new spirit amongst the workers of the world. It is that spirit alone which can bring a victory of the workers over International reaction and Capitalistic interest …

The anarchist movement, with the death of Camillo Berneri loses one of its most devoted apostles. We cannot replace him, but we can learn from his experience and knowledge.

After her father was assassinated Marie Luis joined Vero permanently in England, marrying him shortly afterwards to gain naturalisation and slightly Anglicising her name in official documents to 'Marie Louise' Richards (though she kept Berneri in practice). Her contacts, charisma and intelligence provided a driving force behind the ideas of *Spain and the World* and it was largely through her that the paper remained on the pulse of what was happening in the war.

Especially following her father's death she, and the paper, were heavily critical of compromises being made by the CNT-FAI group that dominated the union's policymaking and which had entered the Republican government in September 1936, placing *Freedom* in conflict with the union's London bureau. It also eventually led to a break with Max Nettlau after an article appeared severely criticising Federica Montseny in particular when she became Minister of Health in the Republican government. Nettlau, very untypically, supported Montseny absolutely uncritically and thus cut himself off from active London anarchism for good, surviving World War II in Amsterdam, largely overlooked by the Nazis, until his death in 1944.

As the war rolled on towards its bitter conclusion the paper railed against French Popular Front collusion with the fascists — uniforms were sent from Levalloi, gas masks from Indre-et-Loire — printed Emma Goldman's optimistic appraisal of the works taking place in revolutionary Catalonia and raised hundreds of pounds to aid the orphans of slain revolutionary fighters. The paper managed to maintain an entire orphanage in Catalonia using this money.

Moving in with the newly-formed International Anti-fascist Solidarity Group* at 21 Frith Street in January 1938, it began commenting on a wider range of subjects and analysing the achievements of the Spanish anarchist communes. The building was owned by Galasso, who ran his practice from the ground floor and offered a peppercorn rent to both the paper and Emma Goldman's campaign.

Spain and the World called for the release of anti-fascist prisoners in Republican prisons and cursed the Communist Party — not least in Britain where the Communist-run *Daily Worker* was faithfully repeating the Kremlin's line about the war. Vero noted in acid tones that, as it became clear the bulk of the revolutionary work was being done by self-organised anarchist collectives, the Stalinists

---

* This was run by Emma Goldman, who was acting as the CNT-FAI's representative in Britain.

were having to change tack:

> Before, the Spanish Communist Party (CP) stated that industries were collectivised by means of violence and coercion. Now, instead the CP has declared itself in favour of them. Even its press has temporarily ceased in its attacks on the anarchists, though, so that this volte-face should not be too obvious, it draws a distinction between the 'good' and 'bad' anarchists. *Humanite* (Organ of the French CP) goes to the trouble of publishing a photo of our comrade Cipriano Mera describing him as a 'good general' etc.
>
> Naturally our anarchist comrades will accept these generous remarks for what they are worth. The true aims of the CP are quite clearly defined in their official organ *Pravda* (December 17th 1936): "As to Catalonia, the purging of the Trotsky and anarcho-syndicalist elements has commenced; this work will be conducted with the same energy as that with which it was done in the USSR".

This along with a series of talks at the old Emily Davis Rooms in High Holborn, featuring speakers such as Jomo Kenyatta, George Padmore, Dianah Stock, Read and Tom Brown, gave the Freedom Group a higher profile but also brought it into conflict with the Leninist left. Outdoor meetings, primarily run by Tom Williams, Patrick Monks and Albert Meltzer, saw several confrontations.

That year would also see the death of Tom Keell, who passed away on June 26th. Oddly, no obituary appears in the following issue, which merely changes the name of the publisher to Sonia Clements (nee Edelman).

Spain and the World collapsed at the end of 1938 as fascists rolled tanks over the bones of revolutionary Catalonia. Most of the London movement, which had sustained itself mainly through supporting the now all-but-defeated anarchist faction, fell into a shell-shocked stupor. Emma Goldman, her campaign at an end, left for Toronto where she worked and lectured through to her death in 1940.

The loss of momentum forced a re-evaluation of the paper, which had continually run with a whopping deficit averaging between £150 and £200 despite a solid sales base and regular donations. In its wake an immediate effort was made to set up on a new footing, leading to the foundation in London of the Anarchist Federation of Britain (AFB). Despite its grandiose name the group was stating intent rather than reality, and when this "new group" set up a replacement paper, *Revolt!*, the names of the core editorial team were familiar ones — Marie Louise Berneri and Vero Richards, joined by Anarchist Syndicalist Union general secretary Ralph Sturgess and his fellow militant Tom Brown. Additional support came from Glaswegian anarchists Frank and Mary Leech, the former editors of *Fighting Call*. Recounting the forming of *Revolt!* in a 1968 article for *Direct Action* Brown recounts:

> The comrades, mostly fairly young, who remained after the end of the Spanish struggle, reassembled; at first only three persons, who made anti-war posters and pasted them in prominent parts of London, then enough to form a group and link with groups in Scotland — the Anarchist Federation of Britain was formed.
>
> Serious discussion produced unanimity on the kind of organisation we wanted. "Everyone was sickened by the coffee-bar anarchists, who specialised in "the Ego", individualism, hating the working class, being "anti-organisation" and forming organisations to propagate that idea, or had a new theory of society every few months. Such persons had created a bad image of anarchism. We all wanted a sincere, responsible organisation. We wanted anarchism to influence society, to be revolutionary, bring about change, not to be just a permanent grouse. We all insisted on syndicalism and internationalism, we were all anti-war.

Revolt! was however also intended to be recognised as a direct successor to the previous paper, and while it branched out in its topics somewhat the position in Spain remained at the top of the agenda. The orphans fund was reopened, and articles lambasting the victorious Franco were numerous. Vero, as he closed the *Spain and the World* press fund in *Revolt's* first issue on February 11th 1939, noted:

> *Revolt!* is a continuation and intensification of this work, and I hope that all our comrades in England and on the continent will give their continued support to *Revolt!* in the same way as they have for the past two years supported *Spain and the World*.

Though a lively read, *Revolt!* Didn't gain the same audience as *Spain and the World*, only running for a few issues before being killed off by fast-moving events — namely the beginning of World War II. The mooted AFB was, too, slightly ahead of its time and Sturgess having left over a disagreement with the editorial line, Berneri, Richards, Brown and Albert Meltzer, supported by the likes of Lilian Wolfe, Peta Edsall and Faye Robertson, were the remaining members of the publishing team when in 1939 they decided to rejig it again to respond to the beginning of a new European conflict, under the name *War Commentary*.

Surviving World War II

War Commentary, an expanded version of a vague bulletin idea run initially from Vero's flat (the official address was a derelict backroom in Newbury Street), was founded in December 1939. It was essentially a wing of the AFB, which had been unofficially running earlier but was more formally, if secretly, founded at a conference on April 28th 1940, aiming to unite the anarchist movement in Britain. Alongside it was an official bulletin of the AFB, *Workers in Uniform*. This incarnation of the AFB ran a programme excluding both pacifists and anyone supporting the war, incorporating mainly comrades in Glasgow and London but also elsewhere.

As an established publisher before the war, Freedom Press was allowed to obtain paper for both the new publication and a number of books and pamphlets. The first issue, consisting of 16 duplicated pamphlet-sized pages and sold in just three bookshops, began what was to be a monthly production until 1941 when six supplements were issued, and from 1942 *War Commentary* appeared twice a month.

Its initial editorial took a strident line against taking up common cause with the capitalists against Germany, consistently opposing fundamental assumptions made in government policies. In particular, *War Commentary's* writers were adamantly against allowing the very warmongering, manipulative, exploitative world powers which had crushed revolutions, enabled and encouraged the rise of a Hitler, a Mussolini, a Franco, to absolve themselves of responsibility and pose as defenders of liberty now that their own interests were at stake:

> That many sincere anti-fascists believe in the "righteousness" of this war, quite independently of the propaganda served up by the Conservative and so called Radical Press, is not surprising. They say: "We, who have always shouted that

fascism must be crushed should, now that an opportunity presents itself, act in accordance with our principles". Their actions are, therefore, governed not by reason but their desire to prove to themselves and to others that they are consistent both in speech and in action.

There are others calling themselves revolutionaries who believe that war creates a revolution. The tragic consequences of the last war have apparently not taught them anything. Today the "strategists" are in good company with the British government which has been doing its utmost to convince the British people that there will be a revolution in Germany before long.

They omit to add that in the event of a revolution in Germany they will crush it with the same ruthlessness that they propose to crush Nazism. Mr Churchill, with his past experience, will see to that.

Finally, there is that vast mass of people with no opinions; who are fed exclusively by the poisoned pens of the capitalist press, and the noble words uttered by their political leaders through that most effective channel of propaganda, the BBC.

All these categories of "anti-fascists", referred to above, are either mistaken or misguided, for in no circumstances can this war be justified; in no circumstances can this war be justified; in no circumstances can it bring peace.

It also pulled no punches over the capitulation of trade union leaderships to the demands of wartime production, with Tom Brown thundering in an April 1941 article 'Trade Unions in the War':

The trade unions were formed as instruments of class war using the strike. They now collaborate with employers and the State and abandon the strike. Most of the war time measures of repression directed against the workers are operated by such trade union representatives as Ernest Bevin (appointed as Minister for Labour and National Service by Churchill), in the service of the State. As all this is done in the name of national unity one might expect it to be applied to all classes, but it is a very one-sided business. Men who have worked all their lives are forbidden to leave work or even the service of a particular employer, but we have yet to see the Mayfair playboys formed into labour gangs.

Workers are being fined and threatened with imprisonment

for refusing to do unpaid fire-watching, thus giving to their employers one week's labour per month without wages. Vet when (Minister of Supply) Herbert Morrison was asked in Parliament if he would conscript directors he declined to do so, declaring they might have responsibilities elsewhere.

The editors were unsure of the new publication's potential reception, but it proved to be popular among peace groups and surprisingly with around 200 serving soldiers (its innocuous name and small format made it unremarkable in the mess hall). Meltzer estimated an overall readership of a little over 2,000 (rising to 4,000 later on) and another 4,000 for *Workers in Uniform.*

The *Freedom* team was also able to organise talks on the experiences of Spain, including to the Peace Pledge Union* and Albert Meltzer credited these with bringing in a generation of militants to the anarchist scene in the 1941-43 period, pitching the press towards a long-running association with the peace movement. A Special Branch report from one meeting in November 1941, reporting that Winston Churchill was being named "as much a brigand as Hitler", noted an attendance of more than 400 people. First among the speakers at such meetings was Marie Louise Berneri, with Meltzer noting her preternatural calm in addressing hostile and rowdy groups on all number of matters — permissive sexuality in front of crews of "lusty merchant seamen", for example.

Early amongst the new intake of writers and backers would be John Hewetson (see People, page 244), with Brylcreem model (later psychologist) Tony Gibson, Elizabeth and Tom Earley, Jankel Adler, Ken Hawkes, Laurie Hislam, Gerald Vaughn, George Melly and many more following suit, largely replicating the situation which had gone on in the 19th century of drawing people into the collective's orbit from other progressive sources. Hewetson in particular became a core member of the Freedom Group and showed a clear-eyed approach to the issue of war in *War Commentary's* October 1940 issue, noting that "everyone hates war, but almost no-one understands it, except the anarchists, who perceive that war is a symptom ... of an underlying disease — the contemporary social and economic order".

As anarchists regrouped around the paper via the Peace Pledge

---

* The PPU was easily the largest gathering of conscientious objectors in the country at the time, though its real membership of 8,500 in 1941 was far lower than the number of supposed pledge takers

Union and to a lesser extent the Independent Labour Party, many people connected to Freedom Press became conscientious objectors* including both Vernon Richards, who worked in a reserved occupation as a railway engineer, and Albert Meltzer who, having registered, never received a solid reply back and found himself essentially blacklisted until near the end of the war. His limbo status would prove extremely useful in the first few months, as he was able to work on both *War Commentary* articles and *Workers in Uniform* out of the lobby of the Strand Palace Hotel until 1941-43, when he moved to Blackpool to work for comedian Roy Barbour.

Not everyone would escape the baleful eye of the State however, and there were some anti-fascists caught up, including Mat Kavagnah who was interned in Essex with a number of fellow anarchists, anti-fascists, Irish rebels, German Jews — and fascist sympathisers. After it became clear what a huge PR disaster it would be for the public to hear that anti-fascists and Jews had been put in camps with actual fascists, most were swiftly released again. A sort of unofficial compromise was reached in this early part of the war which would allow conscientious objectors to remain mostly free, on the grounds that, frankly, the Army didn't want a bunch of anarchists and Quakers messing up their efforts to form a coherent fighting force. Even so, the government wasn't shy of using dirty tricks against activists it felt were problematic and within the pages of *War Commentary* there is a steady trickle of names of people arrested for "refusing a medical examination." Tony Gibson was jailed no fewer than three times before being shifted to ambulance driving and farm work, his fellow conscientious objectors Denis McGlynn and Lewis Gordon were similarly treated.

There was also trouble from the left, *War Commentary* again being heavily critical about the Communist Party's opportunism and adherence to Moscow's line. An article in April 1943 for example notes CP members "blacklegging" on an ASLEF trains strike supporting a victimised comrade, calling strikers "pro-fascist" and demanding "harder work and many more sacrifices".

Once Russia entered the war in June 1941, the Stalinists went from an anti-war position to full flag-waving patriot mode after and had, as recalled by Donald Rooum, since done their best to shop anti-militarists to the police. A short article in the March

---

* Meltzer would later scathingly note that the expertise in securing a non-combat job the movement had acquired would draw many middle class draft-dodgers to its orbit.

1942 issue of *Freedom* meanwhile reports a meeting which had been called by the CP to drum up support for its campaign to lift a government ban on party paper *The Daily Worker.*

> Three members of the Oxford Friends of Freedom Press were selling *War Commentary* outside a "Freedom of the Press" rally organised by the Communist Party recently. The sellers met with great success before the meeting, but afterwards the CP employed its usual tactics in attempting to suppress the right of our comrades to put their case before the workers.
>
> After the meeting one of the sellers stood fast inside the door of the Town Hall while the others sold outside. Immediately the former was surrounded by stewards and without a word of warning, thrown into the street. However, selling continued. Annoyed by this success two CPers, who had been in conference with the stewards, came out and tried to "beat up" one of our comrades, tearing up the papers of another, who was in the middle of selling a copy. A seller of *Socialist Appeal* defended our comrades by calling the attention of those around to the CP's "manifest belief" in the Freedom of the Press!
>
> ...
>
> A very large number of *War Commentary* issues were sold as well as many anarchist pamphlets.

Amusingly the following issue reports a whopping £50 donation from Oxford, mostly from support which had flooded in for *Freedom's* right to tell the CP exactly where it could stick its hypocrisies.

In the face of such early difficulties, increasing sales and support for the group nevertheless enabled the team, by 1941, to open a bookshop with large storage basement at Red Lion Passage, run by Meltzer, with the bulk of its initial offerings being pamphlets from the Whiteway stock. The passage through to Red Lion Street was on the south-east corner of Red Lion Square, just across from Conway Hall in Holborn and known for its second-hand bookshops.

Sadly, shortly after it opened the Luftwaffe would, in one of its last major bombing raids of the Blitz on May 11th, flatten most of the area. One unexploded bomb crashed through the roof of Conway Hall, while another burned numbers 18-21 to the ground, including *Freedom's* premises. Almost the entire stock of pre-war pamphlets that Keell and Wolfe had so carefully kept went up in smoke. The entire street was built over in the 1950s as part of the post-war reconstruction and the old site has been covered by a block of flats and a car park, but the outline can still be seen on satellite photos.

Following the fire the office moved to Belsize Road, which was able to accomodate space for meetings, storage and a small bookshop, this being a period when renting was made far cheaper by the rush to get away from German bombs. Freedom was, despite the fire, prospering through this period and managed to raise nearly £500 in a year to both clear its debts and replace much of its stocks of books and pamphlets. Describing it in the Freedom centenary book, Vero notes:

> Belsize Road was a busy office, for by then Freedom Press publications were appearing in large numbers and the booksellers — particularly W H Smiths and Boots — were desperately short of goods to sell (paper rationing) and their business interests came first when deciding whether to stock anarchist and anti-war literature!

By 1944 a second bookshop had been opened in Bristol at 132 Cheltenham Road* and that same year Freedom/the AFB was offered the chance to take over a near-derelict printing firm, Express Printers. The company, known as a specialist in non-Latin language printing, had been left derelict and fallen to the landlords following the death of the owner, Judah Shenfield. A rival printer lent some money on condition that he could take over the Hebrew type, and the rest of the £500 purchase price, depressed because of the bombings, was loaned by members.

The works were a wreck, covered in plaster loosened by the bombs, with already elderly machines (the guillotine was from 1892) and was only made to run at all thanks to the skills of old Dick Pugh, a conscientious objector from World War I. It was based in two buildings down a cramped old path running off Whitechapel High Street, previously best known for hosting relatively upmarket brothels frequented by 19th century farmers on market day, and in the Victorian era for its proximity to a Jack the Ripper murder. Angel Alley would be associated with Freedom Press for the next three-quarters of a century.

Ownership of a printer helped increase capacity markedly,

---

* Now a restaurant, the site is just a few doors down from what would, 67 years later, become a famous eviction resistance mounted by the Telepathic Heights squatted social centre around the time of the 2011 Bristol riots.

persuading Lilian Wolfe to give up her main income running a shop in Stroud to become a full-time administrator for the Press once more — beginning another 25-year stint. Nicolas Walter writes in the *Freedom* centenary book that:

> Lilian Wolfe was the centre of the administration of the Freedom Press at its various premises in London. She was the person on whom every organisation depends — the completely reliable worker who runs the office, opening and closing the shop, answering the telephone and the post, doing the accounts and keeping people in touch, and generally keeping things going, She maintained personal contact with the thousands of people who read the paper and with many other old anarchists and new ones all over the world.

This stability allowed production of the first new pamphlet since the war began, *Trade Unionism and Syndicalism* by Tom Brown. The same year also saw publication of *The March to Death*, a series of anti-war cartoons by John Olday, a German deserter from the Royal Pioneer Corps (the only regiment Germans were allowed to join), with anonymous commentary by Marie-Louise Berneri. The book was popular given its forthright condemnations of Nazis and Allied oppressors alike, selling thousands as it expressed a widespread dissatisfaction with the old social order.

The press additionally, from 1943-47, took on production of *Now*, a journal hitherto produced by George Woodcock as an open ideas platform (carrying both fascists and anarchists) until he plumped for the libertarian team and turned it into a "cultural review of the British anarchist movement" in 1942. Woodcock was heavily disparaged as a careerist by Meltzer in particular, but his carefully-cultivated connections drew in contributions from a wide variety of people including Alex Comfort, George Orwell, Mervyn Peake, Herbert Read and Mulk Raj Anand. Registering as a conscientious objector when the war began, Woodcock worked on an Essex farm through much of the period, before emigrating to to British Colombia in 1949. His most notable work *Anarchism* was one of the most widely-read explainers of its era, having been produced by Pelican, the non-fiction imprint of Penguin — though it was intensely criticised by the movement itself for a self-indulgent claim that anarchism had "died" in 1939.

Lesser-known, but ultimately more important, was the recruitment (through the AFB) of Philip Sansom (see People, page 278), a commercial artist and conscientious objector, who had been heavily influenced by Read and would go on to become a core member of the Freedom Group for several decades. Writing in *Freedom / A Hundred Years* he recalls the scene as he found it:

> Everyone in the AFB was implacably anti-war; some had already served terms of imprisonment as conscientious objectors — one, Elizabeth Earley, for refusing to be conscripted into war industry. Outside the AFB were a number of Spanish CNT refugees, who had managed to get to London in 1939 and who believed the war was a war against fascism, and that after defeating Hitler, the Allies would march on to Madrid and demolish Franco. These were members of their own group of CNT-in-exile who produced their own little duplicated newsletter, but, while being friends and comrades, could not be members of the AFB because of their support for the Churchill-led British government. As a new boy, I was awed by these experienced revolutionaries, but thought them rather arrogant and slightly contemptuous of our little movement, compared to the massive CNT/FAI."

Sansom immediately became an important figure at the press, forming with Hewetson, Berneri and Richards the core of the editorial group, and later became known as a tremendously talented public speaker. But his mention of the CNT/FAI's opposition to the *Freedom* position on World War II is an important precursor to to a major split (see 'A contigious coup', page 76).

Freedom Press vs the State

For much of the first part of the conflict *War Commentary*, critical though it was of the government remained anti-fascist and had been largely overlooked by the State. As the conflict wound to a close however that line began to be seen as dangerously subversive, particularly when in the Spring of 1944 *War Commentary* turned its attention to the question of post-war demobilisation. The paper was, to put it mildly, blunt on the subject, running an article in its May issue entitled 'Mutiny in the British Army' suggesting that soldiers recall the possibilities raised by similar events at the end of the Great War. Straying into tacit endorsement of mutiny for the cause of winning rapid demobilisation, increased pay, better food and shelter and relaxed discipline, it was setting itself up for a fall with the increasingly nervous Westminster government.

This was supplemented by its clearly waxing popularity,

which saw a Mayday rally and a showing of internationalist film *Kameradschaft* draw more than 600 people. One estimate by Vero suggested that Freedom Press titles were being carried in more than 300 bookshops by December 1944. A crackdown duly began that year, opening with a series of house raids and arrests of supporters. One story told by Meltzer in *Anarchists in London 1935-55* recounts:

> The police broke into the home of Fay Stewart. Her dog, Mickey, either not understanding the legal niceties of a magistrate's warrant as regards unwelcome intruders, or determined to live up to the legacy of Michael Bakunin (for whom he was named), bit a police sergeant in the ankle. Many bones came his way from grateful but more inhibited humans.
>
> Stewart was active in our movement throughout the war; she was tragically killed in a lorry accident at the early age of 30 while cycling to her work as an industrial nurse, in the last days of the blackout. Thanks to her vigilance, the addresses of our soldier contacts were saved from the police when John Olday was arrested. She resorted to the trusted English expedient of making them a cup of tea, taking care to light the fire with her files.

Others, such as Tom Earley and Cecil Stone, were arrested and charged with obstruction for selling literature in Hyde Park. Tom Brown was jailed for 15 months in September for "distributing seditious leaflets". Even the thoroughly harmless George Melly, by this time serving in the navy, was nearly court-martialled (though ultimately let off), for distributing "subversive literature", chronicled in his autobiography *Owning Up*:

> Warrant Officer Perkins approached me with a look of grim satisfaction on his face. I was to come up to the locker flat and open my locker. Why, I wondered? The Commander was waiting there looking rather severe. I smiled at him and he didn't smile back, but asked me to open it up. I did so. Warrant Officer Perkins pointed to the Freedom Press pamphlets. The Commander asked me what they were and why I had so many of each. I told him that they were anarchist literature and whenever possible I distributed them among the sailors. A look of total astonishment passed across the Commander's kindly aquiline features.
>
> Did I realise that these were subversive pamphlets aimed

at undermining the State, the Armed Forces, the Church, even the Navy itself? I said yes of course I did, but ...

There was no but. I was on Commander's Defaulters next day and had better recognise the seriousness of the charge. If proven it could lead to a court martial. Shore leave suspended. Warrant Officer Perkins took the pamphlets, but I asked for an example of each to prepare my defence. The Commander nodded. I took them and went aloft, perplexed, to talk to Felix.

Felix was not perplexed at all. Anarchism opposed, both in general and in detail, the whole structure of society from the Head of State down. It was quite specific in declaring that its triumph could only be achieved through revolution. It dismissed all armed forces as the tools of the status quo and elective representation as a sham. I pointed out that so did Bernard Shaw, and yet there was a complete edition of his plays and prefaces in the ship's library. A good point, Felix conceded, and his advice to me was to spend the evening marking suitable passages on such subjects as royalty, God, the military, politicians and anything else relevant in support of my case. I did what he suggested and, before slinging my hammock, had found a selection of quotes which, taken out of context, made the anarchist pamphlets sound understated.

Meltzer was arrested on spurious charges of desertion (he had for years been locked in an argument over his papers with the government), jailed for 14 months and had his possessions seized. On his release he was drafted into the Pioneer Corps where he served in Egypt until 1947. John Olday meanwhile was sent down for a year for "identity fraud" having refused to speak in his own defence at the court. At end of his sentence he was court martialed and jailed for a further two years. He was drafted after he got out, but given a speedy "dishonourable discharge".

Freedom Press's editors were not spared these unwelcome attentions, with visits being made direct to to the Press's offices from Scotland Yard, with an aim of intimidating the editorial team. Notable in these efforts was a visit in which the editors were pressured to register Freedom Press and Express Printers under the Business Act, as it had not done so since it was first established in 1886, or face closure. Another option would have been to give up some information the police wanted. Rather than inform, Vero and John Hewetson walked down the government office that afternoon and registered Freedom Press in their own names.

A contiguous coup

As the State attack was mounted against *War Commentary* there was also a second crisis for the movement, this time internal. As Sansom and Meltzer previously noted, the AFB, which supported and claimed ownership over *War Commentary*, had over the course of the conflict developed both a strong anti-war line and a base in the pacifist movement despite its constitutional ban on such. George Woodcock in particular is listed by Meltzer (who was no fan) as moving the paper towards becoming an independent collective with an intellectualist nonviolent line, upsetting militant working-class comrades in the AFB.

The other major pole of influence in London however, the Spanish CNT in exile, had been supportive of the war as an anti-fascist one and wished to press for the British government to march on Madrid. Their attitude to the British anarchist pacifists, including in their view the editors of *War Commentary*, was largely hostile. They were increasingly vocally supported in this view by anarcho-syndicalists within the AFB itself, particularly Tom Brown and Ken Hawkes, the latter being the CNT's English spokesman. This manifested over time as an internal wrangle for control over *War Commentary* and the AFB's printer in Angel Alley, as the main assets available to the anarchist movement, and led to an escalating series of heated clashes within the group's Monday business meetings.

The denouement of the argument came in the form of an attempted overthrowing of Vernon Richards as editor. The AFB was, as is fairly common in anarchist groups, run by consensus.

According to Donald Rooum two of the syndicalists (likely Brown and Hawkes) succeeded in amending this to say that if consensus could not be reached a straight majority would be accepted. With the war coming to an end, the CNT comrades were also allowed to join despite prior differences.

Reform in hand, they made their move in December 1944, a month after the Special Branch raids. The addition of the CNT gave them a majority vote, which they used at the end of an AFB meeting, waiting until after the editors had left and introducing a new motion under "any other business". The motion was carried, however in a curious twist of fate, the interference of Special Branch just months earlier when it demanded registration under the Business Names Act served to defeat the motion. Vero, as the newly-registered owner, simply refused to hand it over.

The opposition was furious. The feeling among the anarcho-syndicalists was that they had been victims of a shameless asset grab by pacifists and intellectuals who were out to sideline the class-struggle oriented anarchists and shift Freedom Press towards a more literary, artistic and academic focus. Four men, reportedly including Tom Brown, visited Richards and Berneri at their flat. The tales about what happened next are varied, but David Goodway managed to track down a definite member of the four, Cliff Holden, who recounted that he was the one who put a pistol to the back of Berneri's head and marched her to the bank, acquiring £25 (about six weeks' wages) to start a new anarcho-syndicalist paper, *Direct Action*. The four and two others, six in all, later smashed the printing forme, then met Richards in Angel Alley and beat him up.

The direct outcome of the failed ousting was to split the still tiny anarchist movement straight down the middle. *War Commentary* would now be published by "Vernon Richards trading as Freedom Press" with papers being printed by the linked Express Printers. The scrap killed off the AFB, with the publishers of *Direct Action* going on to name themselves the the Syndicalist Workers Federation (ancestor of the Solidarity Federation) while Freedom Press formed up with the Union of Anarchist Groups.

Meltzer is quick to note that while this proved to be a lasting dispute and for the movement, of more importance internally than the far more famous State crackdown, many of the individuals involved simply got on with things in the aftermath.

Following the split the paper came out regardless of the arguing parties, and he gives credit to three women for that, Marie Louise Berneri, Peta Edsall and Lilian Wolfe.

The Special Branch campaign came to a head in December

1944, when the AFB/Freedom Press office at 27 Belsize Road was raided along with the editors' homes. Warrants were issued under Defence Regulation 39b (against "seducing" members of the armed forces from their duty) and regulation 88a which allowed for the seizure of assets related to such an offence. Large quantities of documents were seized with files, card indexes, typewriters, letters, etc all bundled into sacks, taken away and kept for months. According to *Albert Meltzer*, it was only the *War Commentary* files that were picked up, the files of *Workers in Uniform* having already been burned on the grounds that demobilisation would make them obsolete anyway.

Sixteen-year-old Donald Rooum had taken out a subscription just three months' prior, after coming across anarchism in Kent while on a Ministry of Food placement to pick hops. The teenager wrote to Lilian Wolfe when the next issue failed to arrive and learned that police had seized the subscription files along with everything else. Capturing the files allowed police to go on the rampage and Special Branch officers, led by Detective Inspector William Whitehead*, searched the possessions of soldiers and readers throughout the county later that month, including the home of new 20-year-old writer Colin Ward, at Stromness in Orkney (Ward was already in a military detention camp at the time). Whitehead himself travelled out to Orkney with Sapper Ward in tow to seize the young man's possessions. Active persecution of *War Commentary's* readers was less troubling than it could have been however, according to Philip Sansom, who noted only two other victims, a poet, and a tank driver who was "whipped out of his job and transferred to the Pioneer Corps".

In fact the worst disruption was collateral as the raids led to Freedom being kicked out of its premises. The Bristol shop became the mail orders hub and trade orders were dealt with by Angel Alley until new premises were found in Red Lion Street in 1945. Those premises were slum housing, damp and infested with rats, but remained Freedom's offices until 1960.

After the searches were through, four people were arrested in a second series of 7.30am raids on February 22nd 1945. Vero Richards, Marie Louise Berneri and John Hewetson, now that they had handily identified themselves under the Business Act,

---

* Whitehead, clearly no fan of leftists, had previously been the arresting officer of IRA quartermaster Peter Walsh in 1939, took down Tom Brown during the campaign against *Freedom* and went on to collar Soviet atomics spy Alan Nunn May in 1946

were picked up as the proprietors while Philip Sansom was simply unlucky, having been working in the office at the time of the arrest. They were collectively charged with sedition related to three issues of *War Commentary* — November 1st, 11th and 25th respectively — which discussed the rise of soviet councils in Germany after World War I, soldiers' councils in the French Revolution, and instances off mass union action, linked to the poor conditions of military camps. In addition were the subscriber lists and evidence that new subscribers were being solicited. Most infamous however was a prominently displayed poem:

Fight! What For?

You are wanted for the Army,
Do you know what you'll have to do?
They will tell you to murder your brothers,
As they have been told to kill you,
You are wanted for the Army,
Do you know what you'll have to do?
Just murder to save your country
From men who are workers, like You.
Your country! Who says you've a country?
You live in another man's flat,
You haven't even a back yard,
So why should you murder for THAT?
You haven't a hut or a building,
No flower, no garden, it's true,
The landlords have grabbed all the country,
Let THEM do the fighting — NOT YOU.

The government's direct censorship of *War Commentary* was something of an anomaly. As Carissa Honeywell notes in her 2015 piece on the case for the *International Review of Social History*:

Despite the fact that "the government were involved in a process designed to stifle forms of political opposition more or less continuously throughout the war", both the Chamberlain and the Churchill governments were careful to employ informal tactics rather than public policy methods to control and censor dissident political organisation, precisely in order to "maintain a democratic image", and avoid publicising undesirable views and organisations.

From 1940, though the Civil Defence Committee pushed for direct intervention against anti-war publications, policy was to use other methods such as Section 4 of the Public Order Act (breach of the peace) and covert disruption to achieve the same effect. Hewetson noted in a 1942 letter that then-home secretary George Griffith "does not think ours and a number of other periodicals of sufficient influence to justify any drastic action on his part, more so as he is so unpopular, and presumably does not want to be even more so". This view was supplemented by the assessment of cooler heads in government that *War Commentary* specifically was "confined mainly to pacifists" and overt repression would merely martyr the anarchists.

Freedom Press was kept under surveillance* but as late as May 1944, following another hard-hitting article titled 'Bevin Declares War on Miners' the Home Office was still arguing against arrests, wanting to deny the authors their day in court. Articles addressing the huge and potentially dangerous swathe of often armed, demobbed soldiers as peacetime stripped the State of its "total war" excuses for poor conditions were a step too far however, and the hawks were belatedly allowed to act, just ahead of war's end. Sansom gives an insight into exactly how worried the State really was in a piece written for *The Raven 29* recalling his time in prison, noting:

> Germany was finished by the time the Russians reached Warsaw and the Americans reached Paris; it was only Churchill's stubborn demand for 'unconditional surrender' that kept the Germans fighting. How much the ordinary squaddy knew this, I don't know, but it seems obvious now that fewer and fewer soldiers were prepared to add their names to the lists of late casualties in a war they hated anyway.
>
> Ironically, this was not something we found out until we were actually in prison. Once we got inside, we found the nicks full to overflowing, not with criminals from the home front but with soldiers sentenced by military courts in France, Italy, Germany, for desertion and subsequent offences. When a soldier deserts in a foreign country in wartime, how is he to survive? He has been trained to use a gun, so he survives

---

* Home Office notes suggested keeping a close eye in October 1943 saying "'In view of the fact that Friends of Freedom Press think that they are gaining increasing support in the forces, it may be worth watching to see what line *War Commentary* follows".

by armed robbery, by hold-ups, by black-marketeering, by selling government property and by gun-running. We heard hair-raising stories of the sale of fleets of lorries and masses of material, food, petrol and oil — all of which was in short supply in the countries our boys were 'liberating'. In the process our boys were liberating themselves — until they were caught by the military police. Then they got enormous sentences, of 10, 15, 25, 30 years' imprisonment — and shipped back to England to serve them. Returning soldiers' tales elaborated this story of mass desertions. One ex-8th Army man told us that by the time his unit had travelled from toe to top of Italy, 80 per cent had deserted — and the remainder fell in behind a victory march of Tito's partisans in Trieste to show where their political sympathies lay.

These men were mainly soldiers, but there was a fair sprinkling from the Royal Navy and the RAF, and they were being delivered to the main London "reception" prisons in batches of 20 or 30, two or three times a week. Pentonville, closed in the 1930s, had to be re-opened to deal with the rush. I myself was part of a working party sent over from the Scrubs to clean and redecorate the dirty old dump. In the event, of course, these men served only small periods of their long sentences. They were distributed to local prisons around the country — presumably to the prisons nearest their home towns — and after a few months, quietly given a "special release" and, of course, a dishonourable discharge. The prisons could not possibly have held them all, but back at their units, the sentences were supposed to have a deterrent effect upon their fellows.

Taking place in April 1945, the trial proved to be a case in point for the prior softly-softly approach, as the use of the law to bludgeon Freedom Press sparked what was to become a famous free speech campaign, drawing in a stellar cast of advocates for the tiny paper. *War Commentary* had been publishing roughly the same tone of comment throughout the conflict, but only now was it facing the full force of the law, leading many people to — correctly — surmise that the propagandistic mask of British liberalism as posed against German fascism was slipping.

All of sudden, *War Commentary* became one of the most famous publications in Britain, seen as the key test case against censorship, just at the moment when the State wished it least.

Tabloids publicised the case and the young bohemians and

intellectuals of London lined the public galleries. Public protests saw famous faces issuing damning pronouncements against the government and questions were asked in the House of Commons by Labour MP George Strauss about whether the raid was reasonable and if the seizure of a typewriter was even legal.*

A wide variety of influential figures, many of whom had no particular cross to bear for Freedom Press, voiced their fears over the future of free speech in post-war Britain. Supporters, most notably Herbert Read and George Orwell, put together an open letter condemning the impending charges on March 3rd 1945, which included the names of T S Eliot, E M Forster and Stephen Spender.

By March 31st, this had coalesced into what would become the Freedom Defence Committee, led by Read, Ethel Mannin, Fenner Brockway, S W Taylor and Patrick Figgis. The list of supporters, inspired in large part through Read's motivated efforts, was manifestly impressive including Aneurin Bevan, who was just months away from taking on his most famous role as founder of the NHS, Bertrand Russell, Gerald Brenan, Vera Brittain, Benjamin Britten, Alex Comfort, Cyril Connolly, Clifford Curzon, Michael Foot, Victor Gollancz, Laurence Houseman, C E M Joad, Augustus John, Harold Laski, J Middleton Murry, George Orwell, George Padmore, J B Preistley, Reginald Reynolds, D S Savage and George Woodcock. On April 16th, the day before the trial was die to begin, a defence meeting was held where Read was forthright about the task of the moment: "We will fight; fight the Defence Regulations and that foul and un-English institution, the political police."

Hewetson, Berneri, Sansom and Richards

The law could not, of course, back down once proceedings had been initiated but it became a circus with an all-star cast, the ringmaster being none other than 1st Baron Norman Birkett, a High Court justice who was later appointed as the alternate British judge in the Nuremberg Trials. The prosecution meanwhile was led

---

* A notable gap in the parade of support was, predictably, the National Council for Civil Liberties, which could have been expected to offer aid but was at the time under the control of the belligerently patriotic Communist Party.

by Attorney General Sir Donald Somerville, arguing that the three offending articles, and the poem, connected to show a pattern of *War Commentary* telling British soldiers to hold onto their guns for a brewing revolution. Somerville was however merely the figurehead.

The ever-attentive Detective Inspector Whitehead was the man whose work was at the heart of the case. Whitehead extensively quoted from the paper in his reports, picking out examples of "lessons from 1917", the adventures of French partisans and liberation movements in Greece that could be used to inform modern revolutionaries. That this was allied to a criminally attractive layout and circulated in the forces was, to the Home Office, evidence of an open and shut case.

Some of the examples Whitehead used were entirely silly, such as picking out a headline 'Hang on to your Arms' which was targeted at the Belgian underground, or deciding that Herbert Read's writing on culture suggested the existence of a 'Surrealist Party' at Freedom Press, and these missives were picked apart by some of the biggest names the legal profession had to offer. Colin Ward recalled in a 1974 essay for *Wildcat*:

The defence solicitor was a man named Rutledge, who was overshadowed by his clerk, the genial and flamboyant Ernest Silverman, a tragic character most of whose life was spent in prison for innumerable cases of petty embezzlement (he later died in Parkhurst serving a long sentence of preventive detention). The Freedom Press trial was probably his finest hour. He was certainly a good and honest friend to the defendants, and they in later years made great efforts to alleviate his lot. Ernest briefed some very eminent barristers: John Maude (later a Tory MP and a judge) to defend Hewetson and Richards, Derek Curtis Bennett for Marie Louise, and James Burge for Philip Sansom. Here of course were the tactical dilemmas for anarchists. Having engaged an expensive defence you put yourselves in their hands, and the defence line was that here were four upright citizens (Richards was working as a civil engineer at the time and Hewetson was casualty officer at Paddington Hospital) putting forward their idealistic point of view with no intention of causing disaffection. The four soldiers called by the prosecution (including me) to establish that the offending material had been received by them, testified for the defence that they had not been disaffected.

None of the accused liked the way their case was presented. Marie Louise in particular wanted to defend herself and did not want to rely on the technicalities of the law for an acquittal. On the other hand, if the object of the whole proceedings was to silence the Freedom Press it would have been foolish to strike intransigent attitudes and get, in consequence, far longer sentences. In the event, she and George Woodcock were able to carry on the work of the paper during the period when their comrades were in jail.

The preferred approach from the defendants was to highlight that the paper had never been secret, its paper supply could have been stopped at any time and that its approach had been consistent throughout the war, making it clear that the State had tacitly condoned the existence, and contents, of *War Commentary*. A different approach was put up by the high-powered lawyers however. They argued that not a single soldier could be proven to have deserted or in any practical way become disaffected through the works of the paper. Marie Louise Berneri was disqualified from prosecution as she was found to be incapable of conspiring with her own husband — a woman who had spent the last several years speaking up and down the country and central to the Press, spared prison gruel through the State's own institutional sexism.

Regardless of the arguments, on April 23rd at the end of the six-day trial all three of the remaining editors were convicted. The maximum sentence for the offence was 15 years, but with the spotlight upon him, the gallery full to bursting with the editors' comrades, Birkett offered a blatant sop to public pressure, stating that while "the views expressed might seem strange to many" he believed they were inspired by high motives. He gave each man nine months — just long enough for Vero to form a scratch band playing violin with other jailed musicians.

The defence campaign however continued apace, with Read thundering "There is no longer in this land such a thing as the liberty of unlicensed printing for which Milton made his immortal and unanswerable plea: there is no longer any such thing as freedom of expression which ten generations of Englishmen have jealously guarded."

The campaign would cap a friendship between Read and the editors which saw him writing for Freedom Press for more than 15 years spanning philosophy, education and the arts. With Read regarding it as a new wing of defence for the very heart of free speech in post-war Britain meetings of the Freedom Defence Committee continued through May and June, remaining active until 1948 in a broadened capacity against "our home based fascism, openly and directly".

Read's comments, though rousing, were not accompanied by the end of *War Commentary,* which pressed on under temporary replacement editors, and hit back on May 5th demanding to know who had ordered the arrests. The involvement of the Attorney General suggested ministerial involvement, an intervention from the highest levels.

Special Branch was reputedly furious over the leniency of the sentence, and in a pathetically peevish move, an attempt was made first to jail Sansom for failing to attend a medical examination, and then to draft him after his release in 1946 which was only seen off after a vigorous campaign by the Freedom Defence Committee. He was finally released for good that February. But this would be the last major action by the State against Freedom Press as the war ended and the situation failed to turn into a crisis. The public was largely mollified by the general election of 1945, which defused hatred aimed at Churchill by electing a Labour government. That year was the beginning of a programme of major reforms, culminating in the post-war consensus of NHS, a massive house building programme and the "cradle to grave" welfare state, once again buying off the possibility of mass revolt.

Above and top left, the Committee of 100 mass sit-down in 1961. Top right, Philip Sansom at Hyde Park

1945-1969
Rebuilding a movement

Despite the several successes of the war period, at the end of 1945 we find both Freedom Press and the AFB flat on their backs. Almost every key organiser was in jail, not speaking to one another, had fled or was drafted. Most of the old guard from the 1910s and 20s was dead, including Max Nettlau and Frank Leech, while George Cores was estranged from the movement, dying in 1949.

Beyond Marie Louise Berneri, Peta Edsall, George Woodcock and Lilian Wolfe barely anyone of experience was left to keep the paper running for those next few months until the release of Vero, Hewetson and Sansom in January 1946, and thus almost no capacity or unity remained to take advantage of the paper's newfound fame. On top of that, the feud with the syndicalists was causing a great deal of trouble for Vero in particular, as some of the comrades who had loaned money towards the purchase of Express Printers took heed of complaints that he had carried out an asset grab and withdrew their funding. This was only made up for via an emergency loan from Vero's (non-anarchist) mother, which he found highly embarrassing.

Peace having been established in Europe that May, *War Commentary* was closed in July 1945 and relaunched the next month under an old name, *Freedom*, though at the time the editors stressed this was a "new" publication. Costing tuppence for a four-page broadsheet format, with the end of the war and Labour's electoral triumph in 1945, the anarchist paper, and the remaining movement, were to become very isolated indeed over the next few years. *Freedom*, now based at 27 Red Lion Street, once again found itself on the wrong side of public opinion, being unswervingly hostile to Labour's demobilising programme of nationalisation and welfare legislation. Revelations about the Nazis' concentration camps did little to endear people to a pacifist position, and even on the withdrawal of rationing in 1950 it took a contrarian stance, muttering in June that:

> The whole conception of price control and the attempt to secure equitable distribution through rationing drives from the recognition — belated and incomplete that it is — that all men have a right to at least the necessities of life.

It is unquestionably a progress that such a conception should now be common property. But it is also indicative of society and of the administrative class that this conception is thought to have application only during wartime.

What *Freedom* did have was a selection of very active members, with Herbert Read a particularly loyal figure close to Vero and Berneri, alongside a small number of talented young supporters such as Colin Ward and Alex Comfort.*

Colin Ward, Albert Grace and Tom Earley with a French comrade

How this panned out in real terms is disputed. Tom Brown and the syndicalists, coalescing around what was initially a third AFB and then became (in 1950) the Syndicalist Workers Federation, felt that *Freedom* was now little short of a parasite on the back of the movement, using the radical reputation of anarchism to present an edgy front for middle class intellectuals to show off and build careers. In later years Albert Meltzer and *Black Flag* would, more or less, come to the same conclusion, as would *Class War* in the 1980s.

This was energetically rebutted by Vero and his supporters, who argued both that anarchism needed to establish a rigorous intellectual voice of its own and that the paper must remain an independent production rather than be tied to any one tendency. *Writing in A Decade of Anarchy,* Colin Ward suggests:

I have more than once raised a smile by saying that one of the great periods of *Freedom* was the time just before I was invited to join the editorial group in 1947. But I meant it. Here was a group of like-minded people who trusted each other

---

* Ward's writing for *Freedom* spanned almost the entire rest of the century, with a break in the '70s, and at the time of his death he was widely regarded as one of the few globally influential post-war anarchists to have emerged from Britain. Comfort, best known for his world-famous book *The Joy of Sex*, wrote prolifically for the press around the time of World War II, and a collection of his essays at the time was published under the title *Writings against Power and Death* in 1994.

and brought to the spare-time task of editing an anarchist paper a wide variety of personal experiences. They didn't need to vet each others' articles for ideological rectitude, and they knew that each member would write from a *Freedom* standpoint rather than pursue personal idiosyncrasies. I can only once remember anything I wrote being censored. John Hewetson as a doctor objected to my calling Sir Will Lawther, the miners' leader a "dyspeptic clown" on the grounds that my diagnosis was not accurate.

It is certainly true that a streak of pacifism and artistic liberalism ran through *Freedom's* community in the post-war period. Vero and Berneri for example became fast friends with George Orwell who had gained literary superstardom that year following the propitious publication of *Animal Farm* — Orwell even used his new riches to help the pair set up as photographers, and their photographs of him are among the best available. They were connected to the surrealists through Simon Watson Taylor,* and connections to the Peace Pledge Union continued, leading *Freedom* to become heavily involved with initiatives such as the campaign against capital punishment and later, the Committee of 100.

But in 1946 *Freedom's* content retained a large measure of class struggle focus and an active outward face, organising lectures around the London Anarchist Group (later part of the Union of Anarchist Groups) and maintaining good relations with Glasgow. Beyond its publishing ventures the the collective ran a number of summer schools from 1947 onwards, comprising a gathering in a different city each year, followed by camping holiday. It had motivated, punchy writing and the outstandingly intelligent oversight of Marie Louise Berneri, even if the paper was officially Vero's fief by this point. Indeed a renewal of anarcho-syndicalism as a rebuttal to the "political glamour which has drawn so many millions to tragedy [as] there is no basic disagreement between the government and the opposition" (Feb 1946) is a clear preoccupation of the paper.

The first new *Freedom* in its August 1945 issue does hint at a general direction the editors wanted to move in, opening up a broader approach on anarchism and politics which incorporated

---

* An actor and translator, Taylor had stood bail for Sansom during the *War Commentary* trial and worked with Berneri and Vero to produce the surrealist review *Free Unions*.

thoughts on atomic energy and anarchism, science and humanity — an ambition to take on new trends, technologies and debates in society which it inherited from *Freedom*'s earlier incarnations. Ward, who joined the Freedom Group proper in 1947, recalls his early experiences in *Talking Anarchy:*

> Editorial meetings, every two weeks, were held either in the room behind the bookshop or at the home of Vero and Marie Louise at Chalk Farm, or of John Hewetson and Peta Edsall, first in Hampstead, and after 1918 in Vauxhall Bridge Road and then Southwark Bridge Road, above John's consulting room. Meetings were merry, social occasions, where Lilian Wolfe who ran the bookshop and coped with the mail, would persuade group members to deal with correspondence that needed more than an answer from her and to accept or reject incoming articles and letters intended for publication. Current events were discussed and responsibility to write about them was distributed around the group.
>
> Most of us know, or learned, how to mark up material for the typesetter, how to correct proofs, and how to paste up the "dummy" of the paper ready for Mr. Anderson, the elderly compositor, to insert the headlines, and Hen Chandler, the machinist, to print the paper on the very old printing press that Freedom Press had acquired in 1912 when it became hard to find a printer ready to undertake its work. Within the group there was absolute trust. We did not read each other's contributions to check on their ideological acceptability.

Herbert Read

It's worth noting the strong influence of one writer in particular on *War Commentary* and the relaunched *Freedom* — Herbert Read. The art critic had become a close friend of Richards and Berneri and had been writing regularly in the paper, lending it some academic weight. Read had, thanks to his work with the Freedom Defence Committee, risen to some prominence and, notes David Goodway in *Anarchist Seeds Beneath The Snow*, his approach anticipated and influenced much of the work done by later leading *Freedom* writers such as Alex Comfort, Paul Goodman and Colin Ward. For Goodway, though Read's personal philosophy of anarchism was unexceptional, not moving

far beyond essential Kropotkinist ideas, what he brought to the evolution of *Freedom* was a push for its thinking to become more multidisciplinary while engaging, innovating and extrapolating in both academia and education, as well as drawing artistic circles. This would become a dominant theme into the 1950s and beyond.

If anything, article themes in the 1945-49 period are difficult to pin down politically. They incorporated both a bullish class struggle-focused approach critiquing Labour plans to douse working class self-organisation by providing institutional systems instead, and a desire to establish a respectable intellectual base in academia. This placed *Freedom* entirely outside the bulk of left-wing opinion at the time, which was broadly in favour of increased State intervention and, at its radical end, lined up behind the Communist Party and the Trotskyists, both of which still had wild-eyed visions of capturing Westminster "for the working class". There is a strong argument to be made that *Freedom* was well ahead of its time in this sense, preemptively identifying many of the economic contradictions and problems of inhumanity lurking within faceless State bureaucracy that neoliberalism would so ruthlessly capitalise on 40 years later to eviscerate the welfare state. But few wanted to listen to such cynicism, and Berneri would note in 1949 that "the paper gets better and better, and fewer and fewer people read it".

Freedom's position, both historic and as one of the only remaining anarchist groups left on British soil, did give it some international cachet, particularly through Berneri. At the first post-war anarchist conference in Paris in 1948, the French, Italian and British delegations each contained a member of the Berneri family: Marie Louise represented Britain, her sister Giliana France and her mother Giovanna Italy. Freedom itself would host the next gathering in the 1950s, at the soon-to-be established Malatesta Club. Its international reporting is as a result excellent, with near-unique stories about libertarian struggles taking place worldwide. In 1950 for example it would carry the only English-language report from 1949's follow-up congress where W Karim, general secretary of the General Federation of Korean Anarchists, reported that:

> Around 3,000 active members with influence over a further 600,000 people had in previous years conducted a highly successful anti-imperial struggle to get Japanese oppressors off the peninsular, but had struggled after 1945 as a popular front Workers Union had been largely manipulated and seized on by pro-Bolshevik forces. Shifting to their own groups, including the Agricultural Workers' Party, Independent Workers and the General Students' Federation, the anarchists were at the time of writing running two daily papers and one weekly, using their own presses.

Sadly, Berneri died in 1949 from complications giving birth to her daughter, who also died suddenly shortly after, and that seems to have decided the ultimate direction of the paper. *Freedom* struggled and ultimately failed to reconcile its desire to engage the more forthright militancy of anarchism as a living movement with what became known as the "gentle anarchist" tendency that wound its way into highbrow journals and broadsheet columns.

It's hard to overstate how much of an impact Berneri's loss had on the grouping around *Freedom*, as where Vero was (according to Colin Ward) sometimes a manipulative character prone to high-handedness, she was almost universally loved. The extent of the movement's regard was shown directly after her passing, when a hugely successful fundraising drive allowed for the publishing of *Marie Louise Berneri: A Tribute, Journey Through Utopia* and *Neither East Nor West*, collections of her writing and thought. A summer camp for anarchist children was also established and named after her in 1951 in Italy by her mother and sister, which lasted until 1965.

The proprietor

We should probably take a pause to briefly look at the person who would set the tone at Freedom Press over the next 50 years — Vernon Richards. The post-Berneri era saw Vero throw himself into running the publishing house, selling off the old King Bomba and dabbling in tourist services to Spain and Russia while continuing as a hands-on editor of *Freedom* from 1951-64, stepping back to move to Suffolk in 1969 but wading in if he felt things were getting out of hand until the late 1990s. While the paper retained a broad range of content, he was ultimate arbiter.

Many who remember him best are no longer with us, but several of those who are have useful things to say. Jayne Clementson, who would become *Freedom's* sub-editor and administrator in later years, described Vero's approach to me as "sort of like a shady market stall, money just seemed to appear". Steve Sorba, who helped set up *Freedom*-linked printing project Aldgate Press in the 1980s, reminisces that "Vero seemed to have an inexhaustible fund of old anarchists who had made good." Mo Mosely, who has worked with *Freedom* on and off for decades, remembers a publishing process where Vero would look at a booklet about to go to print, and slap on a seemingly arbitrary price, considering the work as propaganda rather than commercial prospect. Certainly, looking through even the early lists of donations to the paper, it is clear that *Freedom* has had a number of quietly prosperous backers over the last six decades who helped it keep going even when matters were looking particularly grim, and some books such as centenary collection *World War Cold War* (£6.95 for 426 pages) cannot possibly have made a worthwhile profit. In his research David Goodway notes repeated donations to the deficit fund raised by anarchist picnics in the US, ascribing this to "fierce loyalty among anarchists of Italian origin".

Vero's longest-running associate, Donald Rooum, gives I think the most succinct appraisal of how Freedom Press was under Vero, once writing in a brief explainer to the collective:

> "From 1936 until 2001, Freedom Press had a (comrade who liked to pretend he was not the) proprietor, Vernon Richards, known to friends and collaborators as Vero. Partner and latterly proprietor of a prosperous family grocery, Vero paid to revive Freedom Press and then devoted 65 years of his life to it. In his time the publishing part of the organisation was anarchistic, in that all writing, drawing and editorial work was voluntary (production work and some administrative work was paid)."

This he opposes to a "majoritarian democratic" model (practiced in *Freedom* today) with some positions appointed by collective decision, noting that:

> These are examples of two types of equally anarchist organisation, personal "I propose to do so-and-so; would anybody like to help?" and collective "we all want so-and-so done; let us get it done together".

The disadvantage of the personal type is that the originator may feel entitled to go on making unilateral decisions (some people left after minor disagreements with Vero). The disadvantage of the collective type is that paid editors may come to see themselves as employees of a capitalist firm.

In essence, then, *Freedom*'s long-term direction from the late 1940s through to the end of the century was one where people joined the Press understanding that Vero had final say, but contributing to an overall project of promoting anarchist thought. His method of running it meanwhile was often opaque, and drew considerably on personal cachet. As Donald notes, this has some fundamental problems when dealing with anarchists of a more collective ideological bent, or who wished to walk a different path and led to some difficult rows, with even lifelong friend Colin Ward remarking in his obituary for the *Guardian* that:

> Vernon was a quite ruthless exploiter of others. None of the group he had inspired in the 1940s — Sansom, Hewetson, and George Woodcock — were on speaking terms with him at the times of their deaths. Unable to recognise himself as a manipulator, he saw their withdrawal from his circle as proof that they had been seduced by capitalist values.

While in this light he cuts a controversial and at times seemingly dislikable figure* it's important to note that Vero was also well regarded by many and not an irredeemable tyrant. By the 1980s for example former collective member Steve Sorba remembers Vero as being unafraid to make his feelings known but rarely interfering in the paper's editorial line, focusing more on the publishing end where he raised most of the cash and decided what books should be put out. Donald Rooum concurs, also noting that with Vero's move to Suffolk in 1968 it became clear after a while that far from

---

* Not having met him I can go only by the comments of his friends and foes — I have rarely come across such a Marmite response even in the anarchist movement.

continuing to dominate affairs he was only even reading the paper intermittently. After Vero's retirement *Freedom*'s direction as a newspaper was far more heavily influenced by editors such as Jack Robinson, Philip Sansom, John Rety, Nicolas Walter and Charles Crute, who he frequently argued with on policy.

It is also impossible to avoid the fact when researching the history of the anarchist movement that where almost every other paper and magazine produced in the 1951-2001 period flared briefly to more or less effect before collapsing, *Black Flag*, *Organise* and *Direct Action* being the major exceptions, *Freedom* continued its slow burn regardless and helped produce some genuinely outstanding writers. Vero was a primary reason for this, as despite a fading interest in active anarchism after his move to Suffolk, and with every opportunity to simply dump the project, sell the building and mosey off into the sunset, he remained linked throughout his life and using his connections built, with many, many others, one of the largest portfolios of anarchist thought in the English language. And in the end he did relinquish Angel Alley to the movement [page 175].

The million-pound question is, I think, whether Vero's *Freedom*, as criticised over the years for liberalism, individualism, elitism etc, was conducted at an outrageous cost to the rest of British anarchism, or stifled possibilities for something better to emerge. With some reservations, from the safety of distance, I would conclude that it wasn't.

My instinctual sympathies lie with Tom Brown's side of the argument, and Albert Meltzer's, and to a degree with Ian Bone's. In places the old issues of *Freedom* are so dry and dense as to be barely readable to a layperson. There is often listless navel-gazing, sometimes a tendency towards smugness and pontification largely academicised away from anything that would much benefit working-class people. I have a powerful distrust of any anarchist endeavour that can be dictated to by a boss, and of any approach that becomes overly concerned with gaining plaudits from intellectuals.

None of the above however, even in the most villainous renditions, could have significantly slowed a genuine direct action anarchism from re-emerging under its own steam and in fact it manifestly didn't. *Freedom's* longevity (and premises) gave it status as an introductory contact point for the movement for a while, and it clearly had an oversized say in the missed opportunity that was the Anarchist Federation of Britain, but by the end of the '60s this was pretty much over.

Anarcho-punk was an astonishingly successful musical movement which had pretty much nothing to do with *Freedom*, and political squatting was entirely independent of any intervention from Angel Alley. Direct action against Thatcher's road-building and for the environment didn't need *Freedom's* permission. Nor did the paper's infamous slurring of striking miners as "extra thick thickies" stop *Class War* from picking up anarchist ideals and becoming tremendously successful on the picket lines in 1984. The moment there was sufficient resonance for it, the anarchist press went from one paper to dozens, including for individual towns and cities.

Freedom's post-war activity was a different phenomenon from the forces which drive popular movements, involving a coterie of more or less like-minded people, changing over time, who aimed to gain acceptance for anarchism as a mature philosophy. My hunch is that the money it swallowed to publish philosophically-minded journals such as *Anarchy* and *The Raven* would not have found its way to other front lines in the Press's absence. If *Freedom's* position as a first port of call for people interested in anarchism was sometimes annoying and its off and on tendency to moderate intellectualism frustrating for critics it was not as much of a burden as is sometimes portrayed, particularly after the '50s when the movement opened out.

There is a separate value in fostering the sort of thoughtful analytical work that characterises the best of Freedom Press's output through the second half of the 20th century, and at least some in having allies with access to the platform afforded by "respectability" (at least when brave enough to avoid repudiating rabble rousers). *Freedom* also went through plenty of phases under several editorial teams where it went in very different directions from the norm, such as John Rety's punchy editorial turn in the 1964-69 period, and Stu Stuart's weird decision to append his own notes to everyone's articles in the 1980s. As an (always small) paper, for all that it bored some it inspired others to think — including 1984's "most dangerous man in Britain" Ian Bone,* who writes in his autobiography *Bash The Rich* that as a young man at the end of the '60s:

"I noted the address of Freedom Press — 'the anarchist HQ' — in *Punch* and composed a letter to *Freedom* that night, but added a cautious footnote requesting the no-one visits my house ... I needn't have worried that the anarchist movement was that efficient! Three months later, a copy of *Freedom* dropped through my letterbox. I never looked back. For the next two years, I made the solitary trip to London visiting Freedom Press, Indica and Better Books, bringing back to Hampshire Lenny Bruce, Alan Ginsberg, the Beats and incomprehensible copies of *Anarchy* magazine."

Freedom under Vero may have sneered at workers for their foolishness in trusting union officials, but it also ran at least one solid article about workplace struggles on almost every front page in the 1960s.

Pacifism notwithstanding, when Stuart Christie was arrested for trying to assassinate Franco in August 1964 *Freedom* ran two consecutive front pages and numerous follow-up articles demanding his release. Studiedly "independent" though it was, *Freedom* offered regular page space to the new Anarchist Federation of Britain when that formed in 1963. Critical of the limitations of the miners' struggle, Freedom gave NUM activists a free room and phone throughout 1984 to help them organise in Whitechapel.

Ultimately, *Freedom* in the 1951-2001 period was an effort to promote anarchist thought that made some mistakes, had some successes, published both great and dismal political writing, and was neither the parasite nor the struggling angel that its attackers and defenders sometimes draw. The same, I think, is true of Vero's contribution.

* As defined by tabloid *The Sunday People* at the time.

Slow burn

The 1950s, while often considered a slow decade for the anarchist movement, especially when considering the jaw-dropping social changes that were taking place not just in terms of a new social consensus but with the rebuilding of significant working class power in the nation's factories, did have some areas where victories can be claimed. For Freedom Press specifically, the first half of the decade was actually quite productive especially in arenas such as the peace movement, housing, capital punishment and social rights. Solidarity with anarchists on the continent, particularly those in Spain and Italy continuing to feel the heat of State repression, was a standout feature.

In 1950 *Freedom* members resumed a regular speaking and sales pitch at Hyde Park, led by the outstanding figure of anarcho-syndicalist firebrand Philip Sansom, regarded by the anarchists as possibly the finest public speaker of his generation. Groups in Bristol and Glasgow continued to support the venture, and in May 1951 *Freedom* announced it would be shifting gear to become a weekly, costing thruppence for a four-page broadsheet. The move was to say the least an optimistic one, as mentioned in its front-page column on the issue which notes:

> Our financial position does not justify this, nor does the number of our collaborators in producing and distributing *Freedom*. But we feel that the quickening pace of events and the searching for an "alternative" that is to be found everywhere among the politically disillusioned make it necessary for us to try more than ever to influence public opinion and events rather than wait for them to catch up with us.
>
> ...
>
> We do not aim at spreading anarchist ideas by using the methods of mass propaganda, even if they were available to us. But people are not free to accept or reject the anarchist case unless it is brought to their attention and we believe this to be our principle function. And since the subjugation of man today is not only political and not only economic, the scope of *Freedom* includes education, sex, literature and are, and our social environment. For, as anarchists, we are concerned with widening the whole field of human activity.

The state of Freedom's begging bowl has always been a handy guide to its relative financial health and the scale of the funding task for the shift to weekly was clearly formidable, prompting a press fundraiser for the year of £600 which by December had managed a valiant failure of £478. *Freedom* would miss its target by around £100 in both the following years as well, only managing to catch up somewhat in the late 1950s. Notable too are the sources of donations. In the early 1940s, VR and JH (Vero and John Hewetson) were repeatedly putting up large sums themselves. In the early 1950s substantial amounts of the paper's donations were coming from abroad (Australia and the US in particular) but by the end of the decade more was coming from home shores, suggesting increased interest within Britain itself.

Younger comrades also came into their own through this time, with George Melly beginning his rise to stardom as a jazzman, raconteur and flamboyant gadabout and Colin Ward beginning what was to become his long and influential run as a writer for the paper. Having finished art school, Donald Rooum moved south in the early 1950s and immediately got heavily involved with the new London Anarchist Group, which had a great deal of overlap with *Freedom*, while Tony Gibson studied sociology and psychology on his way to becoming a notable voice in the industry. Nicolas Walter, who would become particularly influential in the 1980s, also began coming to meetings at the end of the decade, while Jack Robinson began holding them.*

In an essay for *Black Flag* in 2006, 'The UK anarchist movement — Looking back and forward', anarchist historian Nick Heath notes a theoretical coherence within this London set which he argues grew out of its very particular circumstances, with a core group of trusted comrades left secretive by their wartime experiences. Philip Sansom, in his reminiscences of the period for *Freedom / A Hundred Years* goes into some detail about the activities of the time:

> The Freedom Press Group was joined by a newly-formed London Anarchist Group, and was the foundation of the Union of Anarchist Groups, including a fine group in Glasgow (the best speakers in which had stayed with FP) and a small group in Bristol, where another Freedom Bookshop had been opened. (The Kingston group disintegrated, one of its members going back to being a local councillor!)

---

* From about 1958 onwards Robinson's name is a near fixture in the events lists as the main speaker from the Freedom/LAG groups, talking about a huge variety of topics, continuing into the 1960s.

The London Anarchist Group was what would now, I suppose, be called the "street-wise" group. Its job was to hold meetings — outdoor meetings at Marble Arch, Tower Hill and elsewhere, and the indoor meetings that had been a regular feature for several years during the war.

Membership of the LAG and FP overlapped. Over the years any number from two to six members of the Freedom Group would also be involved in LAG activities. The main activity of the UAG was the annual Summer School, started in 1947 and held as far as possible in different cities each year — London, Glasgow, Liverpool — and usually followed by a camping holiday. These gave great opportunities for comrades from all over the country to get together.

Herbert Read was to be of great use to us again when, in March 1952, Freedom Press organised a very special meeting in defence of Spanish anarchists. News was coming from Spain about a wave of repression directed against leading members of the (then underground) CNT. In Barcelona, men and women were being condemned by Military Tribunals to death by firing squad or to terms of imprisonment of 20 to 30 years.

We decided quite consciously to pull rank in choosing our speakers. They were to be internationally known writers and artists whose standing not even Franco could ignore. Once again Herbert Read used his influence and we had a platform consisting of Jacob Bronowski, Augustus John, Henry Moore, MPs Fenner Brockway and Michael Foot, veteran socialist H N Brailsford, Kingsley Martin the editor of the New Statesman (and no great friend of anarchists, but still ...) and Herbert himself, with myself as chairman. Telegrams of support were received from Bertrand Russell, Lewis Mumford, Aldous Huxley, E M Forster, Benjamin Britten, and others. A couple of weeks later we heard that the wave of shooting had been halted. It's wonderful what you can do with a few big names!

Before the meeting, Herbert Read had written a long leading article for *Freedom* in which he referred to Franco as 'The Ape of Hitler". At the meeting, Bronowski coined a memorable phrase: "Ought you to appear on this or that platform? The grey thumbprint of expediency blurs our conscience". He had appeared on our platform.

Lest you think I was being carried away from the class struggle on a wave of intellectual elitism, I must mention that I was at the time the nearest thing that *Freedom* had to an industrial editor. Within a few weeks of that meeting The Anarcho-Syndicalist Committee, consisting of myself, Albert Meltzer, Rita Milton (see People, page 266) and Albert Grace, launched *The Syndicalist*, a small but brightly produced little paper with contributors from various industries — the docks, mining, engineering — and it lasted for all of a year. It was not a Freedom Press publication, but appeared with its blessing, backing up the regular anarcho-syndicalist articles which the senior paper consistently printed.

It should perhaps be mentioned here that, through Albert Grace, we had established friendly relations with dockers in the East End of London during a massive strike in 1948. The Labour government had prosecuted four dockers under a wartime regulation (1305) for leading a minor strike on a pay issue, and this prosecution brought out the whole of dockland — and Liverpool as well. While three of the accused were well-known Stalinists, one, Harry Constable, was described as an anarchist.

We made contact, only to find he was a kind of maverick Trotskyist, but we got on well and found that the government's stupid action had made the dockers very receptive to anarcho-syndicalist ideas. Comrade Grace was treated with amused affection by the strike leaders, for he was a good trade unionist who was always battling with union leaderships, and I put that in the plural because Albert was a member of two unions — the dockers and the electricians. He would switch from one industry to the other depending on where the action was.

I was surprised, not so long ago, to see an anarchist writer declaring that not much was going on in the movement during the '50s, and another, more recently, that 'the 1950s were a period of somnolence for anarchism in Britain' when in fact the anarchists had a much higher profile in London than any comparable group.

In London's great stamping ground for open-air speakers, Hyde Park, we had a nucleus of able speakers in 1950, which by the end of the decade had grown in numbers and experience so that we were always able to answer requests for someone to talk on anarchism, take part in debates or participate in campaigns.

---

* Grace was also heavily involved in producing *Ludd*, alongside Albert Meltzer.

It is not generally appreciated that the campaign against capital punishment, which so agitated the public mind in the 1950s, began with London anarchists. It might be said anarchists have a special interest since in the past so many of our comrades have suffered from it, but I am prepared to argue that our standpoint was principled.

The initiative in this instance came not from within Freedom Press or LAG, but from two individual anarchists, Kitty Lamb and Gerald Kingshott, who asked us to help in starting a campaign. There had been a very disturbing case in which two youths had been caught in a burglary. One was captured, then the other produced a gun and killed a policeman. The killer, being only 16, could not be hanged and was sentenced to Borstal. The other, who had been in custody when the policeman was shot, was 18; he was sentenced to death and hanged. The general feeling was, if a copper is killed, someone has to die ...

London Anarchist Group organised two large meetings that were held at the St Pancras Town Hall. The first was on February 18th 1953, with Kitty Lamb in the chair, and a varied bag of speakers — Donald Soper (Methodist), F A Ridley (ILP), C H Norman (lawyer), Frank Dawtry (Prison Reform), Sybil Morrison (PPU), myself (LAG) and Sidney Silverman, the Labour MP who was eventually to steer the abolition Bill through the House of Commons.

The second meeting followed quickly with Canon Carpenter, Victor Yates MP, Jean Henderson, Robert Copping, Sidney Silverman, F A Ridley, and myself, a speaker from Norway (which had managed without the death penalty since 1902!) and Gerald Kingshott in the chair. At both meetings the chairpersons read out many telegrams of support from sympathetic writers, politicians, actresses, etc.

By the time of the second meeting, we had given ourselves the name of 'The League Against Capital Punishment'. This was the foundation of the National Campaign for the Abolition of Capital Punishment, launched by Victor Gollancz, backed by Gerald Gardiner QC, Arthur Koestler and many others, and eventually to see the diminutive Sidney Silverman triumphant. In all the self-congratulation of the influential who had joined the campaign after it got going, few, I suspect, raised their champagne glasses to Kitty Lamb and the late Gerald Kingshott, who had sparked the whole thing off by nudging the LAG, with Freedom's support, into action.

No doubt some of our readers are now looking with horror on all this hob-nobbing with MPs, intellectuals and other reformists, and wondering what it has to do with anarchism. Well, this much: if we can reduce even by a little the right (?) of the State to exercise powers of life and death, we are reversing the 20th century trend of absolute state power. I, for one, was not always comfortable in the company I shared on anti-hanging platforms but after all, what we were seeking was a reform in the law which could only be carried out by Parliament. Would it have been better for the gruesome practice of State murder to have carried on?

There have been other campaigns in which Freedom has been so far ahead that it has not been seen to have any part in the popular clamour. Abortion, for instance. The earliest article I ever read on the subject had appeared in *War Commentary* in October 1942, written by our doctor comrade John Hewetson. It did not actually use the phrase 'the woman's right to choose', but that was the gist of the argument. It took a long time for the women's movement to catch up, and even longer for the male politicos. But then, I remember how just after *War Commentary* had published an article on sexual freedom in 1944, a red-faced seller of *Socialist Standard* stormed up to me at Hyde Park and cried "what the hell has all this sex stuff to do with the working class revolution?"

In 1953 we began to publish in *Freedom* proposals for the creation of an anarchist club in London. The number of people we were contacting at our meetings made it clear that the time had come when we should have a place of own instead of relying on meeting rooms in pubs. During the next six months of preparation and the raising of funds — ridiculously small by today's inflated standards — we found a cellar in Holborn, bought the tables and chairs (with the help of a friendly furniture seller in the SPGB), installed a cooker, plumbed a sink, slapped on gallons of paint, and were ready to open on May 1st 1954.

A committee of self-appointed foundation members grabbed the privilege of doing all the work. Every evening a different team of three comrades were in charge of refreshments and whatever activity was going on: lectures, discussions, entertainments, sweeping up, whatever. The voluntary workers came from the Freedom Press Group and the London Anarchist Group, with one or two who would not consider themselves from either.

The Malatesta Club (as we called it) ran for four years, moving from Holborn after two years to Percy Street, off Tottenham Court Road. Activities included hosting an international conference, generating anarchist satirical theatre (ahead of 'the Establishment' or even the BBC's *That Was the Week That Was*) and creating our own trad jazz band. The lectures, debates and discussions were of a high quality, and there seemed a never-ending list of speakers anxious to say their say at the Malatesta.

We also lent our space to such as the great old speaker Bonar Thompson, and to an African group representing the independence movements in Nigeria, Kenya and what was to become Tanzania (with visitors like Doris Lessing and Tom Driberg).

Malatesta Club sketched by Rufus Segar

What some might think a more down-to-earth activity was to establish a street-corner pitch for our platform in Manette Street, on Charing Cross Road, where we held meetings every Saturday night when the West End was thronged with visitors, providing audiences very different from the regulars in Hyde Park. One evening in October 1956 there was a crowd waiting for us when we arrived. It was the weekend of the Suez Crisis, when British troops were invading Egypt and British planes bombing Cairo — while Russian tanks were invading Hungary. The old imperialism and the new — how could the anarchists lose?

We had a splendid meeting — having to despatch someone back to the Malatesta to bring more *Freedoms* — and ended up blocking the traffic in Charing Cross Road with the police standing helplessly by, knowing they would bring more trouble by trying to break it up. (In all modesty, it has to be admitted that this was before the days of the Special Patrol Group and today's riot squads.)

The satirical shows at the Malatesta had some more lasting spin-offs at the turn of the decade when we produced, first an *Election Guyed* for the October '59 General Election, then a *Bombmakers Guyed* for the CND march of Easter '61 and, later, another *Election Guyed* for the 1964 election. These are little gems of satire and surrealistic send-up. I cherish the memory of novelist Colin McInnes rushing into the Freedom Bookshop to buy 25 copies of the 1964 *Election Guyed* to give to his friends.

Sansom, it has to be said, has an element of rose-tinted glasses in his writing when it comes to *Freedom* (returning after a gap in the 1970s he referred to it as his "first love") and is prone to skating over less happy goings on. The early 1950s does seem to have had a lot of energy among the people it involved, but the near-nothingness it was trying to emerge from was formidable and there were setbacks even during this otherwise constructive period. Its relationship with the SWF continued throughout the decade to be poor, with the latter continuing to be of the view that Freedom Press was run by liberal egotists using anarchism to make a name for themselves.

Separate from either group at this point, Meltzer also slightly disputes Sansom's take on the production of the *Syndicalist*, saying that while it was printed free at Aldgate Sansom was not terribly enthusiastic, closing the paper on cost grounds before there was time to properly develop it. Afterwards the Anarcho-Syndicalist Committee became Meltzer and Albert Grace's vehicle as they moved away from *Freedom*'s circles, eventually turning into *Black Flag* and the Anarchist Black Cross.

Strangely, though he briefly mentions Rita Milton, Sansom does not in this writeup expand on the extent of her involvement in *Freedom*. Milton became a core member of the collective throughout the 1950s (and a supporter until her death in 2011) after moving to London in 1946 and meeting Sansom at Burgess Hill school, with whom she became romantically involved for the next nine years. Working with him at Express Printers, where she edited the work of two of its commercial customers, *Sewing Machine Times* and *The Journal of Sex Education*, she became particularly involved with the rowdy talks of Speakers Corner, and elsewhere Sansom describes her as "an effective speaker. Her sharp and aggressive tongue and her jutting chin made up for her diminutive stature and made her more than a match for any heckler."

Notably, she was the first anarchist to appear on British television, appearing on the *BBC* in 1952 to face off in a debate against the Marriage Guidance Council. She wrote later: "I got a lot of letters and it was a bit of fun, but we knew that any immediate propaganda value would be lost when the next programme was switched on". She would appear again on the *Tonight* show in 1958 as part of a special program about LAG and the Malatesta Club, described rather bad temperedly in the July 5th issue:

The comrades who have appeared on this "idiot's lantern" claimed to have had an unfair deal from the proprietors of the peep show. However these were the Other People so whilst we got sympathy from this lot we had no guarantee that similar misunderstandings would not arise.

The whole power lay in the shears of the film-cutters who would prepare our pearl of wisdom for the casting. For his part the producer would work with an interviewer who would ask questions to which we could give pithy answers.

It was pointed out that one of the maxims learnt at mother's knee was "ask silly questions and you'll get silly answers", however it was thought that a rehearsal before the filming would elicit questions and answers that were suitable.

From the start it was insisted that the ideas had to be simple in "terms that the man and woman in the street would understand". It was generally implied that the average IQ of TV viewers was low and the programme could not therefore be pitched too high or our five million captive audience would not know what we were talking about.

The culture clash is palpable, with interviewer Wilfred Pickles struggling to find acceptable questions for the members of LAG who unkindly compared him to "a rather dim AJP Taylor".*

Looking at the output of *Freedom* at the time, for all that it pushed strongly for women's lib there is a distinct impression that the sidelining of Milton in Sansom's recollections was not out of the ordinary. *Freedom*'s pages throughout certainly the 1950s and 1960s are absolutely dominated by male writers, with women's bylines showing up only intermittently throughout the period, most being partners of the main writers. I don't have much contemporary comment available, so can't pin this situation on anyone specifically, but it is certainly of note that the paper originally founded and later rejuvenated by brilliant, game-changing women was by this point a bit of a men's club in its bylines. Admin and distribution on the other hand, boring backroom jobs I'd personally rate as requiring significantly more practical dedication than the reputation-affirming glamour of essay writing, were handled by at least three women, Lilian Wolfe, Rita Milton and Mary Canipa (see People, page 235). Leah Feldman, one of the long-time activists who had supported the

---

* Taylor was an early and far more eminent figure who had worked as a historian for the Beeb.

creation of *Spain and The World* and met Kropotkin, was active at the time as a paper seller during the Hyde Park events.

Also ignored by Sansom was the big scandal of 1953 — Herbert Read accepting a knighthood. Read, always considered on the liberal end of the group, was recognised by the State for his achievements in poetry and felt it only his due to be awarded a gong, but it caused a huge stink. As the best-known anarchist name on the revolutionary left, his decision to kneel for the monarch made *Freedom* a laughing stock, which was not helped by a mealy-mouthed article which subsequently appeared making excuses for his decision. After this point Read mostly stepped back from active involvement, losing his libertarian friends other than Augustus John, Alex Comfort and George Woodcock.*

As to why Read made the decision, biographer James King suggests that the fault was with the poet's wife, Ludo, who was eager to become Lady Read. King notes that Ludo and Herbert were estranged due to a passionate (apparently platonic) friendship her husband had begun with a much younger woman, Ruth Franken, the year before and this was fully leveraged. Read did come from a rural conservative background however, and on his grave is the legend "Knight, Poet, Anarchist", so it seems likely the decision was not entirely forced even if Ludo's wishes were his excuse. In that sense Read joins a political tradition in Britain of drawing from a love of the concepts of liberty, but retaining roots in and a quiet deference to elements of the ancien regime.

The content of *Freedom* meanwhile continued to be a rich mix, but its attempt to meld historic works, sustained solidarity with the struggle against Franco, critiques of social questions and reports on workplace affairs leave it frequently feeling disjointed, as though several specialist papers are trying to cram into one general space. This is a feature of a great deal of the left press, as volunteer writers will tend to focus heavily on areas of interest rather than write on topical matters they're less clear about. But it does mean that in one four-page paper in April 1952 for example you can find nearly three pages of writing about Franco's latest crackdown sat cheek by jowl with a half-page mythbusting piece about the Doukhobors — an obscure group of pacifist Russian Christians with a Tolstoyan communistic bent whose hayday was

---

* Albert Meltzer picks this as the moment when he knew Freedom was irredeemable. Broadly, it can be placed as the start of what was to become an irreconcilible split in the late 1960s [See Albert and Vero, page 143)

pre-Soviet. That same issue carried absolutely nothing about the infamous "gross indecency" conviction of celebrated codebreaker and gay martyr Alan Turing, which concluded at exactly the right time to go to print. When it mentioned the topic of gay rights Freedom was certainly pro, and Jack Robinson held talks on the subject as part of a series of indoor meetings at Fitzroy Square in the early '50s, but the paper's writers at that moment mostly seemed uninterested.

This is possibly a factor in the movement's biggest failure that decade — an inability to profit from the death of Stalin. In March 1953 the terrifying dictator passed away and an internal battle for power began in Russia, laying bare many of the horrors which had been committed in the name of Communism and shattering arguments from the Stalinist left that the USSR was a bastion of socialist ideals.

Though the Politburo forestalled collapse initially by blaming everything on the man they'd worked closely with for decades, it began a trickle of people away from the Communist Party of Great Britain that was to become a torrent after 1956, when the invasion of Hungary proved categorically there would be no improvement under his replacement, Nikita Khruschev. Most of these troubled Tankies did not go to the anarchists however, but rather to more comfortable havens such as Labour or one of the Trotskyite groups, which went forth (international) and multiplied.* Others began a love affair with Maoism. *Freedom* would eventually have an impact on the emergence of the New Left, but this wouldn't manifest until the early 1960s.**

Instead the Press found itself in one of its periodic funks as the decade drew to a close, with the Malatesta Club being forced to shut down in 1958 due to surging rental prices. The Bristol bookshop also seems to have vanished around this time with little

---

* Many apologies to those scratching their heads over this terrible pun, the Fourth International was a Trotsky-backed attempt to build a new Leninist group to compete with Stalin's "deformed" Comintern (Third International). Its history of interminable arguments and splits is extensive and if you think anarchism has a lot of big egos, Trots on tour are a whole different level.

** An exception to this was Nicolas Walter, who was drawn to Freedom Bookshop in 1959 after a period in CND and began attending London Anarchist Group meetings around that time, having been introduced by his father and grandfather. He would go on to write a number of essays in *Freedom* and later *Anarchy*, and became a leading editor in the '70s and '80s.

fanfare. Freedom's major problem wasn't stability so much as a lack of growth since the torrid days of the mid-1940s, alongside increasingly pressing issues with the price of staying in central London. The group had to move out of Red Lion Square in 1960, fetching up at Maxwell Road in Fulham. The site was well set up with office, stock room and even a 200-foot garden, but was outside the beaten track for activists and geographically reflected an isolation that the group felt politically. Launching a reader survey in January 1960, the volunteer editors noted that:

> Every paper, especially every minority paper, has an optimum circulation. It is obvious from the number of readers who got the paper in the first instance by sheer accident or chance, and have then continued to subscribe, year after year, that we are nowhere near the optimum circulation.
>
> Several of the channels through which many of the respondents first came across the paper are no longer open to us. There is no longer a Freedom Bookshop in Bristol.
>
> The big Glasgow anarchist group of the wartime and early post-war years has been sadly depleted by death and emigration. Many of the provincial groups which were active at the same time — in Liverpool, Birmingham, and Chorley — no longer exist, largely through their stalwarts moving to London.

In the March 12th 1960 issue, they mused that:

> Like every other minority paper Freedom suffered a severe drop in circulation in the ten years following the war, and it seems to us that the tide only began to turn after Suez and Hungary.

And in February 1961 wrote:

> Most of us have worked together on the paper for the past 15 years, each with his or her particular way of approaching the problems of propaganda, of organisation; each with his individual interpretation of anarchism. We hope we will not appear immodest when we suggest that to have "put to bed" — as the printing fraternity so quaintly describe the process of getting a paper ready for print — something like 650 issues of *Freedom*, is no mean achievement in the circumstances!
>
> But neither is it unreasonable that some of us, after watching so many millions of words emerge from the presses

over the years, should feel less enthusiastic as to their efficacy, or question the method of approach, or even just feel tired! After all, the results have hardly been brilliant, and the enthusiastic young people prepared to take over for the next decade while we graze, in our old age, on the green pastures reserved for us (on paper!) have not, so far, materialised ...

Some of us think that 15 years of propaganda have been a dismal failure, and among them some think that it has been because we have not succeeded in "putting over the idea" while others maintain that if the public won't respond there is nothing much that you can do about it. In the third group are those who think that we should intensify our propaganda whether the public is apathetic or enthusiastic. None of us, however, doubts the "rightness", the validity, of anarchism.

A modern eye might look at such sentiments and detect burnout — but surprisingly nothing could be further from the truth. In fact, the survey being undertaken was a precursor to one of the most ambitious and productive periods in *Freedom's* history.

Anti-war, anti-nuke

The reasoning for the *Freedom* survey of 1960 was not just navel gazing. The editors had seen the possibility of a renaissance of anarchist fortunes from the public's reaction to the Suez Crisis and Hungary, which they identified as a potentially pivotal moment for the British left.

They were absolutely correct in that assessment. Not just from a perspective of competition against the other left factions, but more importantly a whole set of social issues which *Freedom* had, in its lonely way, been banging on about for years were on the cusp of going spectacularly mainstream as hippy culture razed so many regressive values to the ground. Free love, experimental education, peace activism, *Freedom*'s outsider lecturing put it well ahead of most of the rest of the press. When the oral contraceptive finally arrived on the public scene in 1960 for example *Freedom* had already been reporting on its progress for three years, the only non-medical paper to do so.

The social revolution that took place through that decade was somewhat paralleled by rising class power at the workplace (though that wouldn't really peak until the '70s), and a drive against the drab alienation of the post-war consensus which reached across Europe.

Such social revolts would eventually find their high water mark through America's Summer of Love in 1967, the convulsions of 1968 in France and Italy, and in Britain, everything from free festivals and peace to squatting and anti-nuclear direct action.

Freedom's survey was a precursor to working out a strategy for engaging with this process, which would transform anarchism from a near-forgotten political rump to the philosophical hub of an entire socio-cultural shift, and a number of useful tips to the situation the Press was in at the turn of the decade can be extracted as a result. From the start, for example, a large number of *Freedom's* newer readers were identifying as former Communist Party or Labour — the beginnings of a refugee process from discredited Statist machinery.

The readership was primarily in their 30s and 40s, alumni from the wartime and peace movements with only a very few left from the older generation — less than 10% of *Freedom's* audience was over 60 and able to remember the optimism of the pre-war years. Individualists, philosophic and pacifist readers were the three largest constituencies, leaving syndicalists and anarcho-communists trailing.* Readers reporting about the impact of the paper on their lives often cited its challenges to traditionalist concepts such as the nuclear family — though the proud comment by at least one anonymous correspondent that it had helped him feel less guilty about cheating on his wife was likely an unintentional consequence. Others admitted to having harboured political ambitions as MPs and diplomats before being persuaded otherwise by *Freedom's* arguments.

The biggest complaint was that the paper lacked "a clear policy", and it is certainly true that there were moments of some confusion as competing tendencies within the movement played out across the newspaper's pages. In one case for example the paper, largely pacifistic in its everyday publishing, backed rebels in Algeria, while another particularly controversial headline about a farmer's failed attempt to shoot South African Apartheid Prime Minister Dr Verwoel simply read 'Too Bad He Missed'. This caused uproar which would dog the letters pages for months to come. Similar arguments would take place throughout the decade.

In the main however a relatively stable collective was still in place with clear political lines over the first few years of the '60s,

---

* This was particularly clear in the letters pages, which politically were total bedlam, with an individualist-pacifist lean

particularly involving Vernon Richards, Philip Sansom, Jack Stevenson (see People, page 281) and Jack Robinson (see People, page 235), with John Rety also becoming heavily involved shortly after. They were supported by a recurring cast of writers, most reliably Arthur Moyse who turned in both cartoons and an acerbic exhibitions column for decades, continuing to help out with *Freedom* projects into the 1980s.

Alongside solidarity notices for the victims of Franco's purges in Spain — one petition was signed by up to 100 prominent figures including Iris Murdoch and Benjamin Britten — the group's main focus continued to be the peace movement, and 1960 proved to be a key year in that campaign. It started with a major series of arrests, as 82 demonstrators linked to the Direct Action Committee were collared at Harrington missile base. The rally and its aftermath, initially disavowed by CND, was an early example of the sort of non-violent confrontations that would characterise much of the rest of the decade. Having already been heavily critical of the "lollypop waving" CND's endless solemn marches, *Freedom* was supportive of this new development. In an April 16th article, 'Is Aldermaston Enough', for example an editor wrote of the annual big anti-Bomb march:

To our minds the only effective function of an organisation such as the CND at the present stage is that of provoking more independent thinking among the people. This, as we who are engaged in just such a task with *Freedom* know only too well, is much more difficult than organising spectacular demonstrations which appeal to the emotional temperature of the moment, but which leave little trace once the organs of mass communications cool off and the provocative incident has been relegated to a paragraph in history and replaced by new provocations ... let us face the fact that something more is needed is we are to build up a spontaneous movement of the people which will also be able to influence the course of events.

And in the same paper 'Are You Marching For Kicks' by 'G' lauded the younger attendees' "avoidance of the 'holier than thou' attitude that afflicts a certain section of all movements of social protest." Those relative newcomers went on to participate in sit-ins and taking more serious direct actions, following the founding of the anti-militarist Committee of 100 later that year which featured several prominent anarchists and fellow-travellers. This attitude was to prove extraordinarily valuable for *Freedom*, as it was able to connect directly to the new wave of activism being undertaken by young people who had run out of patience with the dignified but almost entirely ineffective softly-softly approach being employed by CND.

At Aldermaston alone more than 1,500 copies of the paper were sold and such numbers, which made a dramatic impact on Freedom's ever-ailing finances, marked the start of a long upswing in both readership and publishing activity on the part of the group. Looking at the fundraising column, annual shortfalls drop over the course of the decade from £800 a year to near enough break-even in 1968 despite significantly higher expenses, primarily due to a substantial rise in subs income. In 1961 for example annual expenses were around £3,500 (about £74,000 today), rising to £4,500 in 1967, but subs income more than doubled over the same period from £1,600 to £3,764.*

It was the following year however when *Freedom*'s contribution to the shape of that decade was really nailed down. On March 4th the paper showcased a major redesign, its first since 1945, raising prices to 4d and announcing the forthcoming launch of a new journal, *Anarchy*. The paper would come out 42 times a year while the 32-page journal would produce 10 issues annually, edited by Colin Ward with front page designs by Rufus Segar. The new system offered a dramatic improvement over what had gone before, allowing Ward to build up a reservoir of intelligent essays at a reasonable pace without having to vie for space within the more news-oriented paper, and through to the ending of its first run in 1971 *Anarchy* would help relieve *Freedom* of at least one of the many tensions which stretched its column inches, between the desire for slower, thoughtful analysis and engagement with the issues of the day.

---

* It's worth reiterating that throughout, these figures included few paid positions, virtually the entire sum being spent on non-editorial matters such as printing costs, distribution and rent. Even the mailout was done by volunteers, which is a remarkable amount of drudge work to do for free.

Anarchy

Some of its work dates badly, but *Anarchy* has generally retained a good reputation for both its beautiful cover art and the quality of its essays.* Ward's sources and topics were extensive, from carpenter James Lynch writing on workers' control in the building industry of the 1920s to *Joy of Sex* author Alex Comfort musing on sex and death. Also of note were Ron Bailey, whose related 1973 book *The Squatters* was picked up by Penguin and Jim Radford who was involved in the later Centrepoint occupation. *About Anarchism* by Nicolas Walter also came out of this series.

With issues themed around a specific topic, Ward took a microscope to education and British institutional processes in particular, but also dedicated substantial efforts to international analysis such as imperialism in Africa and dictatorship in Spain. Writing in *History Workshop*, former *Freedom* member David Goodway notes:

> As editor of *Anarchy* Ward had some success in putting anarchist ideas "back into the intellectual bloodstream", largely because of propitious political and social changes. The rise of the New Left and the nuclear disarmament movement in the late '50s, culminating in the student radicalism and general libertarianism of the

---

* Notable exceptions here are Albert Meltzer, who wrote that Anarchy "helped, as much as anything, to reinforce the myth of a non-violent, sanitised 'anarchism' that could help capitalism out of its difficulties", and Ian Bone, who deemed it incomprehensible.

'60s, meant that a new audience receptive to anarchist attitudes came into existence.

My own case offers an illustration of the trend. In October 1961, a foundation subscriber to the *New Left Review* (the first number of which had appeared at the beginning of the previous year) and in London again to appear at Bow Street after my arrest during a Committee of 100 sit-down on September 17th, I bought a copy of *Anarchy* 8 at Collet's bookshop in Charing Cross Road. I had just turned 19 and thereafter was hooked, several weeks later beginning to read *Freedom* also. When I went up to Oxford University 12 months later, I co-founded the Oxford Anarchist Group and one of the first speakers invited was Colin Ward.

Ward himself penned a full analysis of *Anarchy*'s impact in the June 28th 1969 issue of *Freedom*, summarising its first 100 issues under his editorship and his perspective on how it did in achieving its original aims, reproduced below:

Anarchy, like *Freedom*, is a propagandist journal. Its purpose is to convince people of the validity of the anarchist point of view, and to persuade them to initiate some kind of anarchist action. This is the aim against which its success or failure should be judged. So perhaps the first thing to say about it is that from the acid test of sales, it has not been a success. The two dozen or so issues which have completely sold out have sold 2,800 copies. Every other issue has sold less than this. In an early issue, suggesting that it would be a useful exercise in mental self-discipline if we anarchists, instead of aiming at infinity, were to calculate what we might expect to achieve by 1970, I said that I aimed at a circulation for *Anarchy* of 4,000 by that date. How wildly optimistic was that modest ambition! Most anarchist publications have suffered from the fact that, with their limited human and material resources, the effort to produce, the goods absorbs all their efforts, and nothing is left for marketing. Obviously both *Anarchy* and *Freedom* desperately need to find someone who will see it as his or her unique and indispensable task to push sales and find new readers.

The only consoling feature of the sales situation is that, as we all know, the minority press is much more intensively read by the people who do read it than the large-circulation journals are.

People who bother to seek out and subscribe to the minority press are often people who exercise an influence in society greater than their numbers. They are often opinion-formers and activists.

One of *Freedom*'s great editors in the past, Tom Keell, declared that "Our propaganda is necessarily for serious people in their most serious moods. If it is merely glanced through casually and cast carelessly aside, like the ordinary daily paper, nothing is accomplished". Seen in this light, *Anarchy* has a certain amount of success. Material from it has been reprinted all over the world and translated into many languages. The anarchist press throughout the world has used articles originally published in *Anarchy*, and, perhaps more important from a propagandist point of view, it has also been reprinted, quoted and commented on in many non-anarchist periodicals and books.

Nor has *Anarchy* hesitated to reproduce articles from elsewhere (sometimes eliciting more response for the author from his readers than in the original place of publication). This has been partly because of the policy of one- topic-one-issue, and partly because so much is published which is too good for our readers to miss just because they don't read every periodical.

The one-topic-one-issue policy which I have tried to keep to as far as possible has been intended to make the journal a monthly pamphlet to fill the gaps of contemporary anarchist literature. I am convinced that this is the most effective way to use an anarchist journal as propaganda and I am sorry that more use has not been made of it in this way by the anarchist movement.

The besetting editorial problems of any periodical of a minority movement are parochialism and sectarianism. You, as a curious outsider, pick up a magazine put out by some other minority and find that it is full of references which the uninitiated do not understand, and has a background of in-group feuding in which X is getting at Y over some historical or doctrinal difference which you can't comprehend, *Anarchy* has tried, not always successfully, to avoid this: to take it for granted that anarchism is in the mainstream of modern social ideas, and to address itself to the outside world rather than to the ingroup. This has involved going outside the usual circle of contributors to the anarchist press, and accepting the fact that their opinions are not always 'ideologically correct' even though the general tenor of their contributions is sympathetic. This is the policy which was followed by some of the great anarchist journals of the past — for example *La Revolte* in France and the *Revista Blanca* in Spain. It involves using the journal as a kind of anarchist shop-window, displaying to the world the quality and range of goods which the anarchist approach can offer. Looked at in this light, I think that readers will agree that an extraordinary range of anarchist insights and applications have appeared in the course of our 100 issues. The raw material for the individual propagandist is there, waiting for use.

Any editor, unless he happens to be a prolific writer is at the mercy of his contributors and what they will write for him. There are very many topics which should have been discussed from an anarchist standpoint in *Anarchy* and have not been. On the other hand, several of the themes which have run through the hundred issues have taken root and blossomed elsewhere since *Anarchy* began. Take the idea of workers' control of industry. When *Anarchy* 2 was devoted to this topic in 1961 we called it "an idea looking for a movement". By the time of the Fifth National Conference on Workers' Control 18 months ago (1967), Geoffrey Ostergaard, writing in *Anarchy* 80 felt able to describe it as "an idea on the wing". Or take education. No journal has published such a budget of authoritative material on the progressive movement in education. Today we have a growing questioning of the foundations of the education system, a movement for "pupil power" in schools, a Libertarian Teachers Association, and a groundswell of interest and concern of an essentially anarchist kind.

Take crime and punishment. No more devastating enquiry into the nature of delinquency and the penal system in our society has appeared in any journal as in *Anarchy*, and a whole school of criminologists has emerged in the last few years, whose outlook is essentially anarchistic (see for example *Anarchy* 98 on 'libertarian criminology' and *Anarchy* 101 which will examine detention centres and approved schools).

Finally take housing. *Anarchy* has continually come back to this topic, advocating a new squatting campaign. Over the last six months, it has happened. The London Squatters' Movement has not developed in the way in which we all hoped. It has not been emulated everywhere into a nationwide campaign of direct action. But Ron Bailey and Jim Radford and the handful of people who have thrown themselves into this campaign, have provided an inspiration which is not going to be lost in the future. The battle that has been played out in suburban streets between them as responsible citizens, and the authorities who have destroyed houses rather than risk their being occupied by the homeless, and have hired strong-arm men to throw out squatters because they couldn't legally get the police do do it, seems to me an object lesson in the truth of everything the anarchists have ever said about the nature of authority and the necessity of resisting it. If *Anarchy* has contributed anything to these four areas of social concern, it will not have been a wasted effort.

A New Series of *Anarchy* would follow in 1972. Helmed by Phil Ruff, this was spun off and became an independent production, briefly working out of Angel Alley again in the 1980s.

As *Anarchy* prepared for its first outing, the new-look main paper was handed a happy coincidence to kick off with — the inaugural sit-down protest of the Committee of 100. Chaired by the world-renowned philosopher Bertrand Russell, a lifelong anti-war activist who "had the tendency" with his libertarian leanings, it was counted a huge success, harbouring anarchist ideals which would dominate the group for most of the decade.*

A follow-up demo the next week against the Polaris nuclear programme in Holy Loch, Scotland, saw direct involvement from LAG members and *Freedom* covered the Committee's activities extensively as an escalating series of non-violent direct actions took place — the first sustained use of such tactics. In September Bertrand Russell himself was detained, along with 32 others, under the ludicrous charge of "inciting breach of the peace." The discomfort of police and their initial inability to work out how to handle such tactics subtly was clearly refreshing to a peace movement which had been painting by numbers for some time, and by December a National Civil Disobedience Day called by the committee drew over 6,000 people nationwide with 850 arrests being made. Freedom's response to this heavy backlash was cautious, praising the year's events overall but remarking both on the need to think in broader terms and tread carefully in encouraging particularly young people to risk imprisonment. An unsigned editorial, likely by Vero, is heavily critical of a lack of appreciable planning by the Committee over what was to be achieved by civil disobedience:

> There can be no doubt whatever as to the importance of the activities of the original Direct Action Committee in shaking off some of the apathy, the hopeless fatalism and defeatism which had enshrouded the more or less progressive, thinking, elements in this country. But it seems to us that the kind of useful publicity that the National Press could be expected to give to the activities of the Committee of 100 are now exhausted.
>
> ...
>
> This writer has all along supported the initiatives taken by the Committee of 100, without sharing their hopes in a non-violent social revolution and firmly disassociating ourselves from the muddled thinking of their chairman, who we deeply respect ... the sit down demonstrations they organised served to break

---

* This event would also be the last action attended by Augustus John, who died a month later.

down the blind acceptance with which the majority of people swallowed the orders and policies of the government in office.

...

[But] demonstrations which involve the possibility of arrest, police violence, and imprisonment must not be treated lightly, as a weekend outing. Because we consider them as serious non-violent threats to authority, we felt that the Committee of 100, when they originally stated that their acts of civil disobedience would take place only if a minimum of 2,000 people pledged themselves to take part, clearly valued the person of the demonstrator as highly as his "witness". A demonstration of 2,000 had the possibility of success so far as its limited objectives were concerned, or failing that, ensured either immunity from arrest or mass arrests which would cause a breakdown of the Court machinery and of the prisons if demonstrators refused to pay fines.

Russell at a Committee rally

This was a reasonable supposition perhaps a year ago. It no longer is. Knowing that there was a reception committee of the Establishment of some 3,000 military and civilian police at Wethersfield, that the coach company had refused transport facilities the Committee of 100 should, at its eve of the demonstration briefing, have held a secret meeting with its Wethersfield marshals calling off that demonstration and asking them to intercept would-be demonstrators at the London Station and on the highways and suggest they join the Ruislip demonstration.

This it seems is the old guard at *Freedom* making an effort to dredge up lessons of yesteryear to pass on to the enthusiastic youth surrounding Russell in the face of mass arrests and escalating police repression. *Freedom* was at this stage, while active in the peace movement, not entirely at its heart and the conclusions its veterans had drawn from the second world war about sticking your neck out with no plan were not necessarily common currency among the influx of new activists.

Nevertheless, *Freedom*'s holding later in the year of an October Ball, reported in its November issue, offers a sense of the growing optimism in the anarchists' ranks. Booked at Fulham Town Hall and headlined by the indefatigable George Melly, it celebrated 75 years since *Freedom's* founding and drew more than 300 people. The paper gives a quick overview of the sort of people who were involved at the time:

> There were jazz-men and musicologists, production engineers and demolition men, psychologists and beatniks, a girl from the San Francisco to Moscow march, luminaries of the Committee of 100 fresh from jail, a troupe of novelists and poets — Charles Humana, Alan Sillitoe, Christopher Logue and writer Colin MacInnes, actor David Markham, students, physicians, meter-readers, Freedom's machine-minder and one of its typesetters, a gaggle of architects, and the only pacifist bouncer in London's nightlife — not that he was called upon to perform, for this was an anarchist, and not a law-abiding assembly."
>
> Among the anarchists who couldn't be present, we most of all missed Lilian Wolfe; who has been engaged with Freedom Press activity for 50 of its 75 years. We send her our affectionate greetings. We were sent greetings from Alex Comfort, Charles Duff, Doris Lessing, Compton Mackenzie, Ethel Mannin, Herbert Read, and other absentees, including Augustus John.

Melly at the event

The event was successful enough to prompt a second ball the following year, though Philip Sansom noted ruefully that it made no money, as the bar franchise was held by someone else. This was particularly unfortunate given the cost of moving to Fulham, redesigning *Freedom* and launching *Anarchy*, which had collectively blown an £1,800 hole in the group's finances.

The next couple of years saw a rapid rise in the number of new faces, and 1962 saw the forming of the London Federation of Anarchists, which would incorporate LAG alongside anarchist groups from Notting Hill, Woolwich and Enfield, as well as the Iberian Federation of Youth, meeting weekly in Monmouth Street. Further afield, *Freedom's* 'Contacts' section saw groups springing up in Edinburgh, Bristol, Oxford, and for the first time in many years, Glasgow. This quickly led to the first calls for bigger ideas, such as the resurrection of the Anarchist Federation of Britain, which started getting mentioned in the letters pages early in 1963. Later that year, at LAG's annual summer school in Kent, Jack

Stevenson was appointed co-ordinating secretary to organise the first AFB conference since the end of the war.

Projects which anarchists had been key in such as the League Against Capital Punishment also saw substantial progress and reports such as Shorten The Rope' (April 15th 1961) reflected a campaigning atmosphere which could be found in ongoing Hyde Park talks and public meetings, led by regular speakers such as Philip Sansom and Jack Robinson. Under sustained pressure from LACP's successor, the National Campaign For The Abolition of Capital Punishment, the State would cease hanging people in 1964. The Committee of 100 too came up with a number of innovations in its direct action, moving from sit-downs to more proactive fare, such as ploughing up an RAF V-bomber base at Swaffham in October 1962, then coming back the following year to "auction it for scrap." Hundreds of arrests continued to take place, and *Freedom* began to carry regular fundraising columns for the detainees.

In February 1963 the Committee came under significant pressure with the emergence of Spies For Peace, a group which broke into a government bunker near Reading, stole secret documents outlining preparations for a post-nuclear war scenario, and published 3,000 copies, sending them to MPs, celebrities and protesters. In later years Nicolas and Ruth Walter would admit that they were involved and after his death, daughter Natasha described the raid in the *New Statesman* in 2002, conceived after contacts hinted at the existence of a secret site:

They drove for hours over ice-covered roads, and tramped over snow-covered fields. At the east end of a village called Warren Row, they found a fenced-off hill with a padlocked wooden gate, and an unmarked hut. They climbed over the gate to find a brick boiler house and a wide concrete ramp leading into the hillside. Radio aerials stood a little way off, their cables leading into the hill. One of the explorers tried the doors of the boiler house and found them unlocked. The four of them went in.

Inside, they tried another door on what looked like a cupboard. This was also unlocked, and swung open to reveal a steep staircase leading into an underground office complex. They ran down the stairs, their feet clattering in the silence, and snatched what papers they could from the desks. Then they rushed out and drove away, hardly able to believe their luck.

It led to major protests and humiliated the secret State, which knew this could not be the Soviets' doing as the documents had been made public to all. Raids and questionings duly followed, including against future *Freedom* editor Bill Christopher, but no-one was ever charged. Such activities only served to fuel the continuing rise of the movement at large, and *Freedom* was by this point enjoying a weekly circulation of around 3,500 alongside healthy sales of *Anarchy*. Writing in defence of *Freedom's* independence from control on May 9th 1964 on individualist grounds (it had been suggested the paper become an official organ of the AFB once again), the editors noted:

Peace protest, 1963

The situation today is that over the past 12 months a number of anarchist groups have formed themselves (with no direction from anybody else) and have quickly become numerous enough to feel that there is some advantage in federating — presumably for mutual aid. The personnel of these groups consisted mainly of anti-Bomb militants disillusioned with the political slant of CND who realised that the logical development of the practice of direct action was the acceptance of the philosophy which went with it.

Further, they saw that the Bomb is not an isolated factor in authoritarian society and that the struggle against the Bomb led inevitably to a struggle against the state. So we got a great increase in the number of people calling themselves anarchists, some of whom were (and are) pacifists first and anarchists second.

These new comrades accept the relevance of anarchism to their primary interests but reject the traditional revolutionary attitude which the anarchist movement as a whole has represented. Besides these, there was a tougher leavening of militants who thought in terms of mass revolutionary movements and, rejecting the fragmentary Marxist groups, found their answer in the ideas of anarcho-syndicalism.

This again hints at a "nice problem to have" complaint common to many moments of extraordinary growth — the difficulty of dealing with success as new people with broad-based and sometimes messy or simplistic politics upset existing stability and push through changes, sometimes to the good, sometimes repeating old mistakes.

Alongside this confusion of minor successes there was another issue at hand for the burgeoning movement. Spies for Peace, as well as a spate of anarchist-led protests against repression in Greece and Spain, and especially following an occupation of the Cuban Embassy in July 1963 led by Philip Sansom against Fidel Castro's repression of anarchists there, had placed the libertarian left square in the sights of the press and police. This led *Freedom* to start carefully judging its words in defending libertarian activities.

When Committee of 100 secretary Michael Hardwood started panicking in print about "unruly elements" for example *Freedom* was quick to reassure readers that the movement remained "non-violent with some dissenters". And in a front page article on July 13th, noting a warning from Special Branch in the *Sunday Telegraph* about potential anarchist violence on the streets, an editor accurately predicted:

> One can expect that the tactic of the press will be to seek to work up fears of insecurity in the "respectable" middle classes, and to divide the movement loosely joined around the nuclear disarmament movement by scare stories and suggestions that certain "undesirable" elements are infiltrating the movement and driving out the moderate elements.

With the State once again taking notice, it would be no coincidence when LAG member Donald Rooum was arrested in the infamous Challenor Case — prominent anarchists were seen to have been courting a backhand from the police for some time. More broadly, London's Special Branch of protest observers and spies were already taking the situation seriously enough to begin a major reorganisation and would keep a close watch for the next four decades.

This included an edge of horror as it descended into the depths of manipulative undercover officers having children with their unsuspecting targets [see the Spycops scandal, page 173].

Donald Rooum, Frank Leech, Arno Pomerans, Tony Gibson and Leah Feldman at Glasgow anarchist summer school in 1951

Donald Rooum and the mystery of the missing half-brick

Greece in the 1960s was the victim of a strategy of permanent tension (which also played out in Italy), with a half-crushed left struggling against the ascendant monarchist right, which would lead to the coup of 1967 and the installation of a near-enough fascist junta, with 10,000 leftists arrested and widespread use of torture.

In 1963 the situation was precariously balanced and Greece's Queen Frederika had become an international lightning rod for left activism due to her hard-right views. A former Hitler Youth member in Austria, she consistently used her position to attack left politicians and in April 1963 had been chased down the street by protestors during a visit to London as a result. A month later, Greek peace activist and MP Grigoris Lambrakis was assassinated, meaning that when she returned to London from July 9th-12th demos were well mobilised at Claridge's hotel in Mayfair, where she was staying. The Met, having been unprepared for the reaction to her last visit, went mob-handed, led by the notorious Harold Challenor. Donald recounted his subsequent experience in "A Personal Story" (*Freedom*, August 17th 1963):

I first met Detective Sergeant Challenor at about nine o'clock on the evening of July 11th. The previous evening a large crowd had booed the Queen at a theatre, and the Home Secretary, a man usually noted for his imperturbability, had been reduced to trembling with rage. So the police were taking no chances. The Queen was to arrive at Claridge's Hotel, and a huge area surrounding was being cleared of all but police and a few press photographers.

A Committee of 100 briefing instructed demonstrators stopped by the police to sit down; but sit-down demonstrations have become rowdy and undignified over the past year, and besides, I hadn"t time to get arrested. So I was playing it legal. When the police told me to move, I moved, but in a circle, in the hope that if I could stay in the neighbourhood until the royal party arrived I might be permitted to stand silently holding my innocuous paper banner.

So there I was at about nine o'clock in South Molton Lane with Peter and Anne, who were trying the same tactic; not indeed, within hailing distance of Claridge's but well within the evacuated area. The police had stopped us again and one of them had taken my banner and was making a great show of reading it (it said "Lambrakis RIP") when four plainclothes men came up and took it off him.

"Can I have my banner back?" I asked when they'd all read it.

The biggest one stepped forward. "Can you have your what back?"

"My banner."

He smiled at me. "You're fucking nicked my old beauty." he said and gave me a terrific clout on the ear. Then he grabbed me by the collar thrusting his knuckles into my skull and bustled off towards Claridge's.

"Please, officer," I protested, "I'm coming quietly."

"Don't say please to me, my old darling, I've got a stone 'art." At least he is not a hypocrite; from the beginning he acted like an antagonist.

Round the corner was a bus full of uniformed policemen, presumably reserves. My captor pushed me up the stairs and we sat in an empty seat. But there was no driver and after a while we moved to a police van, also full of uniformed men. I collided with one of them as I hurtled in but he was a pleasant bloke and took no offence.

"Sit down there," said the big plainclothes man, indicating the floor, "That's the best place for you, isn't it?"

"If you say so, sir," I said affably. No point in arguing.

Round and round went the van, slowly past the endless police barriers, past groups of jeering marching kids, on Oxford Street I think, where the big bloke and some of the uniformed ones got out and walked behind the van. Apparently we went in a big circle: cries of "Blimey, Oxford Street again!" Then after what seemed a very long time we stopped at the back of a police station.

We got out, the two of us. He pushed me up the few outside steps and let go. There were two or three corridors and a flight of steps. I opened by mouth to ask which way, his voice behind me roared "Gerrup them stairs" and Wham! Another great clout on the ear which knocked me flying. I got up them stairs, naturally, as quick as I could. But at the top of the stairs was another landing with corridors and more stairs going up ...

Wham! "Gerrup them stairs," and at the top of these stairs, another landing with corridors and stairs ...

And so on. I can't remember how many landings and flights of stairs. Perhaps there are only three. But memory is confused by a dream I had, lying with my sore ear on a coir bolster in a cell, of stairs and landings which went up and Wham and ouch and up indefinitely.

Sooner or later we reached the charge room, and the big bloke called out 'I've got a desperate one 'ere," which someone took as a signal to open a cell door. The big bloke frogmarched me in and the door was locked on the pair of us.

He pushed his face into mine.

"Boo the queen, would you?" he snarled.

"No," I said quickly, "not at all."

"Eh?" he looked slightly worried. Then craftily. "But you sympathise with 'em, don't you?"

"No," I said. (Strictly speaking the answer should have been "it depends what you mean by sympathise," but this did not occur to me at the time). So he didn't beat me up after all. Just three more clouts to the ears, which were rather an anti-climax after the softening-up on the stairs.

"There you are my old darling," he smiled at me sitting on the floor, "'ave that with me. And just to make sure we 'aven't forgotten it ..." From his pocket he took a screwed-up newspaper which he slowly and deliberately undid, turning it in my direction so I could see that it contained: a broken brick. "There you are, my old beauty."

Later I was called before the duty officer and the big bloke charged me with carrying an offensive weapon, to wit the brick. The story he told need not delay us except for the significant detail that he found the brick in my pocket.

Thanks to that small oversight Donald had a trick up his sleeve. Realising that Challenor had never actually placed the evidence on him, upon being bailed he ran directly to the office of a commercial scientist who proved in exhaustive detail that not a speck of brick dust could be found in his pockets, or anywhere else.

At trial, it was a legal massacre. Rather than Donald it was the officer who looked to be the defendant, and Rooum was acquitted. Challenor was himself sent to trial the following year charged with conspiracy to pervert the course of justice and made an, astonishingly, successful bid to escape justice for his crime by having himself diagnosed with paranoid schizophrenia. Three of his fellow detectives went to jail.

Eventually a full Parliamentary inquiry was held over the case, the first held under the 1964 Police Act, which also found Challenor innocent. The result was widely decried as a whitewash of blatant corruption and for many years afterwards "doing a Challenor" became police slang for avoiding justice by claiming illness and retiring without consequences.

While Donald was dealing with corrupt coppers, the anarchist revival was gathering steam. With *Freedom* behind it and Jack Stevenson organising, the Anarchist Federation of Britain held its first formal gathering that April, which saw strong support from *Freedom* but was primarily organised by Bristolians Digger Walsh and Ian Vine. The conference had plenty going for it, bringing together *Freedom*, the SWF* and others for the first time since the war. Chaired by Arthur Uloth and Malcolm Keith, it had about 80 delegates and set up a secretariat to maintain communications, co-ordinated by Tom Jackson. Extensive coverage from *Freedom* followed in the next few years, outlining the paper's intended (independent) relationship with the movement.

Alongside *Freedom's* audience of approaching 4,000 another four publications were now being published, *Direct Action, The Bridge, Anarchist Youth* and *Anarchist International*, with another, *Germinal*, on the way. By the end of the decade there would be *Solidarity, The Anarchist, Cuddon's Cosmopolitan Review, ABC Bulletin, Community* and likely others not mentioned in *Freedom's* pages.

The introduction of small offset printing had a lot to do with this, as it brought costs down significantly, but it also reflects increased interest in anarchist ideas. The Committee of 100 too became more overtly anarchist, publishing its 'Third Policy Statement' in the August 8th issue of *Freedom* saying outright:

> It is not enough to be merely anti-war. We are interested in the problems of building a new non-violent society. We think it essential to undertake this even under the shadow of war and war preparations. We are, for example, actively involved in new thinking and action about education, housing, health, communications, transport and industrial relations.
>
> We have broken with party politics. We believe in the day-to-day mutual accountability of individuals and groups. We have ceased to believe in dependence upon representatives and officials. We are, in consequence, opposed to the present trend towards the centralisation of government. We urge new experiments in regional, local and functional administration in which the importance of the individual counts more than the importance of "the machine".

---

* The SWF hit its high water mark in the mid-'60s with a membership of around 500 people, according to Nick Heath.

That same month a big story hit the headlines, as an 18-year-old Scot was arrested in Madrid, his rucksack full of dynamite, for trying to assassinate General Franco. Stuart Christie had recently become active with the anarchists, involving himself with the AFB conference. While that had been enough for many new activists however, Christie had already become obsessed with deposing Franco and made useful contacts towards that end through Acracio Ruiz, a CNT-FAI veteran active with a group charged with killing the dictator — Directorate of Defensa Interior.

The attempted attentat is more fully described alongside extensive background information about the post-war struggle against Franco in Stuart Christie's memoir *Granny Made Me An Anarchist*. But in sum, the young militant wished to strike a blow, and organised to go to Paris, telling friends including John Rety that he was going fruit picking for the summer. Instead, he met up with Defensa Interior operatives and picked up a bagful of explosives.

From there, he hitchhiked to Madrid, where he and his comrade Carballo Blanco were detained, having been clandestinely followed by a Francoist agent. When word filtered back to Britain, it emerged that he was facing 30 years or worse, the garotte. In the *Freedom* centenary Philip Sansom (somewhat defensively) describes the response back home when the news came in:

> Immediately the story broke, the comrades of the Freedom Press group swung into action. Four members formed the nucleus of a Defence Committee, which organised meetings in Conway Hall and at Trafalgar Square addressed by representatives of Freedom Press (myself), LAG, the Syndicalist Workers Federation, CND and others.
>
> One member of LAG, John Pilgrim, appointed himself press relations officer and manned the telephone in the committee's office day and night, to ensure that any news we had from Spain was immediately available to the British press, and everything published about Christie was as true as we could make it. Pilgrim had also acted as press officer for the well-publicised Freedom Press/LAG occupation of the Cuban Embassy, following the execution of some Cuban anarchists.
>
> Establishing what was true was the difficulty in the Christie case. In the light of a telegram, "Please believe in my innocence", *Freedom* at first took the line that the whole thing was a frame-up by the Spanish police. But when the trial

came on, it was found that Christie had confessed "freely" — having been caught red-handed. The sad thing was that a Spanish comrade, Fernando Carballo Blanco, had been caught with Christie and ended up with 30 years against Christie's 20 — of which he served three.

What is even sadder is that the effort *Freedom* put into supporting the Christie-Carballo Defence Committee has been denigrated by techniques of sneer and smear, and reduced, in the minds of some who do not take the trouble to check what actually appeared in print, to the dread "liberalism". What *Freedom* actually printed on August 29th 1964, when we were asked to believe in the frame-up line, was: "If Stuart Christie is, as we suggest, innocent of the charges made against him, there is no question but that a campaign on as wide a scale as possible on his behalf must be organised. But if he is guilty? Then, in our opinion, the efforts of all men of goodwill must be redoubled, irrespective of whether they approve or disapprove of his methods. For what will count, what will remain in people's minds, is the noble intention".

Some liberalism! The then-editor who wrote those lines was Vernon Richards.

Freedom did publish copiously about the Christie case over the next three years of his incarceration, including prominent articles every week for the first month, fundraising columns, and even a regular filler simply noting: "Christie still has X weeks to go, what are You doing?" Conversely, unmentioned by Sansom are the sometimes toe-curlingly bad arguments which went on the inside pages.

The worst of these was Nicolas Walter vs John Rety, which saw the frequent *Anarchy* contributor and future editor write in on September 19th accusing Christie of being a part of anarchism's violent wing and demanding that the paper cease defending him as an innocent. This was, probably unwisely, printed and then retorted to by Rety, sparking a long back and forth about the case which did Christie himself few favours.

In the event however not much of this actually reached Christie, whose contact with the British movement was limited mainly to the occasional letter. He notes: "Catching up with it later, it was par for the course, more or less what I'd expect from the editors, especially Vero Richards and Nicolas Walter. No surprises there, but I did get on with Walter, more or less — Albert didn't, couldn't stand him".

Vero's 'retirement' and a move to Angel Alley

As it turned out, the Christie case would be the last major story of Vero's first stint as editor. After 30 years, he seemingly saw his chance to get out from under the masthead and quietly announced his decision to retire from the paper. It's easy to see why. Beyond his personal wish to move to Suffolk with his partner Peta, the growth of the movement and the re-founding of the AFB came alongside a move into financial stability for the Press, which featured a reliable collective of editors including Philip Sansom, John Rety, Jack Stevenson, Peter Turner, Mary Canipa, Roy and Barbara Fisher ready to take up the baton.

He had intended to leave without a fuss, but was stymied in this by Philip Sansom, who unbeknownst to him inserted a farewell article in the December 26th 1964 issue, lauding his efforts and defending him against his critics:

> During VR's editorship, *Freedom* has been committed to anarchism not to any single facet of anarchism. This has been the strength of the paper, but it has of course frustrated those who narrow their anarchism down to a part instead of the whole. Ironically, it was the generosity of his attitude in allowing full expression to all points of view (while retaining the right of full editorial reply!) that gave rise to criticism from those who think that an anarchist paper should plug a line (their line), not give space to argument and discussion.
>
> On the personal level, VR's very qualities of being able to treat with dignified contempt personal attack and ill-will were bound up with what (in my opinion and in the context of work in a propagandist movement) were his defects of not being extrovert enough to meet and talk and relate with people in a public way. But then, he has never wished to project himself in a personal way. A belief in anonymity, a desire to be just a back-room boy, led to VR being almost unknown in a movement in which, by virtue of his work, he has had great influence.

With Vero gone, the lead figure for the following 1965-9 period is generally given as John Rety, who was most often the one making editorial decisions and replying in the paper's columns. With the New Year also came a new redesign, with the distinctive lined logo replaced by a more compact, tabloid-style masthead and a whole new back page section dedicated solely to industrial news with the subhead "for workers' control". Almost certainly the work of Sansom and Stevenson who both had strong syndicalist sympathies, this would continue to push a radical line on workplace affairs for the rest of the decade.

The change in tone was immediate, and initially drew criticism for being too doctrinaire, but the readership stayed stable and the punchier new tone drew new writers, including Bill Christopher, an anarcho-syndicalist who worked as a carpenter and would later become a core editorial figure. Peter Neville, highly active in Birmingham, was also a regular. The letters pages became significantly more diverse, not always for the better as it included an influx of people whose politics were very much in flux. As the decade went on support for Irish nationalism, the Viet Cong and even suggestions to join a Red Front appeared and sparked heated arguments. This was in stark contrast to the historic content of the paper, which tended towards debate within a much stricter framework. Rety's reputation in the movement was strong and his policy of printing whatever got sent in was popular, allowing him to draw in a good variety of otherwise critical writers and the paper even at one stage gave over its pages to a Scottish group once a month.

John Rety

As they got into their role the post-Vero editors had an initial filip when the first major confrontation in what has since become a five-decade long campaign to close down Faslane Naval Base took place in March 1965, a year after its establishment, and *Freedom* got something of a scoop as the direct actionists wrote in to describe their actions.

> We broke onto Faslane ... we then immobilised a truck and a pneumatic compressor which works the cement silo. We removed 50-100 wooden levels (this means the whole of the new road will have to be replanned). Our purpose was to halt or to slow down building of the new road for as long as possible and to be as much of a nuisance to the building of the base as possible. We will continue to do this for as long as we can.

Scots Against War (though this was never the name of any truly organised grouping) had opened a new phase in the campaign, going well beyond the Committee of 100's strategy with a daring piece of sabotage which would be pushed even further two months later when Ardnadam Pier, part of the Holy Loch Polaris missile base, was torched. The pier saw its officers and huts burned to the ground, followed shortly by the pier itself and the two incidents shook the State in a way that mere sit-ins had ceased to. Raids were carried out nationwide against Committee of 100 members, such as noted Scottish pacifist Walter Morrison, though arrests never materialised. The Committee leadership was spooked by the actions and publicly disavowed them, but its own star was already in marked decline, with the group slowly losing impetus until it finally collapsed in 1970. The SAW incidents would mark the beginning of a rising tide of direct action going beyond prior pacifist approaches that would peak over the next decade.

The AFB meanwhile grew that year to include around 120 delegates, and *Freedom* started regularly running a column of groups — though even at this early stage it was starting to become apparent that the federation was lacking in organisational structure. Multiple attempts to improve the situation would fall short over the next few years. In 1966 it would fall back to 100 delegates as people questioned the need for an organised AFB presence, and by that August the secretariat was essentially gone, with *Freedom* acting as the main throughput for individual group contacts. Nick Heath describes the scene in *Looking Back and Forward*:

Each conference of the AFB attracted all and sundry. On one hand anarcho-syndicalists and anarchist-communists, on the other individualists, radicalised liberals and pacifists and prophets of the counter-culture. These conferences were glorified talking shops where few decisions were ever agreed on, and even fewer carried out. There was no structure as such. Positions became shared by default. They were not usually discussed at the conferences, adopted or agreed upon, as there was no recognised way for doing such a thing. These gatherings were large and attracted representatives from many local groups like for instance the Harlow Anarchist Group, the Manchester Anarchists and the Brighton Anarchists, who were very active.

It was no surprise that many who had been initially attracted to anarchism were deterred by its chronic disorganisation and lack of effectiveness. Some of these turned to groups like International Socialism (precursor of the Socialist Workers Party) and the International Marxist Group. Digger Walsh, active in the Black Flag group of the period, was to be quoted in a national paper as lamenting the fact that 800 militants had gone over to the Trotskyists.

The AFB would potter on into the early 70s, topping out at around 85 active groups in 1968, but never managed to get itself organised and remained mostly a gathering of politicals rather than a political gathering.

An effort was made to create an internal bulletin, the *AFBIB*, which was sent all over the world and made it to foreign luminaries such as Noam Chomsky, but that this was the main function of the effort was a direct contributor to difficulties which young Ian Bone in Swansea found were allowing the Trotskyists to sweep up the student radicals, simply through superior discipline. The regionalisation of media would prove of more interest over the rest of the decade, producing papers such as *Liberty* in Yorkshire and the *Red Paper* in Ipswich. A shortlived London Industrial Shop Stewards Committee was also announced by Peter Turner which managed a surprisingly strong turnout for its inaugural meeting in June on incomes policy, drawing 200 people.

In London, LAG had grown to a stage where once again tensions were being felt and in the September 30th issue of *Freedom* people signed a letter calling for the founding of LAG2. It would broadly mark the boundaries of the 1945 Freedom/SWF split, and appears to have been an effort to keep co-operation going without rendering the group dysfunctional. This bigger London movement was showcased at probably its largest point by the third and final anarchist ball in Fulham in 1966, drawing around 480 people. Learning from previous errors, Freedom Press turned the event into a major boost for its finances, enabling the first eight-page paper since the 1930s on September 17th. Provocatively, this issue led with a splash on the this-time successful assassination of Dr Hendrik Verwoerd in South Africa titled 'Shed No Tear' and contains a summary of recent goings-on in the anarchist sphere which notes:

> Recently, Donald Rooum set in train the exposure of Det Sgt Challenor, and Stuart Christie was arrested in Spain and tried by a military court on a charge which could never be substantiated in open court. Anarchist influence has been present in the Committee of 100 and the campaign for King Hill homeless. Recently anarchists have been active in the field of education and a Libertarian Teachers' Association has been formed.
>
> Bombs and anarchism have outlived their old association, true there were anarchist assassins but their belief was in propaganda by the deed. The nature of the deed has changed

but anarchists do not repudiate the effectiveness of the elimination of tyrants. In 1960 we printed a headline 'Too Bad He Missed!' That error has since been rectified.

Inevitably there was a backlash, and this would in many ways mark a watershed moment for the paper.* It was suggested by Albert Meltzer in his autobiography many years later that Pete Turner, and Verwoerd splash writer Bill Christopher, who had both gone into the editorial game to push practical anarchism and class struggle, would instead be "overcome" by *Freedom's* ingrained liberalism. This was probably unfair overall but contained a kernel of truth — *Freedom* would go on to be widely considered the voice of boring intellectualism as the direct actionists moved elsewhere, due in part to a clash between the "direct action class strugglist" and "gentle anarchist" wings of the movement which has persisted in one form or another for nearly as long as *Freedom* itself. Writing in the February 26th 1967 issue, Jack Robinson neatly summarised the problem:

> With *Freedom* the case is sometimes violently put. "Why should we workers have to worry about the intellectuals' problems about censorship?" "Why should we intellectuals worry about the workers' struggle?" With such a small paper one is inclined to resent the limited space being given over to topics which have for us only an academic or limited interest.

When the direct actionists finally abandoned ship for good in 1968-9 following the release of Stuart Christie, setting up the Anarchist Black Cross and founding *Black Flag*, it did make an impact. However before that fateful split, normally identified as being between Albert Meltzer and Vero Richards but somewhat wider in terms of solidifying two very separate political camps, there were three more major events of note for *Freedom*.

On February 27th 1968 Freedom Press was raided for the first time in two decades when four plainclothes officers led by Sergeant Ian Ferguson, but directed by the CID's "anarchist specialist" Sergeant Roy Cremer, marched into *Freedom's* offices with Stuart Christie in tow. Mary Canipa** and her partner Jack Robinson,

---

* Nicolas Walter would make a different kind of splash when he heckled Harold Wilson at Canterbury Cathedral in November. He got two months in prison for that.
** Mary was the main person at Freedom's bookshop by this point, continuing until the mid-'70s.

as the only people in at the time, were told that the building was being searched for bombs. According to Christie, he had been told that the raids were related to a possible bomb attack on the Greek embassy, making it likely that *Freedom* had remained on the police radar since Donald Rooum's involvement in the Challenor case. Writing for its March 9th issue Mary Canipa reported:

> In the office they went through our book of postage stamps. They went into every part of the premises, and looked in many of the hundreds of packages and behind some of the books. One of them asked Jack who did the embassy bomb, and was asked if he expected an answer.
>
> They showed interest in a small back room where the duplicator sat and which is staked with great piles of old magazines, rolls of wallpaper and tins of paint left by the previous occupant, and remnants of gardening stuffs lying under the dust of the many years since the back garden was tended. One officer was interested in a dusty leaflet printed in Italian. As nobody read Italian the packet was opened. It contained beans.
>
> ...
>
> A large dusty box was brought down. "Hello, what's this?" It contained something heavy, black and iron. It was a hand-printing machine. There were a few unoriginal references to bombs and where do we keep them, and the equally unoriginal rejoinder that "I wouldn't know what a bomb looks like if I saw one, except the ones that are dropped from aeroplanes," was answered with "No, but you'd know if they were mixing powder here."
>
> "Who's they" went unheard or unanswered.
>
> There was a momentary flurry of excitement when one of the men found on the table a small bottle half-filled with bright pink liquid, and two of the others gathered round.
>
> "It's stencil correcting fluid" they were told.
>
> "I know what it is, dear, but ..." All three heads concentrated around the now opened bottle and sniffed.
>
> "Nail varnish — remember?", and its half-emptiness regarded. Within seconds a second half-empty bottle of the same was picked up.
>
> "Well, why have you got TWO bottles?"
>
> They were told there might be half a dozen, and were given the, rather patient I thought, explanation that when they get half-used the stuff gets too gooey to use on stencils being

cut, but could be used for dabbing out any odd spots of ink coming through on stencils on the machine.

Clambering over some of the piled up packages (and mountains of empty cartons) in the stock room one remarked hopelessly: "I didn't know there were so many books about." After a quick tour round a shed at the back (also stacked with unbound sheets) and a glance at the burnt rubbish in the garden bins, they left, the sergeant satisfied that there weren't any bombs, another officer "satisfied they hadn't found them".

In reply to a parting civility from the sergeant, Jack assured him "Last time you did raids we were left out and we felt snubbed; we had difficulty in explaining it to our friends".

Political police raids had become entirely common by '68, not least because of a rise in trouble over Northern Ireland and paranoia about red insurrectionism — even the AFB secretary at the time, peace activist Peter Le Mare, was detained at one point to see if he was linked to the (Maoist) Red Army Fraction.

Freedom was by now already on its way out of its Fulham base, as it had been told to vacate the premises late in 1967, and this led the group to move to an old location — Angel Alley. The "new" home of Freedom Press had already been the premises of Express Printers since the 1940s, so when the notice came to quit it was pencilled in as an emergency replacement venue. And in one of those twists of fate which lead more spiritually-inclined people to nod their heads knowingly, this emergency coincided with a hugely fortuitous opportunity.

Early in 1968 the owner of 84b Whitechapel High Street, where Express Printers had been working for decades, passed away, leaving both that and 84a to his son. He had not raised the rent in all that time and the son felt he could not simply kick the group out after 25 years, so he offered the sale of 84b to the printers, if it could be afforded. Both lots were put up for sale, and while that was in process Vero borrowed money in his own name to buy 84a as well on the other side of the Alley. 84b became the new home of Freedom Press, while 84a (since demolished) was resold to and then swallowed by Whitechapel Art Gallery, helping fund the project. Over the next few months Freedom worked out of 84a, with Express Printers in the basement, while 84b's floors were strengthened to take the weight of book stocks and to facilitate moving the print shop over to ground level — marks from old machines can still be seen on the floor of Freedom Bookshop today.

The move was not without its problems. Beyond a dispute with Albert Meltzer over roomspace (see Albert and Vero, page 143) there was also a near-disaster linked to the very success Colin Ward was most proud of from his work with *Anarchy* — the arrival of the squatting scene.

Campaigning squatting had begun to kick off in earnest in the late 1960s with the Family Squatting Movement, and was paralleled by a rise in student and hippy squats, some very large indeed. Shortly after moving in, a particularly unfortunate run-in with the students was reported in the paper's October 25th issue. Hundreds of people had been evicted from the London Street Commune that September and organisers, eyeing the empty ground floor at 84a, were granted temporary leave to stay (though the Press was under no illusions that refusal would have made much difference).

The floor was occupied on October 4th, but due to what the editors referred to as "the nocturnal habits of hippies" the building was largely open 24 hours a day, and with organised crime at a high in the East End* what happened next was largely inevitable — a group of heavy-set lads (described as "Hell's Angels" types) walked in, past the squatters, over to the iron-barred grate down to the printers, and smashed the place open. They stole large quantities of type metal, including for an upcoming *Freedom* supplement, and even stripped the windows of their lead. The financial impact was substantial, leading the editors to post an emergency appeal in 1969 for £1,000 on top of the original £500 moving fund, having found themselves with a £1,300 black hole in the accounts.

Amid all the other shenanigans of the year, it is frankly amazing that *Freedom* managed to write anything substantial at all about the final big event of 1968, the May Days in Paris. Nevertheless, *Freedom* was absolutely obsessive on the subject. After a slow start on May 11th with its first report, *Freedom* opened its coverage properly with a May 18th splash headline, 'Vive Etudiants!' And ran front pages on the revolutionary riots until well into June. The libertarian character of those protests and the clashes they turned into was obvious, and the editors latched onto Daniel Cohn-Bendit (also known as Danny the Red), a charismatic member of the Nanterre anarchist group who had become a leading face in the crowd, as evidence.

---

* Ronnie Kray had carried out his infamous murder of George Cornell just a few minutes down the road at the Blind Beggar two years prior, and had only finally been arrested in May of '68.

The tone of the paper is euphoric in May 25th's article 'New Revolutionary Movement':

These events have smashed the talk put about by liberal sociologists and Maoists that the workers of the Western World have become too corrupted by increasing prosperity to fight capitalism. Within a fortnight the demands of the students unleashed forces that officially are out of date in the era of the Welfare State. Barricades have been built in Paris, buildings seized, and bosses taken prisoner. Official reaction has been predictable. The brutality of De Gaulle's CRS has been completely naked and unconcealed.

...

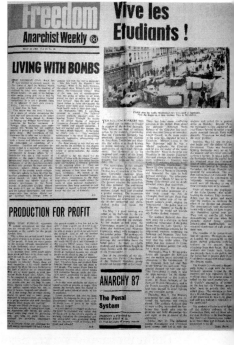

The French workers and students have demonstrated the insecurity of the system which we fight. All over the Western world a new revolutionary movement is being built. In Germany the SDS is the only real opposition to the coalition. In Poland demonstrations have shaken the Gomulka regime. In the USA the government arms itself for war in the cities this summer. And in Britain events such as the Grosvenor Square demonstration have shown that the potential for a similar movement exists. Soon, perhaps, it may be Wilson's turn to tremble.

Even when it became clear that the moment was over, as the summer slid past, the paper remained upbeat — if furious with inevitable betrayal by the "big fat rats" of the French Communist CGT union which had helped put the brakes on:

This has been the great surprise for the world and perhaps even for the French people themselves: the extent of discontent, even of hatred for the regime, that exists under the surface of an apparently stable and orderly society.

And the great achievement of the French students has been to bring this out into the open, to carry their own struggle into the factories and workshops, to offer a great gulp of fresh air to the French workers and deliver a great kick to the fat backside of French bourgeois society. The regime can never be the same again.

These days would be the high point of *Freedom* under John Rety. 1969 would see a descent into bickering as, despite the sudden rise of a fascinating nationwide squatting movement which made a temporary home in *Freedom*'s columns, the combination of a boom in small magazines, the rise of what became *Black Flag* and the paper's financial crisis all bit into its situation. A full-blown crisis would emerge as a feud blew up between *Freedom* and Albert Meltzer (see below), but the paper was also damaged from within. An angry editorial in October, 'The Cost of Being Anarchists' bitterly complained about the break-in and blamed the squatters, prompting a furious reply from John Rety in which he revealed he had been away ill and castigated the remaining editors as a clique.

By the end of the year he was gone (though would continue to write, on and off, for many years to come), along with a number of other figures, leaving just four main editors to finish the year with an editorial titled 'With friends Like These — Who Needs Enemies?', Bill Christopher, Jack Robinson, Philip Sansom and Peter Turner.

Sansom would also disappear shortly afterwards, to be replaced by a more full-time effort from Nicolas Walter alongside John Lawrence — artist Clifford Harper would also begin to get intermittently involved at this point, though less with the paper. Colin Ward and Rufus Segar meanwhile would both step back from *Anarchy*, which would briefly begin a second series in 1971 under Phil Ruff before being spun off on its own, and Donald Rooum would drift away until the 1980s, though mainly because he was dealing with career and family issues. Even Lilian Wolfe, that endlessly patient and stalwart presence, left due to "personal differences".

And so we come to the end of, if not *Freedom's* golden period, then at least an event-packed silver in terms of its activities and influence. The paper has had its ups since, but seems unlikely at present to regain such a position of note in the dead centre of an epochal change in Britain's zeitgeist. With the end of the Swinging Sixties came a new, more physically confrontational era for which *Freedom*'s direction and audience were not well suited, and the Press would remain in a relative holding pattern in decades to come.

Albert and Vero's 30-year feud

When Freedom Press republished one of Albert Meltzer's memoirs, *Anarchism in London 1935-55* in 2018 I was accosted by several people who opined in a sort of amused way that Albert, Vero or both would be "turning in their grave". That this was still the response more than two decades on from Meltzer's death is a handy illustration of just how poisonous the feud had become, though its prominence in the activities of both sides is largely overstated, never escalating much beyond rhetorical barbs in their respective outlets.

What the exact cause was has been disputed, but the story comes into some focus through the course of reading 1950s-60s issues of the paper, particularly the many hints which can be found between the lines of reports on the London Anarchist Group and Anarchist Federation of Britain.

The short version, as told by the pro-Vero camp, is that following a turbulent move to Angel Alley a letter arrived from Meltzer, suggesting that Wooden Shoe Press should hire a room in the newly-owned building, contributing to the mortgage repayments.

Unlike the new Freedom Press building, Wooden Shoe's premises had a shop window. Jack Robinson, who was managing Freedom Bookshop at the time and earned his living as a second-hand book dealer, visited the empty premises to ask about taking on the tenancy, and was told Wooden Shoe had paid no rent for the three years and was being evicted. Vero — already struggling with mounting debt — wrote a waffly letter about avoiding quarrels among anarchists, turning down Albert's offer without mentioning the real reason, sparking the feud.

Meltzer himself meanwhile said it was the political character of *Freedom,* its elitism and prostration at the feet of academia which drove him away over time, and the final nail in the coffin was an article suggesting a whip-round for a policeman who fell off his horse at a protest. This appears to be a reference to a letter in the April 20th 1968 issue, which was actually objecting to the anti-police tone of a Vietnam protest report by then-editor John Rety. Geoffrey Featherstone's call to raise cash for the injured officer prompted a reply the next week signed by Meltzer, Christie, Adrian Derbyshire, James Duke, Ross Flett and Martin Page in which they charged:

> *Freedom* must choose; it cannot be both a paper for anarchists and for non-violent authoritarians, including police sympathisers ... the sickening adulation of [the recently deceased] Martin Luther King by Jeff Cloves on your front page and 'collect for a cop' within, makes it look as if you <u>have</u> chosen.

The longer version seems to suggest a slightly different process. The key political note is in Meltzer's biography *I Couldn't Paint Golden Angels*, in which he talks about publishing *The Syndicalist* with Albert Grace:

Albert Meltzer

To produce it we sought the co-operation of Freedom Press. I still hadn't learned my lesson, and supposed it to belong to the anarchist movement, if in practice under the control of Richards. They however still recognised some sort of obligation and it was printed free at their printing press by Philip Sansom ... I had not realised that the Freedom Press Group, since it had broken away from the old Anarchist Federation, was degenerating into a privately-owned publishing house. Any venture like *The Syndicalist* only boosted their reputation.

Given the level of anger which had been generated in that original 1945 split, and Meltzer's veteran position in the '50s, I'm not sure I entirely buy the tale of trust betrayed. Meltzer comes across as a canny political operator, and I suspect his early collaborations with Freedom in the 1940s-50s period were more tactical than portrayed, taking into account the extraordinary smallness of the movement as a whole and his poor relations with the SWF. But his description of Freedom Press as morally belonging to the wider movement, his disappointment in its refusal to fully commit to that role and his critique of its individualist-intellectual-pacifist streak is remarkably consistent, even in *Freedom's* own pages.

By the early 1960s Meltzer was primarily active elsewhere in London, while maintaining some cordial links. He had for the most part stopped bothering to write in *Freedom* other than with letters to occasionally solicit new recruits. Collaboration didn't entirely cease through the decade however, and he remained friendly enough with some *Freedom* regulars, alongside contact with the London Anarchist Group.

Meltzer was scathing about most of the peace movement, agreeing with *Freedom* that the CND was a waste of space but also critical of the Committee of 100 for its single issue pacifism. While *Freedom's* analysis of social issues placed it in a good position to be part of the wave of New Left activism, Meltzer was largely dismissive of what he saw as a fundamentally middle class phenomenon dominated by students, refocusing the left away from working class self-activity and more insurgent methods.

Nevertheless, he was impressed enough by the resurgent energy of anarchist politics in London to re-engage in 1964 with LAGs 1 and 2. While he was still not entirely a fan of the latter SWF-dominated group at the time, he was pleasantly surprised to meet a sympathetic character in Australian activist Ted Kavanagh and they formed a small LAG 2 caucus. Through LAG he also engaged with the formation of the Anarchist Federation of Britain, and was enthusiastic enough, at least in its early stages, to volunteer as the AFB press officer in August 1965. That same year he launched, with Kavanagh, *Cuddon's Cosmopolitan Review* and opened the Wooden Shoe bookshop. Relations seem to have temporarily improved over the period, possibly due to the elation of being part of a growing movement again, to the point where *Freedom* editor John Rety, along with supporters Michael Duane and Arthur Uloth, could be found speaking at LAG 2 meetings in 1966.

The events of 1968-9 were likely of *some* importance in killing off this more convivial atmosphere, inasmuch as Meltzer was having a tough time of it when Vero told him there was no room at Angel Alley. A succession of unfortunate events had wiped his finances out and Meltzer could have very much done with a bit of help, which perhaps he hoped would be forthcoming from those who were still, at that point, his comrades. But if anything, it would have been the last straw rather than a simple disagreement getting out of hand. As Stuart Christie notes in Meltzer's obituary:

> It was his championship of class-struggle anarchism, coupled with his scepticism of the student-led New Left in the 1960s which earned Albert his reputation for sectarianism.

Similar scepticism, along with anger at *Freedom* generally, comes across in the AFB report of October 12th 1968, noting that *Freedom* was heavily criticised and "an absent comrade", likely Vero, denounced as "bureaucratic deadwood ... totally uninterested in the anarchist movement." These complaints were only quietened by the announcement of "something little short of miraculous" by the *Freedom* members present — likely the buying of 84b.

By the end of 1969 however Meltzer was in a position where he had been snubbed by people he already felt offered little to the movement, but also had other opportunities. The Anarchist Black Cross had just been founded, and the establishment of *Black Flag* as its bulletin in 1970 would finally provide his politics the outlet he felt they desperately needed. Fundamentally he no longer had to play nice — so he didn't. And the rest is anarchist folklore.

As much as *Freedom* supporters have sometimes suggested that the group held itself above the subsequent plethora of snide comments in *Black Flag* over the next 30 years and just got on with things, the feud was fairly tit for tat. *Black Flag*'s 'Liars and Liberals' supplement in 1986 for example was aimed squarely at *Freedom*. But equally there's no mistaking who was being portrayed by Donald Rooum's "fat rat" character in his *Wildcat* cartoon strip, while the 1970s and '80s issues of *Freedom* contain a wide variety of minimally-veiled, scathing references to "the self-appointed ideologists of the movement" and so forth.

That being said, Vero himself seems to have been less aware of the depth of the issue than could perhaps be expected, possibly because he was not regularly reading the anarchist press through much of the worst of it. Both Donald Rooum and Dave Peers have separately recounted that when Vero appeared at the London Anarchist Bookfair in 1995 he walked up to Meltzer, hand outstretched, seemingly expecting little more than a lively bit of argument. When Meltzer turned away instead this affected him strongly, and he complained afterwards of feeling hurt by the snub.

The low point of the argument occurred a year later, when Vero's infamous 'Instead of an Obituary' appeared in the May 18th 1996 issue of *Freedom* directly following Meltzer's death, accusing him of being a fantasist and a liar who damaged the movement.

It should never have been penned and reading the article back, including Vero's execrable 'ner-ner you died first' finisher (I should note that this has also been characterised as banter by Vero's friends), it's easy to sympathise with at least elements of Acrata's retort in *The Albert Memorial*:

The vindictive pursuit of the departed, the insult to the grief of those who mourn, the abuse of the fondest and most cherished memories of the man and his works — these are not the doings of even half-decent people.

There is significantly more written of Meltzer than of Vero here, and this reflects their relative positions. Meltzer considered Vero to be a cuckoo in the nest, sucking resources into a project which excluded his own political tendency and pushed a line he felt little affinity for. There were real philosophical disagreements underlying his antipathy towards Freedom Press, which directly manifested in the 1970s when his and Stuart Christie's work on *Black Flag* made so much headway within that generation of young militants.

For all that I have suggested elsewhere that *Freedom* was not ultimately much of a block on the emergence of other anarchist strands, there is an entirely valid argument to be made that *Freedom's* position in the 1950s, amid a general collapse in the movement, was pretty hegemonic in London particularly. It held tangible assets, it was usually first station on the line, it had the biggest voice — almost the only one outside *Direct Action.* Some of that undoubtedly carried through into the mid 1960s, given its prominence in Anarchist Federation of Britain discussions, though a subsequent expansion in new anarchist publishing quickly rendered such advantages moot.

For Meltzer it must have been extraordinarily galling to see much-needed money appear as if from nowhere to continue the existence of *Freedom*, a source of nothing but dreary radical liberalism in his eyes, while he and his wing of the anarchists struggled along with mountainous debts trying to produce a worthwhile paper. *Freedom's* own hostility in the other direction needs less explanation. When you feel you're trying your best, only to be accused of ruining the very movement you work for, it is tempting to lash out in kind. Vero, as noted earlier, was prone to dismissiveness against his critics and getting into fights even with his friends, and he surrounded himself with people who were more than capable of putting a degree of venom into their copy when required. He and many of his fellow editors were also, politically, no fans of Meltzer's tactics either, feeling them to be largely a matter of braggadocio drawing from the fetishisation of violent action.

A step back could maybe have provided both sides with the possibility of a gentler relationship, but as with the devastation of the 1920s, the feud's principle antagonists were survivors of an era in which the movement was smashed, not just in Britain but everywhere. Their and their comrades' sustained efforts to drag anarchism back to prominence were both a horrendous slog and for a long time quite isolated endeavours undertaken by people damaged by war and loss. When added to their undoubtedly large egos* and the gulf in their respective politics, this made for a flammable mix.

---

* This is not meant as criticism, a robust ego is almost always implied if you think you can personally change the world.

~ An endnote ~

There are people on both sides of the divide who are still alive, and in some cases who seriously disagree with parts or all of the characterisation above. Acrata responded to this section for example by noting that:

> Albert didn't stoop to public personal feuds. And there was no poison in Albert. His courage and commitment had no need of it ... Whatever his shortcomings, those who worked with and knew Albert well saw his politics as motivated by his love of freedom, his generosity, and human solidarity.
>
> What moved Richards to antagonism seems to have been more like the defence of the egotistical personal boundaries within which he, Richards, withdrew in the pursuit of a vision of some rarefied eclectic, personal political creed, itself constantly threatened by ex-comrades like Albert, Ken Hawkes and Tom Brown and their associates; these comrades' own plain dealing and decency were dire threats to Richards's deluded, ever-manipulative, divisive self-seeking.
>
> Just as Spanish workers in July 1936, beginning from almost nothing materially, rose collectively and spiritually to the sublime heights of libertarian communism that are a matter of unchallengeable historical record, so Richards and his clique plumbed the depths of division and personal acquisition, command and control.

I include this because it's important to illustrate that *A Beautiful Idea*, while attempting even-handedness, cannot offer a definitive assessment of the characters of two men who died before I got involved at Freedom Press and of course my writing most likely suffers from source bias, so is best read in conjunction with memoirs of the time.

Both Vero and Meltzer inspired, and continue to inspire, extraordinary loyalty in their friends and heavy criticisms from their opponents, making the job of assessing them difficult.

Above, Mary Canipa and Jack Robinson. Top, a joint rally called by ABC, Centro Iberico, ORA, Oxford Anarchists and the SWF at the French Embassy protesting against arrests in France.

1970-1980
Out in the cold

As the '70s arrived a lean time began for the press, particularly in the middle of the decade, with Vero having temporarily retired and a skeleton crew working on bringing out the paper. Initially, a minor redesign aside, it continued on much the same path as before, but with the collective having dropped mention of the paper's broader financial situation from the deficit fund it becomes impossible to tell exactly what was happening in terms of sales and debts.

It is clear that a financial crisis had evolved, as alongside major debts accrued from the move to Angel Alley there was also a decline of interest in *Freedom*'s brand of politics, driven by two main factors — aw moving of young energy towards the direct actionists around *Black Flag* alongside a broader shift from primarily the student movement/ New Left towards Trotskyism.

The former problem was worsened by the burgeoning *Freedom* vs *Black Flag* feud, which initially included accusations that Vero was hiving off assets for his own eventual gain. While doubtless the remaining group at Freedom Press coveted pole position within the movement, the idea that it was about money seems unlikely, mainly because *Freedom* didn't pay the editors and tended to be a sink for cash rather than a producer of it. And from the '80s onwards, neither the building nor the printing presses were in Vero's hands. Nevertheless a poor impression left across the international movement led to some funding falling away, according to Donald Rooum.*

Freedom's rhetorical clout was also largely broken, with the AFB having mostly collapsed and those who wanted to take direct action moving over to *Black Flag* and other publications, leaving *Freedom* largely out of touch with events as they moved into a new, more explosive phase. Albert Meltzer would later recall in *I Couldn't Paint Golden Angels* that after an escalating series of bombings by the Angry Brigade, an unnamed *Freedom* editor came along to an

---

* It is important to note that regardless of the differences between the two two sides, co-operation did go on. Freedom Bookshop continued to sell *Black Flag* for example, and reps from the magazine were present for at least one attempt in the mid-'70s to build a new anarchist federation.

Anarchist Black Cross meeting and demanded "this sort of thing has got to stop", oblivious to how sidelined they'd become.

Momentum had also been lost more broadly in the student movement, which for the most part rejected the old peace campaigns and as non-violent hippy activism fell out of vogue with the ending of the Beatles, Leninism took root on campus. The Trots made themselves the major players, building off a major propaganda coup scored in 1968 when a 10,000-strong anti-Vietnam War rally kicked off,* with 200 arrests made — directly leading to the establishment of (now disgraced) police undercover unit the Special Demonstration Squad. This was bettered by a rally drawing 25,000 people the same year. The New Left faded into this milieu, and for many years to come the Trots would continue to outmatch any libertarian presence in academic circles. As far as the hard left goes, the '70s would be their decade as the largest groups went from hundreds to thousands of members across the country.

Similarly, the centrality of peace movement organising and political vagueness which characterised the anarchists through the '60s had for the most part cut little ice with the labour movement. Union militants were busily building significant power for the most part without the aid of syndicalists — though many excellent militants were present and grassroots organising always had the tendency — and would peak at a membership of around 13 million people at the end of the '70s. Despite Hungary and the invasion of Czechoslovakia in '68, union structures would remain something of a bastion of Communist Party influence in middle to upper tiers until the rise of Eurocommunism** cracked that organisation like an egg in the '90s.

It was in this setting that the price of *Freedom* rose from 6p to 9p and, as a result of the loss of Philip Sansom (who had proofed every paper), a reduced and more error-prone collective was trying to make its mark. Only in publishing was the old hand still at play, with around 10 books being produced through the period, three of which were by Vernon Richards with some classics and others from writers such as Steve Cullen (*The Last Capitalist*), Colin Ward and a translation of Gaston Leval's excellent *Collectives in the Spanish Revolution*.

---

* Though it may be claimed as a Trot-led demo, longtime *Freedom* supporter Ernest Rodker was there and recalls John Rety "in heroic mode", being "one of the first to burst through the heavy police cordon surrounding Grosvenor Square".

** A strategic shift which sought to reject the USSR, engage with social movements such as feminism and fully embrace the democratic route to change.

Note: *This is the point at which a larger number of the people mentioned are with us and often still active, meaning not only are there memoirs and histories yet to be written, making cross-checking more difficult, but many individuals will have significantly more technicolour memories of this period can be portrayed here. A future, more leisurely edition may be able to incorporate those but in the meantime, heartfelt apologies to all involved for any mistakes, misrepresentations and unfair monsterings that occur, as well as to anyone who feels left out — it's not a deliberate snub.*

Boom and bust

Of the illegalist revolutionary groups to emerge in Europe in the late '60s and early '70s, including the Red Army Fraction in Germany and Red Brigades in Italy, the Angry Brigade was the only anarchist-aligned group identifying itself as such, running a campaign of mostly small-scale bombings and actions from 1967 to 1972 with a focus on non-lethal property damage against institutional powers.

A significantly more nebulous phenomenon than the press would have liked, the 1968-71 period saw 1,100 bombings cross the desk of Woolwich Arsenal labs chief Major Yallop, only 25 of which they were able to tie to the Angry Brigade. Most of the "Angries'" attacks were aimed at industrial targets or in solidarity with international causes, such as the Department of Employment and Activity, or the firebombing of Glasgow South African Airways. The incidents nevertheless caused an atmosphere of complete media hysteria, and even *Freedom* was eyeballed as potentially complicit, solely because it was one of only a few anarchist institutions known to the press.*

---

* This is a regular pattern, as for the most part reporters sent to cover "the anarchists" don't know their arsehole from their earhole but have to pretend expertise. Examples of this include "leading members of the WOMBLES" being cited as causing disturbances years after the group broke up in the early 2000s, or the time anthropologist Chris Knight was splashed in the *Sun* in 2011 because the firm's "journalist" had credulously swallowed a line from Whitechapel Anarchist Group that Knight was their dear leader.

The paper would subsequently blast a front-page denunciation:

> Even the bombing campaign carried out by the Angry Brigade which was technically brilliant ... achieved absolutely nothing because, in direct contradiction with their spoken ideals, they were trying to act as an elite vanguard leaving ordinary people as passive spectators of their actions. Far from this resulting in an 'awakening' of the masses' it resulted in a fear of anarchism and anarchist ideas which has significantly contributed to our current impotence.

The idea that the Angry Brigade were the ones responsible for the movement's "impotence" was, frankly, wishful thinking. By this time the AFB for example was essentially over, the Organisation of Revolutionary Anarchists having split off to try and put together a more coherent effort with no input needed from the Angries,* while the SWF had already been 20 years in relative obscurity and *Freedom*'s own woes were almost entirely unrelated.

Unlike with the attentats of the previous century, the brigade bombings threatened no loss of life, and while off-putting to peaceniks, were popular with militants on Meltzer's wing and even occasionally with the general public, when aimed at hated groups like property speculators. The various people involved were significantly more thoughtful in their approaches than they were given credit for in the pages of *Freedom*, drawing from its own prior philosophical challenges against the dull conservatism of family life alongside the class struggle orientation of the anarcho-syndicalists and direct actionists.

Across 13 communiques they show solidarity with the Basque struggle, against the Industrial Relations Bill, for a deepening of militant trade unionism, against police brutality and the alienation of everyday existence. A mix of the situationist, the liberationist and the insurrectionist, their politics weren't easily defined through gnomic public communiques alone, and *Freedom*'s connection with them was not good enough to offer many insights. It was thus left hectoring from the sidelines while the more overtly supportive group around ABC and *Black Flag* (to the point where they were criticised for "uncritical cheerleading") wrote blockbuster articles

---

* This lasted until early 1974, when the platformist group was shut down by a further split (with many of its members joining Trotskyist micro-sect Left Tendency), re-emerging as the Anarchist Workers Association

about the group. Anarchist historian Nick Heath's assessment, from a bit of distance, offers more nuance on the Angry Brigade phenomenon in *The UK anarchist movement — Looking back and forward*:

"The general illusion that there was a mass movement capable of carrying out a revolution, common in many quarters, led these libertarians, active in claimants and squatters struggles, to engage in a number of attacks on property, including the homes of Ministers and capitalists seen as instrumental in bringing down repression on the working class. The Angry Brigade's activities were meant as supplementary to the actions of the mass movement. However they had failed to understand the nature of this movement and had overestimated its revolutionary capabilities."

The first arrests of what would eventually become known as the Stoke Newington 8, those few ever accused of membership of the Angries, took place in 1971. Chris Bott, John Barker, Hilary Creek, Anna Mendleson, James Greenfield and Stuart Christie (once again on the receiving end of a lack of police imagination) were picked up in August, while Angela Weir and Kate McLean were detained in November and December.

Their trial, which *Freedom* largely missed out on, ran from May 30th-December 6th, the longest criminal case in British legal history at that time. The story was letched over by the tabloids, with one *Sun* writer losing their composure entirely and penning a feverish imaginary number about the defendants holding deviant anarchist parties involving turkey sacrifice titled 'Sex Orgies at the Cottage of Blood'. In the end no-one went down for any late-night poultry experiments, and of the eight detainees, four were instead jailed for "conspiring to cause explosions likely to endanger life or cause serious injury to property". Barker, Greenfield, Creek and Mendleson all received 10-year sentences and were bundled with a fifth man, Jake Prescott, who had been sent down the previous year, when backers formed the Stoke Newington 5 Committee to support them.

Freedom's reaction was not of an order with previous incarnations, and even core team member Mary Canipa, by now on her way out of the bookshop to be replaced by the more taciturn Jim Huggon, was moved to write in and complain on August 4th 1973 that coverage in the paper had been minimal and confusing. This was accompanied by an article from Nicolas Walter which denied the

Angry Brigade even *were* anarchists, insisting instead that they were "a combination of situation and syndicalism", seemingly attempting to disqualify them through definitional pedantry. Walter went on to express annoyance that focus was on the ABC and Stoke Newington Five Committee while leaving those "opposed to the technique of terrorism" out, writing: "The development of a libertarian consciousness has been retarded rather than advanced by this tragic episode".

This approach, needless to say, went down extremely badly in the wider movement at a moment where support was needed and made for a particularly odd intervention given that *Freedom* was already offering solidarity to many others across Europe who were engaged in direct struggle a little further from home, especially in Spain, France and Portugal. That same year *Freedom* did offer significant backing for jailed CND co-founder Pat Arrowsmith whose politics, while progressive, never made it within a country mile of anarchism. The backlash was hugely damaging to *Freedom*'s reputation, with erstwhile writers from the '60s such as Jerry Westall (not generally a prominent anti-*Freedom* partisan) pitching in via *Anarchy (Series 2) No.12* in 1974 to say:

Recently *Freedom* has completely alienated a fair section of active anarchists in Britain, mostly young, mostly working class, who have established a number of periodicals: *Black Flag, Libertarian Struggle, Black and Red Outlook, Inside Story, Anarchy* — all libertarian, none friendly to *Freedom* and it is most encouraging to have anarchist views available from a number of sources. Yet these events have largely occurred as a reaction from *Freedom* because the paper was failing the anarchist movement.

In the last few months *Freedom* has taken to publishing letters which other papers have chosen not to print — one which *Time Out* in fact used and a telephone call would have established that they were going to do so. It is worth mentioning because if anyone collected together the letters not published by *Freedom* it would take several volumes to facilitate publication.

I can remember three particular times when *Freedom* has not published letters of mine which caused some consternation on my part. Both Jack Robinson's articles on the Angry Brigade, which between them were possibly the most disgraceful writings ever attributed to an anarchist in Britain, received replies from my pen.

Neither appeared, but I was allowed to criticise Nick Walter whose views the editors of *Freedom* share.

...

The third example of Freedom's nonpublication consists of a reply to Walter's claim that he had criticised the Angry Brigade but had never attacked those standing trial as the Stoke Newington Eight. Nick ... is a very confused individual. Trialists at the Stoke Newington trial expressed sympathy with the Angry Brigade, in the public mind (rightly or wrongly) they were seen as the Angry Brigade and the position of Walter and *Freedom* subverted the spirit of those who were supporting people faced with 15 or 20 years in prison if convicted. Whilst this sniping was going on *Freedom* claimed to be assisting the Stoke Newington Defence Committee.

In order that in the future and internationally today anarchists shall know that *Freedom* has been discredited within the anarchist movement we must write these words and publish them.

...

So, is *Freedom* run by an elite who are out of touch and steadily grinding to a halt? Is the initiative of anarchism in Britain passing away from *Freedom* to a number of other sources? I'd say "yes" to both those questions.

By 1973 *Freedom* was experiencing many other issues beyond its treatment of headline events. Printing costs were running high and even with a 50% increase in cover price sales were not so spectacular that debts were being paid off. As a result, the collective decided to stop using the machines they had carefully moved over just five years prior and opted for the new, cheaper offset litho techniques already in use by their rivals. The new system saw articles set on a typewriter and then sent to Vineyard Press in Colchester. Even here however there were problems over time, when after three years a union dispute came along, described by Vero in *Freedom / A Hundred Years*:

Unfortunately, at a certain stage the National Graphical Association representatives, acting on instructions from above, declared that Vineyard could not print Freedom from pages that had not been pasted up by NGA members. Charles, while recognising that commercial firms should not get their camera-ready material done on the cheap, defended non-profit setups like us doing their own thing, and told us that he would get another printer to produce the paper. However the NGA managed to block that arrangement as well. On to the stage [in 1976] came Ian King — 'Ian the Printer' of Magic Ink — who had no union axe to grind, and for five years printed *Freedom* in Margate, for a time with help from Women in Print in South London.

And with a new system came a new redesign, which was a bit of a dog's breakfast. The format had switched to an eight-page A4 magazine with left-aligned text, selling for 5p. It was difficult to read while also being intensely space hungry, with up to 1,200 words shovelled onto a single page and overly wide letter spacing with usually little imagery beyond the occasional cartoon from Philip Sansom (signed 'Skitz'). Articles spill randomly over onto second pages, no sections are in place and no thought whatsoever is given to making it a pleasant reading experience. Within the paper a quite amazing amount of grumpiness was to be found particularly in the letters section, with one exasperated missive from Dave Poulson on the subject noting that the September 22nd issue had spent a full quarter of its limited resources giving over space for people to be rude to one another. This tendency was heavily criticised by the remaining rump of attendees at that year's (final) AFB conference.*

Decent writing did go into this period, loosely definable as the Robinson-Turner-Canipa editorship after its three most active members. David Goodway remarked in his article 'Freedom: an obituary' for *History Workshop* in 2014 that to the end, the paper usually had at least one interesting article in every issue — and this was still the case in the 1970s. *Freedom* continued to produce some worthwhile writing from the likes of Paul Avrich and Peter E Newell (who later authored one of Freedom

---

* Attempts to keep networks going did continue after this point, for example in December 1975, with Philip Sansom leading an effort to establish a London-wide network involving Freedom, LSE Anarchists Group, East London Libertarians, Harrow Anarchists, International Times and West London Anarchists

Press's best modern titles, *Zapata of Mexico*) while its news section was in some ways occasionally superior to the 1960s, in that it more often tried to report what was happening rather than simply commenting about it. An early essay from John Quail in 1975 on the history of anarchism in Britain to 1919 offers an intelligent precis of his historical classic *The Slow Burning Fuse* and is followed up by an equally useful response from Nicolas Walter correcting some of his assumptions (August 2nd). Walter's analysis in *Freedom's* June 26th 1976 issue of the idea, popularly held in intellectual circles thanks to George Woodcock, that "traditional" organised class struggle anarchism had died in Britain by the end of the second world war is a standout exercise in devastating an academic opponent.*

But *Freedom's* content was for the most part lacking charisma and the trend was downward. A December 29th 1973 article from the editors sums the period up perfectly in a simple headline: 'We Survived!' Such survival seems to have been the best the press could manage at the time, with most of the

Nicolas Walter

interest and vitality of the movement being elsewhere. Martyn Everett, who became interested in anarchism in 1973, recalls a gloomy atmosphere in the alley:

I read a pamphlet on anarchism and liberalism written by a prominent young liberal named Simon Hebditch. I also read copies of *Peace News* which was stocked by a local newsagent, in which anarchism was mentioned and saw a TV programme in which a number of anarchists were interviewed on the television in the wake of the Angry Brigade trial — and the critique of capitalism seemed to make a lot of sense. They mentioned Rising Free bookshop, so not long

---

* Walter's great strength was in the obsessive precision with which he approached his subjects of research — though it sometimes became a weakness when applied to squabbling in letters pages, which he indulged in often. His essay *About Anarchism* is widely considered a classic and has been translated into many languages.

afterwards I visited Housman's and Rising Free, which were at the time just around the corner from each other. Among the publications I picked up was a Solidarity pamphlet on sabotage, which discussed exactly the alienated experiences I had while working in a number of factories.

Eventually I got around to visiting Freedom Bookshop. Angel Alley was gloomy and depressing, and if the doors were open to the room downstairs it was possible to catch a glimpse of the (what seemed huge) printing machines — I was quite interested in them as I had worked for a printing firm and in print -related jobs for several years ... up the rickety stairs, which made me feel as uneasy as David Balfour climbing the stairs in his uncle's house in *Kidnapped*. The bookshop seemed terribly disorganised and dusty, and Jim Huggon, who seemed to spend most of his life in the bookshop, didn't really seem interested in chatting to people at all. The only part which was worse than the bookshop was the toilet — the whole thing was really Dickensian, but luckily there was a fantastic array of anarchist papers from many different countries and books about many different aspects of anarchism, and biographies and histories of anarchist movements in other countries. I became a regular visitor, and later an occasional contributor.

1974-5 was mostly more of the same. The movement's more general problems were strongly highlighted by a protest at the French embassy on August 3rd at which a joint rally of most organised anarchist groups, including both the Anarchist Black Cross and *Freedom*, which drew just 70 people who were absolutely surrounded by more than 600 police officers (see page 150).

Of more note was the occupation of Centrepoint on New Oxford Street, London, involving *Freedom* writer and peace activist Jim Radford. Radford, one of the original Aldermaston March organisers in the 50s, was heavily involved in squatting advocacy and with Ron Bailey and Jack Dromey engineered an audacious takeover of the 33-storey tower in January 1974.

Centrepoint had, since its completion, become an icon of landlord profiteering, having been left to stand empty for ten years while thousands of people in London remained homeless. The meticulously-planned operation to make an example out of it saw people get jobs with a firm handling the building's security, and then on January 19th two men simply walked in, used the keys to open up, and around 100 people flooded through the doors to occupy the space. The crack took just minutes, and the squatters stayed in for a symbolic two days, prompting massive press coverage, ending with a rally which drew several thousand people. Police went in swinging and arrested 18, injuring one and seeing seven of their own number hurt. Within the year the building had found a tenant. Today it has been converted to luxury flats with asking prices of up to £5 million each, in a new round of the housing crisis.

Direct actions aside however *Freedom* had been earning itself as reputation as a dull read and in October a note on the state of the Press remarked "Our circulation is a disgrace, fully low". The remaining collective was clearly struggling to fill space, with a great number of classic essays being recycled throughout the year and existing supporters such as Arthur Moyse, who started once again sending in his satirical sketches, getting more involved. 'HB' and Alan Albon (who would later co-found *Green Anarchist*) would also start appearing more frequently.

Other ex-*Freedom* activists meanwhile, including Nicolas Walter whose writing slackens off in the paper around the mid-'70s, were trying out a new magazine for size with Wynford Hicks's *Wildcat*, a far brighter and more graphically able effort which opened with a special issue on the occupation of Northern Ireland. Hicks was an SWF veteran and not much impressed by *Freedom*, though had briefly written its 'Fifth Column' on the strength of John Rety's editorship in the '60s, the title being a play on the fact that he spent a good deal of time criticising the paper.

End of a weekly

By 1975, keeping up a weekly schedule in which barely three to four regular writers were active was becoming more and more obviously unsustainable, and even with prolific work from Turner, Robinson, 'HB' and 'DLM' there was a great deal of filler going in. International articles were a favourite, usually cribbed from the more active anarchist press on the continent, alongside a lot of analysis of government policy and miles upon miles of classic works. The paper continued to complain about the new wave of paramilitary leftism, writing of the kidnapping in Germany of mayoral candidate Peter Lorenz by the 2nd June Movement:

> We do not question the activities of these groups from a pacifist standpoint. In an extreme situation, under a totalitarian government with awareness and co-operation from a

substantial section of the population such bank robberies, kidnappings and even assassinations can be condoned and indeed, even expected. But the situation in West Germany is far from extreme. The majority of the population is apathetic and the bourgeois effects of the "economic miracle" have not yet worn off.

Similarly repudiated were the works of the Baader Meinhoff group as "alienating the working class on whose behalf these acts were presumably performed."

In February, a price rise for stamps forced *Freedom* to float the idea of going fortnightly while doubling in size, following similar moves by *Peace News* and *Freethinker*, noting: "Anarchist papers like *Anarchy*, *Black Flag*, *Direct Action* and *Wildcat* dependent on postal subscriptions will find this 60% increase a hammer blow." But it coincided with a malaise that was already afflicting the paper and the following month the collective was unable to bring out its regular weekly. *Freedom* formally switched to a 12 pence fortnightly in April, taking the sensible decision to include an "anarchist review" supplement of eight more pages rather than simply expand the paper. This allowed a newsier approach in the front half of the paper, though it still suffered from a notable lack of strong activism-related content. Clear sections of analysis and reviews in the supplement meanwhile allowed for a better standard of writing with more time to solicit copy.

Of the writing through the mid-'70s iteration of *Freedom* by far the best frontline work came from Stepney Squatter, whose reports on the London scene chart the highs and lows of a movement which was vastly larger than today's post-2012 anti-squatting Act landscape. In one block alone in Corfield Street, round the corner from Bethnal Green, more than a third of the 30-flat block was squatted in January 1975. Stepney Squatter recounts:

> As soon as the squatters moved in the council rushed through a demolition decision and a £76,000 demolition contract with Sqibbs and Davies Ltd. About 6pm on Wednesday February 19th, over 25 demolition men descended on Corfield Street and began smashing up the flats on two staircases that hadn't been squatted yet, and all the next building (80 flats). A squatter who tried to phone the press was hauled out of the phone box by three men. Bethnal Green Police Station — 300 yards away — took an hour to send someone. Sinks, windows, and lavatories were smashed, but the men left after about an hour.

After they left, 40 squatters invaded the Tower Hamlets Council Housing committee meeting that was going on at the time. The committee denied any knowledge of the demolition gang's activities. Police arrived within minutes this time. A lady councillor told squatters there wouldn't be such a problem if they didn't have so many babies, and advised them to go to a family planning clinic!

Another try by the demolition men was foiled the next day when three flats in the path of the wreckers were squatted. In the resulting confrontation, and with the press present, the police and council told the demolition men to stay out of the Corfield building.

Fires were "mysteriously" set at Corfield after this, water mains were broken, flats mysteriously trashed, and so the conflicts went on.

Even in such straightened times *Freedom* was also still capable of being a little disreputable now and then, and on September 27th 1975 the paper includes a page on which the single paragraph is stamped:

> The item which should have appeared on this page was refused by the printers on legal grounds. Readers will find it has been duplicated by the Collective and is inserted in the current copy.

Sure enough, inside there is a two-page essay detailing the best way for discontented soldiers to avoid being deployed to Northern Ireland (the editors were careful to note that this didn't mean they were supporting nationalism). The article had previously been published by *Peace News*, resulting in a raid at its Kings Cross offices by Special Branch and the arrest of 14 people under the Incitement to Disaffection Act 1934. Amusingly, the next issue contains a report from Dennis Gould* telling of his efforts to sell the offending text to punters outside the Old Bailey while the BWNFI 14 (British

---

* Gould, a lifelong peace campaigner and supporter of *Peace News*, published Freedom Press poetry book *Visions of Poesy* alongside Clifford Harper and Jeff Cloves in 1994.

Withdrawal From Northern Ireland) stood trial for disseminating it just inside. He was initially told to move on before eventually being allowed into the courtroom to watch the trial. All the defendants were eventually acquitted, and Dennis never was censured for encouraging disaffection outside a disaffection trial.

Special mention should also be made of *Freedom*'s punchiest front page of the period, marking the death of General Franco. On one half was a list of the Spanish dictator's crimes. On the other, a tribute to CNT fighter Cipriano Mera who had died at around the same time.

Freedom continued to benefit from just "being" — as in a solid point to which new people could flock and, through its listings a place where more isolated anarchists could keep an eye out for new contacts in their areas. New people did eventually get involved and from 1975 or so, things initially picked up slightly with regular writers turning up, including Gillian Fleming (under the pseudonym 'Gaia'), Nino Staffa and Dave Peers, all of whom went on to be part of the editorial collective. Colin Ward also returned both as a writer under various pseudonyms and for publication of his book *Housing: An Anarchist Approach* in April.

Colin Ward, from a picture card set produced for Freedom Press by Clifford Harper in 1994

Several of his other books, most notably *Anarchy in Action* and his updated selection of Kropotkin's essays documenting the possibilities for communal production *Fields, Factories and Workshops*, were subsequently reprinted by the press over the next few years. *Freedom* remained out of the loop on developments in Spain, which were better covered by the far more connected *Black Flag* collective, but as political punk started to enter the scene there did seem to be more vitality in the writing, even if it initially remained dominated by Jack Robinson and Pete Turner filling space. Staffa's clearly-written articles on the 'New Bosses' were of particularly good quality.

Writing in *Freedom / A Hundred Years* former editor Dave Peers describes his recollections:

On occasional visits to London [in the early 70s] I eventually located Angel Alley and met Mary Canipa and some of the then collective. A couple of pieces I posted in were published, a dizzy experience for a young lad. From outside, *Freedom* seemed a solid establishment.

I moved to London in 1976 and went along to help fold and despatch, The weekly routine helped outsiders to make contact, something which has since been List. I was encouraged to contribute, and I had some inside information on a topical event (the attempt to nationalise the ship-building industry). I produced an over-extended, rambling piece (a habit which was to become repetitive). The next week I was amazed to find it on the front page. Emboldened, I submitted something to the next issue, turned up for the Thursday folding session and walked into what was then called a "heavy atmosphere".

Most of the collective had walked out in a dispute over responsibilities, decision-making and established power (a lesson which were to repeat. They went on to launch *Zero*, which fell prey, among other things, to similar mistakes.) I was enticed into the inner sanctum to help the rump with the next issue and I haven't escaped since. Thus are innocent young people ensnared.

The people who left represented most of the younger new members. Richard Schofield, Peter Webb, Adam Flowers, Geoff Ingarfield — even Nino Staffa and Philip Sansom showed interest, though they didn't go through with it. *Zero* ran as an anarchist/anarchist-feminist magazine from June 1977-August 1978. A couple of other people went over to *Solidarity*, the influential libertarian socialist group led by Chris Pallis, leaving behind a tiny collective with Jack Robinson retiring in 1976 and Peter Turner drifting away in 1977. Peers continues:

The next period was frantic. The production collective was down to three. We were producing a section weekly (eight pages A4, perhaps 8,000 words), setting it ourselves on battered IBM typewriters whose only concessions to modernity were electric power and proportional spacing. We then relied on the State, BR Red Star parcels, to get the completed artwork to our old friend Ian the printer (RIP) in Margate and bring back the paper. Gillian Fleming did most of the typing on one floor, Francis Wright most of the paste-up on another and

I scurried between, doing a bit of each, writing last-minute fillers and acting as intermediary. Mary Canipa still worked in the bookshop and helped with the typing. There was too much pressure to bother with too many ideological disputes, and enough to give a few personal ones.

Talking in 2018, Peers told me a bit more about the process at the time, which involved the tortuous regimen of putting everything together on a Sunday and putting it on a train to Margate on the Monday, then waiting for the train back with 2,000 finished papers which then had to be shunted across London, using the Underground, back to Angel Alley for fold and dispatch.

I was also a member of the South London group set up to organise a May Day picnic, and later secretariat for the Federation of London Anarchist Groups.* Alan Albon and I managed to fit in an educational and enjoyable trip to a festival of the re-expanded CNT in Barcelona. There were a couple of anti-fascist riots that summer.

Pressure lessened as more people joined, including Steve Sorba [in 1977], now with Aldgate Press, and Philip Sansom, rejoining what he has called his "first love". Freedom still gave an impression of impenetrable solidarity. The Hastings Group, producers of one of the first of the welcome wave of local publishing, turned up to a readers' meeting to slag us all off and show us the error of our ways, and were astonished to find that the monolith, the "Establishment" of British anarchism, was half-a-dozen people struggling along as best as possible, much like them.

By the late 1970s we were a group of over a dozen. The big issue of the time was the Persons Unknown case** and a couple of us, including me, worked with the support group. Our own problem was lack of clear structure.

---

* This group formed in 1977 in an effort to make up for the collapse of the London Anarchist Federation. Several attempts were made to build new federations, including the Confederation of British Anarchists in 1976.

** A political trial in all but name, Vince Stevenson, Iris Mills, Ronan Bennett, Trevor Dawton, Stuart Carr and "Taff" Ladd were initially charged with making bombs but then with "conspiracy to rob" after it became clear the charges wouldn't stick. Ladd skipped bail and went on the run, eventually being jailed for separate offences. Carr pleaded guilty and was sent down, everyone else was acquitted.

We had grown haphazardly, coping as we could, and things were still so conducted. There was enough work power for production to proceed but this was sometimes more by default than by intention. Several people who had just turned up were good-naturedly included, leaving no clear distinction as to who was an 'editor'. There was enough surplus energy to form factions.

Freedom's involvement in the Persons Unknown case led to something of a culture clash for some of the returnees, Sansom in particular. One fundraiser put on at Conway Hall for the accused, headlined by Crass, saw a neo-nazi invasion partway through the night and a fight broke out, trashing the venue. Peers remembers: "When Philip Sansom turned up with his partner later in the evening I introduced him to defendant Taff Ladd. We were standing knee-deep in broken glass and blood and whatever and Philip was saying 'oh this is awful we never had this in the past'. Taff was agreeing and they commiserated for a while until they realised they were at cross purposes — Taff was actually outraged about having lost his dope".

As the collective entered the 1980s though it was in slightly better shape that when it had started that decade, looking more the part of a modern paper and with a larger group around it while remaining somewhat out of the activist loop. It had few strong connections with the awakening of political punk, though it was slightly better-linked with the anarcho-pacifism that swirled around the phenomenal success of the band Crass. It had been mostly left out of the creation of the Direct Action Movement (DAM) when that was formed in 1979 between the last remaining SWF branch in Manchester, *Black Flag*-linked groups and others.* So it would initially be the publishing arm driving Freedom Press in the '80s rather than the paper, which from 1982 would drop to a monthly, with a readership falling towards the hundreds rather than thousands.

---

* Through the '80s and early '90s DAM was the main anarcho-syndicalist grouping in Britain. Though it managed several successes particularly in anti-fascist organising, the group suffered from a lack of focus which led it to being refounded in 1994 as the Solidarity Federation.

From top left,
Philip Sansom
in Aldgate Press,
Alan Albon, the
front page which
prompted Vero's
return (page 185),
and the London
Bookfair in 1987

1980-2001
The long goodbye

If the '70s had been a decade of Trots in the university and militancy in the unions while anarchists found their action in squats and bombs, the '80s and '90s saw an anarchist resurgence quite different from what had gone before. The late 1970s had seen Crass and political punk storm into view, and presaged the rise of a new scrappier breed of troublemaker whose name would set tabloid hearts a-flutter throughout the '80s and '90s — *Class War* was on its way.

Alongside them, though often separate, were the fluffies, non-to-less violent direct actionists coming out of the mid-'70s green and anti-nuclear movements who were soon to rejuvenate the peace camps and cause endless trouble for Tory road-building schemes. Such groups strongly engaged with CND and environmental groups such as Greenpeace* alongside more radical groups, and even the apocalyptic views of primitivism, forming a force which continually harrassed the State. The tight organisational and membership strategies at play were extremely effective, especially the confrontational tactics of the anarchist-influenced Animal Liberation Front, but cell-structured groupings and what tabloids termed the new wave of "professional protest" led to accusations of elitism from other anarchist strands and eventually, intervention by the State as it drafted punitive laws and sent in spies who lied their way into friendships and even family relationships with unsuspecting activists.

In Britain's wider social struggle meanwhile the stakes were about to get very high indeed. In 1979 Margaret Thatcher was elected, and would wage the most comprehensive war against working class power of the modern era. Multiple historic strands converged at the turn of the decade, lined up for a struggle which would set the direction of Britain in stone for the next three decades until the onset of the 2007 banking collapse brought neoliberalism to crisis point.

---

* This was sometimes complex — London Greenpeace for example was not affiliated to the international body, operating independently, and was the hub for much more direct action-oriented activities.

The miners' struggle in 1984, Wapping, the fall of the Berlin Wall, the Poll Tax riots and the Criminal Justice Act, through to wars in Iraq and Bosnia would all take place in this 20 year period.

At *Freedom* the start of the decade would march to a beat set by the return of a seemingly reinvigorated proprietorial figure in the form of Vernon Richards. From 1980 the old editor began to re-involve himself with the Press, just in time to see Jack Robinson, Peter Turner and Mary Canipa step back, replaced by more anonymous articles and a very obvious change in tone. While the newspaper would continue to slowly decline in readership throughout the period for a variety of reasons, it would revive the idea of a quarterly journal via the *Raven* and significantly up its publishing game, bringing out around 80 books over the course of two decades until Vero's death in 2001.

One factor in this relative wealth of new publishing would be the existence of A Distribution, which from November 1980 took over the task of actively selling Freedom's output, producing some of its most commercially successful efforts and maintaining a long association with the Press as the group took over an office in Angel Alley. This would lead, in 1981, to Freedom being directly involved with the setting up of the first London Anarchist Bookfair, which would become the movement's biggest annual get-together until at least 2017. After a period of upheaval in the 1980s which saw multiple collectives come and go, the '90s under Charlie Crute would see *Freedom* settle into a sort of grandad role, stable but often criticised for not engaging with the militant activism taking place and (at least according to a survey undertaken in 1992) increasingly talking to to roughly the same, now much older audience that it had been addressing in the 1960s.

Printer paper distro spy

At the beginning of the 1980s, although rhetorical hostilities continued with *Black Flag*, the two papers were both fortnightlies, publishing on alternate weeks and with joint weekend meetings to deal with subscriptions. Vitality in the movement however was starting to move in a different direction to both publications. While *Class War* only formally emerged in 1983, its key players were already around, viewing *Black Flag* as having a "fixation with international terrorism and worshipping at the shrine of the Spanish syndicalists" and regarding *Freedom* as a "fucking boring, liberal irrelevance of a paper".

Peace movements would also kick off again in 1980, With a massive CND demo bringing that organisation back to public notice following Thatcher's go-ahead for Cruise missiles to be based in Britain. The movement quadrupled in size by 1983, holding the largest anti-nuke demo ever and pouring new energy into the radical non-violent direct action movement which would fuel the Stop the City rallies of 1983-4, sparking two decades of upheaval.

This period saw the founding of most of the first major anarchist distributors, including AK Press, Active Distro and A Distro, reflecting an increasing amount of libertarian literature emerging from the movement at large. The latter of these groups would be particularly important for Freedom Press, as it would go on to have a long association with the group including opening its office in Angel Alley. A dynamic force in the movement, A Distro was a prime mover behind the London Anarchist Bookfair's establishment in 1981, with Freedom being involved from the start, and helped shift the books being produced, building up a publishing arm to offset losses from the paper. Offering some memories from his time around the building, A Distro and bookfair founder member Martin Peacock writes:

I've been coming at least once a month to Freedom for just under 50 years. When the movement gets round to producing medals I would like one.

It's a lot friendlier than it used to be. I know, but it always had an association with old people's weariness and cynicism. I may be part of that now. It almost felt like Freedom's duty was sapping the energy and optimism of the youthful anarchist. Obviously that has totally changed.

In the early days Freedom fitted perfectly into a barren waste of dead factories. Now I quite like the island in a sea of gentrification. There is a lot less urine and fewer used condoms. I'll probably miss it sitting amongst a sea of towering financial institutions as the city expands east.

I remember sleeping in the building one night and being woken in the early hours by two men trying to smash their way into the building. It was pre-shutters days. They were repelled by books dropped from the third floor. I particularly remember Leval's *Collectives in the Spanish Revolution* doing significant damage.

I remember my first ever *"Freedom-folding"* (an ancient ritual) with Pete who was one of the first to be killed by AIDs. Just ghosts in the building.

Revolutionary optimism fluxes and wanes but it is worth pointing out transformations linked to Freedom. Issues such as freedom of sexuality and identity, ecological awareness, mental health have gone from concerns accepted by people at Freedom to mainstream concerns. I'm not saying that battles have been won, but the debate has massively changed and Freedom has always been around 20 years ahead. From sandals (honestly a revolutionary concern once) to non-binary. Child sexuality has been quietly dropped though.

Freedom has always been about the printed word. When I first arrived Freedom's ground floor was a refuse tip of a long-gone anarchist printer. Then it became Aldgate Press until they outgrew the space. Then a storeroom for Freedom's books. Today it's the bookshop.

Printing and shifting the anarchist classics and the other stuff. It's interesting how that hasn't disappeared with our ebooks. Maybe that's connected with Freedom as museum: the yellowing posters, the titles centuries old, the old gits hovering around.

It's more than that though. It's not just the police infiltrators that believe in its revolutionary potential. It's a hub, to work out those connections: linking the liked, dividing yourself from those you like less, doing things together, going to the pub and talking about doing things together. The whole revolutionary spectrum is there!

I would say that Freedom has often been marked by the most intense ideological disputes. Only they're not: they're personal rivalries, competitions and feelings just couched in ideological terms. They linger for years and then decades later you rack your brains for the cause. They're still not talking to each other though. Bless!

I'm often struck between our image of a self-managed society without privilege and coercion, where we all work as one to raise that barn, to the reality of Freedom. Don't forget that it was built as an oligopoly founded on inherited wealth. Freedom doesn't have to be a museum, a refuge for alcoholics, an oligopoly, a home to internecine clique warfare. Personally I'd like it to be an advert for anarchism.

Breakout: The spycop: Roger Pearce

At the time of writing Freedom is a core participant in the Undercover Policing Inquiry, following official confirmation that Pearce had operated as "Roger Thorley," a former writer for *Freedom* under the moniker RT. Pearce penned a series of articles over the course of the period 1980-81 and then joined a fact-finding mission to Belfast, before disappearing from sight.

Most of these essays were heavily critical assessments of the policing and justice systems with a focus on the situation in Northern Ireland, suggesting among other things that IRA members detained by Britain should be treated as political prisoners — a major and controversial demand of Republican combatants at the time. Pearce qualified as a barrister with Middle Temple in 1979, meaning he was ideally placed to act as an "expert voice" on such matters when putting forward such articles for publication.

The strong implication is that Pearce was using the paper as a way to contact and assess British connections with the radical community in Northern Ireland in a period of crisis. Freedom had received several articles from and was cordial with the Belfast Anarchist group.

Anarchists who were active at the time do not, for the most part, remember Pearce well — he seems to have kept a relatively low profile — and as far as can be told he was never an active editor. Some memories do survive however, which fit with what we now know to have become the standard operating procedure for Met infiltration.

Dressed up with Trotskyish glasses and a goatee, Pearce was conspicuously "useful" as a car driver prepared to give people lifts and one comrade remembers he was the "unofficial chauffeur" of Leah Feldman.

When inquiry head Mitting defined Pearce's writing as "virulently anti-police" he wasn't exaggerating — and it was specifically in favour of the IRA. In one article, 'Prisoners of Politics' (1980 Nov 8th) the editors debate "RT" over his demand that IRA detainees should have political prisoner status, noting that "all prisoners are political".

In another he attacks the arrest of Peter Sutcliffe, the Yorkshire Ripper, as "difficult to evaluate in terms of sheer blatant prejudice and hysteria," comparing him to Provisional IRA man Gerard Tuite.

But it is R.T's final article which should raise the most eyebrows. In 'The Not So Distant Struggle' (1981 Sep 26th) he reports back from a fact-finding mission to Belfast that he had inveigled himself onto. The London police spy's empathetic report on the Troops Out phenomenon notes:

> Within a short distance of Britain we are daily witnessing a most repressive regime whose intensity supports no comparison with life in London; a regime where there is near total monitoring of movement day and night, where constant use is made of the Prevention of Terrorism Act to detain and prosecute 'political offenders', where the overt presence of armed forces often reaches saturation point, where prisoners are condemned by juryless Diplock courts, and where widespread condemnation has been directed internationally, particularly from America.

This was a man so embedded in the heart of that "repressive regime" he would become ringmaster to the many other liars and manipulators of that force. A paid-up member of the British state writing to the public that:

> Ideological scruples must not be allowed to erode the clear responsibility of focusing attention on what has become the embodiment of the repressive state visibly at work in utilising all its resources, using the streets of Belfast, Derry and elsewhere as a prime testing ground for future urban unrest in Britain.

It's an analysis many anarchists would agree with, then and now. But for an agent of the Crown, misleading would be an understatement. Pearce's actions manipulating the Freedom group were sadly among the less vile taken by the officers of the Special Demonstration Squad which would sneak into and ruin the lives of so many for the crime of being political.

By the 1980s, with a decade-long pseudo holiday under his belt, Vero was increasingly getting involved in the Press again, and would work with A Distro to bring out a wide array of titles both classic and new over the course of the next two decades. He had already published two of his own works, *The Impossibilities of Social Democracy* and *Protest Without Illusions* at the end of the '70s and would see him experience a second wind through the next few years, publishing some of his best projects including *Lessons of the Spanish Revolution* and *Why Work?*, both of which have been updated and reprinted in recent years, as well as titles by Colin Ward and Donald Rooum. His major move however was one which would secure the future of Freedom Press for many years to come — he gave 84b away.

The start of the decade was to see major changes at the building, as in 1981 Freedom Press finally cleared the last of its debts related to the original purchase of 84b 13 years before. Following this, Vero re-established the Friends of Freedom Press as a dormant limited company, comprising mostly close allies of his publishing ventures over the years. The original members comprised Mary Canipa, John Hewetson, Olive Markham, Geoffrey Ostergaard, Vernon Richards, Philip Sansom and Colin Ward, with their *Memorandum of Association* making it clear what the function of the group was to be:

- Non-profit, with no remuneration going to members
- Assist financially and fundraise for the publication of Freedom and associated works
- Own the building on behalf of the movement
- Distribute remaining assets to the rest of the movement in the event of collapse
- Build and maintain a library of anarchist literature

1981 would also see the establishment of Aldgate Press as an independent firm with enduring ties to *Freedom*, which for the next three decades would be the group's printer through arguments, fire and raids while also providing a backbone service to many groups in the wider movement, including *Black Flag* and *Direct Action*. Steve Sorba, who moved over from Freedom Press to the new company, recalls:

> Vero wanted very much to bring the printing back in house to make the printing cheaper both for the paper and for other publishing projects. One aim, from the very start, was for AP to make enough money to be able to print *Freedom* for free —

which we do to this day! It was also a way of setting up a co-op to show that you don't have to run business in a capitalist fashion. Which again we do to this day. (At the time there were probably a dozen print related co-ops in London)He raised £20,000 from a supporter who I seem to remember was either Swiss or Italian. I never met him and don't remember his name.

I went to LCP (now LCC) for a year to study printing, and at the same time I emptied the bottom of 84b of all the old printing equipment and lead type etc. Then along with Dave Elder and Alan Albon we put the place back together. Installed a heating system and built the dark room. Dave McCabe (who was on the Ireland trip with Roger Thorley) also helped as well as sundry others. Aldgate Press had already been registered as a name by Vero so we used that.

We bought a second hand press Rotaprint R20 with help from Magic Ink, a flatbed camera and a guillotine and started working. We used to dish develop negatives it was that long ago ... and then it all began ...

Vernon Richards himself noted in *Freedom / A Hundred Years* a few years later:

Once again costs had escalated. Apart from the fact that Freedom Press books were being printed in Aberdeen and Nottingham, getting the copy to Margate and the proofs back, and the same procedure with the artwork and the printed copies of the paper, all made it clear that the time was ripe to think again of setting up our own printing press with the new technology on the premises. One of the most generous Friends of Freedom Press was impressed by the proposal to set up a new print shop in 84b and replace all the old plant, and provided the means to do so. A number of volunteers got the ground floor at 84b ready, and Aldgate Press has now been operating for five years as we had hoped it would when the name was adopted more than 20 years ago.

As changes went on at Freedom, a buildup had been taking place in Brixton which was to explode into the national consciousness in April. In a rare scoop, a correspondent from the anarchist squatters active in the London borough wrote to *Freedom* at the time with their take on the situation. The tone in the May 1st 1981 issue is a significant departure from the norm of the paper, that of a local writing about their part in a major riot, presented unvarnished.

A massive surge of adrenalin. War whoops. Class war whoops.'Whoops! Class War!' A scramble for bricks. 'I must have a brick. Where are the bricks?' A hail of bricks. The cops are confused as they realise they are no longer in control. Puppets without a role. They look at us, at one another and around themselves.

Them. Run. Away. Down Mayall Road, leaving their vehicles in our hands. In the twinkling of a rioting eye the vehicles are smashed up and turned over. A light is instantly provided and poof! Up goes a cop's van. Wild cheers. Laughter, Dances of joy. I see a comrade and we beam solidarity at one another.

It's the sort of front page that an editor usually dreams of. Active, raw and powerful frontline reporting from someone directly involved. But for *Freedom* it hinted at problems in the collective. By this time, the new influx of people at the end of the decade was having its standard "good problem" effect with the paper's prior consistent (if often criticised) line deploring riot cheerleading clearly not coming into play. Internal arguments were starting to build between what amounted to *Freedom* "traditionalists" and a younger group, broadly around Aldgate Press. The presence of such difference may have been picked up on even before that point, as on April 1st Angel Alley was visited by nine members of the Anti-Terrorist Squad, led by Detective Inspector Gibb-Gray. The next issue reported:

> The four people in the building at the time were arrested and taken to Leman St Police Station. Quantities of printed matter and printing materials were also taken by the police. The four arrested were held in the cells for four-and-a-half hours during which time they were interrogated in turn. They were then released without being charged.

This catch-shake-release approach was part of a much wider campaign by police against what seems to have been considered a threatening growth in anarchist activity, as several threatening visits were also made to individual readers of both *Freedom* and *Peace News* at the time by Special Branch officers. In Glasgow, ten anarchists were arrested in connection with the local paper *Practical Anarchy* while in Birmingham eight people headed to a demo were put on trial on ludicrous charges of "going equipped to cause criminal damage and conspiracy to commit a public nuisance", using the evidence of a can of paint found in the boot.

The police were also mobilising much more broadly than merely making an effort to scare anarchists, having been put on high alert by the scale of the anti-nuke marches and CND's sudden growth to more than 300,000 members as part of what's now known as its "second wave" of activity, including the establishment of Molesworth Peace Camp in 1980 and what would become Greenham Women's Peace Camp in September 1981.

They had good reason for doing so. The re-ignition of CND once again connected isolated groups across the country and brought many people into its orbit who would go on to be active in activism for years to come, often with the anarchists. At one of the first big demos at Molesworth for example, Martyn Everett recalls:

> I was standing by the main gates when a load of young anarchists came almost from nowhere and gathered round a skip by the gates and started drumming on it, gathering more interest, then setting fire to the contents, before they (I had joined them at this stage) rushed down the fence away from the main gate and started tearing down the fence. Inspiring stuff!

Scotland Yard took a particular interest in the political punks who had so energetically entered the nation's cultural consciousness, and tended to focus heavily on them at rallies. A June 11th issue of the paper covering one such CND march noted the panic that gripped officers when 300 anarchists broke from the main body of the demo and marched into Oxford street, headed towards the US embassy. It was turned over by what was essentially a test run of new quick-response riot units alongside the Special Patrol Group.

Freedom's evident interest in such events was rewarded by an increasing number of direct action reports sent in from across the movement, from peace marches to Animal Liberation Front actions and anti-nuclear power activities. The contacts lists once again grew significantly, and there was a significant uptick in the deficit fund income to £1,624 (from around £1,000 in the late '70s) A censorious streak did remain though in some of the people writing in to the paper, with one for example indignantly telling off the punks for being "too scruffy". Opinion from other quarters became more positive for a time, with an editor of *Direct Action* (revived as the organ of the Direct Action Movement) writing in on May 29th 1982 to enthuse:

> *DA*'s editorial collective do not view *DA* as an alternative or rival to *Freedom* (or any other anarchist publication). As far as we're concerned, the more anarchist papers there are,

fulfilling a myriad of needs, the better. The fact that there is a growing number of both local and national anarchist papers is, we believe, a sign of a healthy movement ... because we are only too aware of the problems of producing a paper, we would never criticise *Freedom*, the editors of which are doing a good job.

With the collective still experiencing tensions between its newer and older members however this uncomfortable balance wasn't to last long. Things began to fall apart again in 1982 with spiralling internal arguments, the expulsion of Gilian Fleming from the collective* being the precursor to a much more comprehensive break. Writing in 1986, Dave Peers recalled:

> With a change in format and with the launch of Aldgate Press absorbing energy, things had already gone too far by 1984. Nobody quite knew what was happening. There were two undercurrents, more or less breaking down into the traditionalists, Alan Albon, Philip Sansom and others, against the people grouped around Aldgate Press. Some would feel that they were being left to do the necessary work and then criticised for any shortcomings, whilst others thought that things were done behind their backs. These contradictory emotions circulated through the group. Eventually came to a head and people just said they didn't want to bother any more. I was the only one left!**
>
> So, there I was at a historic moment. I brought out an an issue. This image of heroic splendour is not actually quite so stark; Veronica still produced the subscription labels and Mo, who had just taken over the bookshop, helped with some paste-up, but allow me my moment. Meanwhile, sympathisers set up a new group to exclude all remnants of previous tensions.

---

* She had been inserting articles in praise of the Animal Liberation Front and the Irish Republican Army without telling any of the other editors.

** Albon's departure is notable for resulting in the launch of *Green Anarchist*, which was founded following the Stop The City protests and would initially see contributions from the likes of Colin Ward, Crass and Class War. Albon dropped out of that paper when fellow editor Richard Hunt started extolling violence. *Green Anarchist* would move in both a primitivist and insurrectionist direction over the course of the next decade before being brought down by Operation Washington in 1995 and the subsequent GANDALF political trials in 1997 against green and animal rights activists.

As I hadn't been part of them (which I called tolerance, and somebody else fence-sitting), I was included.

The nominal list soon reduced to a couple, which is frankly not enough, especially as a disproportionate amount of work falls on the one who can spend time in the office.

There are obvious lessons in this. I joined in the aftermath of a split and we are still reeling from the next. The obvious dispiriting point is that it happens too often. So many initiatives, projects and groups splinter in comparable fashion. It's not only anarchists, it is apparent in all voluntarist activity whether Marxist, Nazi, Labour Party or stamp-collecting societies. It is also apparent in non-voluntarist activities, such as formal jobs, but these hold together simply because there are not the same opportunities for walking away.

The difference should be that we base a philosophy on mutual aid. An essential is mutual goodwill or, at least, toleration. This can rapidly become strained, for example in a self-contained group within a self-marginalised subculture. What should be resources of strong-minded individualism can resemble petty- minded egotism. It is trite to point to the theory; we all know about open decision-making and consensus. It is easy to find those with special skills, or simply more time, getting on with the work. They start to resent it whilst others resent what they increasingly see as exclusion. It doesn't take long for such a polarisation to become established.

Freedom was never the monolith of its image. Far from being a centre of Establishment power it is a few people juggling resources of time, energy and money.

Stu notes

The second person in that couple of editors was Stu Stuart, who joined in 1984 around the time the miners' strike began. It's difficult to know where to start when writing about this phase in *Freedom*'s existence, as Stu and Peers took the paper in a drastically different graphical direction, making a fairly substantial splash with a totally redesigned look and layout that was light years of anything Freedom had previously managed, but carrying a tone (mostly from Stu) that would frequently verge on trolling.

The typesetting was done by Jayne Clementson, who would have a 30-year stint at Angel Alley working across nearly every part of the group at one time or another, particularly in the 2000s running the admin and paper distribution. She recalls of her experience:

> I started out working in the top room working for Aldgate as a typesetter, but as Freedom was in the same building you just sort of interact and just end up doing mostly Freedom Press stuff, but initially I was the bright young thing around all the old codgers.
>
> One of my jobs was doing an editorial column on a Tuesday, so I'd be typing that up and it'd be hot off the press — it was kind of a jobshare. I transitioned over to doing layout along with changes in technology, learning Cora 5 to send to the printers and getting faxed galleys back, a sort of long-term process as the industry changed. Then once computers came in I could do layout, but before then it was just galleys.
>
> With the admin I ended up taking on individual jobs when people dropped out simply because no-one wanted to. Then I started doing mailout when no-one else would do that either — there were piles of cheques which had to go to the bank. The general chaos after Vero died in 2001 made mailout an issue, as it was difficult to tell how many were actually getting to people.

Stu gained temporary control, as often happens in such periods of collapse, by virtue of being the only one other than Peers who was prepared to put in the legwork to keep *Freedom* running — everyone else was commuting in from outside London and of limited real help in production. As a result it largely became his baby from 1984 to late 1986, but he was not well regarded by either those he worked with at *Freedom* or by their comrades at Aldgate Press. As time went on articles began to be accompanied by "Stu notes" where he would critique or retort to what everyone else was writing. Donald remembers being contacted at one point by Jayne saying she wouldn't include this or the other missive, only to find that it had gone in anyway as Stu had intervened with the printing.

Amid an uptick in activity more generally, including Stop the City (one and two) in 1983-4 which foreshadowed the new movement's 1990s high point, and the beginning of the titanic miners' struggle against Thatcher's plan to close the pits in 1984, *Freedom* experienced, for a while, a marked increase in new writers.*

---

* Though apparently not readers. An 1985 editorial note estimated international sales at 250 made up 35% of the subscriber base — implying a total of 750-800.

Stop the City was a major milestone for the new wave of anarchism, drawing together multiple strands of activism into a crowd 3,000 strong at the London Stock Exchange (more outside the cordon), overwhelming an underprepared police force despite the use of military trucks blocking the streets. A stockbroker who tried to ram his car through the protest saw it turned over, windows were smashed and, in the view of Iain Bone at the time, the pacficist approach to resistance was essentially upended. Martyn Everett recalls that:

These early actions gave the anarchist movement a lot of self-confidence, and brought the new-wave of CND anarchists into contact with the anarchist movement. The independent anarchist May Days grew out of this experience.

The monthly's approach to the miners' strike specifically has interesting parallels with the paper's approach to the Great Unrest so many years before in that it was strident in criticising the limitations of the struggle, which was certainly not the most popular move it could have made. That popularity was instead reserved for the newly-formed *Class War*, and to a lesser degree for *Black Flag*, both of which saw a surge of interest on the picket lines, the former shifting tens of thousands of copies each issue at its height with funny, confrontational splashes. *Freedom* did offer practical solidarity for the miners throughout, most notably by giving over office space and a phone to Bates Pit National Union of Miners (NUM) for fundraising, regularly printing fundraising appeals and running a support page for jailed pickets, but refused to support a leadership which it characterised as "conscious 'vanguard Marxists'".

It was uncompromising in attacking the strategies and cult of personality built around NUM leader Arthur Scargill and this position may explain why some characterised *Freedom*'s position as primarily being about looking down on the miners as dupes of the Leninist left and trade union authoritarians. The counter position to this from the editors was that the miners deserved an honest perspective, and that solidarity which merely followed the river to defeat without trying to divert its flow was no true solidarity. In one peevish aside, a columnist suggested that Albert Meltzer might be expecting a ministerial post in a future Scargill government.

Regardless of the ins and outs, *Freedom* was continually rubbing many in the movement up the wrong way. Stu often tried for irreverent but all too frequently fell into outright obnoxious behaviour, being prone to a brand of snarkiness as well as sometimes childish sectarian flourishes, such as printing a report on a DAM conference next to a cartoon of a brawl (page 188). Paper donations fell to £818, a worryingly low figure compared to just a few years prior particularly given that Angel Alley was now listing up to 70 groups in the paper and hosting PO Boxes for *Class War*, DAM and a dozen other groups at a time of enormous growth for the wider movement.

As January 1985 rolled around *Freedom* made a quite startling graphical change, running with a shiny A4 magazine format. The impression is of a much more friendly and readable layout, with articles cut to length rather than spilling their pages and graphics used liberally to break up the text — though front page cartoons were hit and miss. One from August '85 featuring a discussion on porn for example was simply an erect cock and balls framed by peacock feathers, which entirely predictably led to the paper being removed from shop shelves. The following issue complained mightily, and apparently with genuine anger* about censorship, especially by co-operatives:

The Real CNT Stands Up
Anarchy, Porn and Repression

> Censorious retailers reading this might pause and consider in what way they are different from other authoritarians with control over the media. What is; the real difference between those bastions of the status quo we expect to censor us and your local trendy bookshop! Oh yah, you're probably a co-operative, with consensus and no shareholders, and super, you carry all the terribly important small press titles, and gosh, look at that window full of social concern posters, okay? All of this just seems to amount to fashionable changes attributable to the generation gap. Your basic attitudes have not shifted. Meet the nouveau petit bourgeoise, same as the old petit bourgeoise.

---

* I must admit I find this baffling, given that even today a giant front page penis wouldn't make the proverbial cut at most stores with any interest in making sales to family clients.

That some censorious retailers claim to be libertarian in philosophy simply marks the high refinement of their hypocrisy. Once more we are forced to consider the honesty of blatant pornographers, the openly philistine attitudes of major distributors, and contrast it unfavourably with the covert authoritarianism, displayed as repression and confusion, by those who should be our allies in changing society.

Phallic experiments aside, supporters from the time did include excellent artistic contacts who were brought in for the monthly production allowing full front-page cartoons for the first time. Alongside the first 'Wildcat' strips from Donald Rooum (this would run into the 2000s, and has been reproduced as the *Wildcat* comic book series), the '84-86 period saw other cartoons of varying quality such as the 'Kronstadt Kids' and 'The House Next Door' with a number of decent-quality artworks by 'Nick' and 'CAM'.

With a temporary emergency price rise to 75 pence thanks to increasing print costs and a robbery which had taken place towards the end of the year, the Jan/Feb 1986 issue's editorial team was joined by Donald Rooum, who added some much-needed support towards making the paper happen. In a mark of the flourishing of wider anarchist media, the bookshop was able to announce it had gone "fully anarchist" with Mo Mosely, arriving for a temporary stint as main co-ordinator, drastically reducing the non-specialist stock while retaining similar sales.* Even with more support coming in however, Stu continued to wind people up until April, by which time Vero had had enough. Donald Rooum recalls that Vero, on his way in to the Press to depose the wayward editor, happened upon a scene on the ground floor in which one of the printers was pinning Stu against the wall, threatening to beat him up, and the situation had to be defused so that Stu could walk away.

The next issue politely announces his "retirement" and Vero quickly installed new editorial staff, Francis Wright and administrator Charlie Crute joining Dave Peers and Donald Rooum. The collective also booted out a number of groups from using its premises, particularly for mail, including the independent *Anarchy* magazine, which had been hostile towards the group for some time. A major new project was set in train as well, with Vero commissioning Heiner Becker to produce a centenary book (*Freedom / A Hundred Years*) and getting financial support to enable the printing of a series of related works, including *A Decade of Anarchy* and edited compilations of writing from around the post-war period. Many other books would follow, including reprints of several classics, *Talking Houses* by Colin Ward, and, going into the '90s and increasing number of new titles. The early part of that decade would see Freedom publish writers such as John Griffin, Michael Duane, Tony Gibson, Peter Marshall and long-runing writer Harold Sculthorpe (who also served as secretary of the Friends of Freedom Press from around that time).

The tribute to Freedom's past was in some ways rushed with Becker, supported by Donald Rooum soliciting copy from groups around the movement, struggling to put together the issue in time for its October launch. But it went off largely without a hitch and interest from many major papers meant that its 3,000 run sold out in short order. Several other events marked the centenary including a group celebration at Rita Milton's house in Golders Green and a public birthday party held at Covent Garden Community Centre, featuring Vi Subversa, Richard Famous, Riffraff Poets, Street Accord, the Anvil Quartet, Janet Ahmed and Adrian Mitchell. In his own contribution to the book, Vero described the scene at Angel Alley that year:

On the ground floor is Aldgate Press which was launched by funds from the Friends of Freedom Press but which operates

---

* Mo, who has since returned as a member of the collective, went on to run Phoenix Press publishing a number of classic titles, including Tom Brown's Syndicalism as well as the Anarchist Yearbook series in the 1990s

most successfully as an autonomous, commercial printing partnership. All the old machines are gone. On the first floor the large room is the bookshop, with a comprehensive stock of anarchist literature as well as a selection of non-anarchist titles. Open Tuesday-Saturday 10am-6pm. On the same floor is the Freedom office.

On the second floor is the Freedom Press stock room with some 25,000 books and pamphlets and the Aldgate Press office and typesetting department. On The third floor A Distribution have their stock room and Freedom Press have the accumulated materials, books, journals, files etc for the Freedom Library that has still not materialised.

There is a clear element throughout the year of Vero progressively cleaning house of tendencies which he felt ran counter to the aims of that post-war group he had helmed in the '50s and '60s and this became most evident to readers at the end of 1986 in the form of a redesign. The November issue of the paper came out featuring a CAM artwork involving a skeleton wearing a santa hood with the title 'Seasonal Greetings' (see page 168) and this had been enough for Vero. He put his foot down and a new version of the paper appeared the next month with no graphical splash pages and a huge reduction in cartoons and pictures generally. Both that and the next redesign in 1990 would move *Freedom*'s look back towards its early period. The direction of the paper was essentially reset by the start of 1987, reverting to its previous consistent line and with the price dropping back to 50p. This manifested in *Freedom*'s approach to the Wapping printers' strike against Rupert Murdoch that year. Class War in particular had been highly active supporting the pickets and Ian Bone tells in *Bash The Rich* of their early-morning adventures disrupting distribution of Rupert Murdoch's scab papers, but the new-old look *Freedom* front page sets a more sedate analytical pace without frontline reporting:

While we were pleased to learn that anarchists were at Wapping on Saturday January 24th, modesty forbids us from claiming all we were credited with by police, press and parliament. The mass picket held at Rupert Murdoch's News International plant was on the first anniversary of the dispute over the sacking of 5,500 employees,members of Sogat '82 and the National Graphical Association, and exceptionally large numbers were present — about two pickets for every man sacked. As television viewing voters saw, there was also a massive police presence. One half of one per cent of those present were arrested, and over a year the dispute has involved 1.2 million police man hours at a cost of £5.3 million.

Police made allegations of missiles thrown, unions claimed police provocation with mounted police launching an unprovoked attack on demonstrators.

And why were the police there? To uphold 'law and order' — that is government legislation. Since Mrs Thatcher has said that she believes the majority of trade unionists agree to her legislation, that 'they themselves didn't like the power of the trades unions over individual members, they don't like the dosed shop, it becomes necessary to deny that militants are ordinary trade unionists, to drum up scenes of 'violence' and then blame it on "extremists".

Similarly with the Broadwater farm riots that happened that April:

The first achievement of the Broadwater Farm riot was expressed by a local councillor, 'the police got a bloody good hiding'. This of course is not a long term political achievement, but neither is a riot a long-term political campaign. A sudden spontaneous uprising can only have immediate, simple objectives, and at Broadwater Farm the objective was attained — to take revenge on the bullies.
...
The accidental, long-term achievement of the riot is that judges and legislators have come to recognise that their power is being usurped by the police, who are supposed to be their servants. Already the Metropolitan Commissioner, who at first blamed the riot on 'anarchists and Trotskyists', has sent officers from other London divisions to investigate the methods used in Tottenham to get confessions. Already there has been a discernible diminution of police power in Tottenham.

Evidently this made a significant impact in terms of re-engaging with *Freedom*'s donors, as deficit fund receipts shot back up to £1,600 again in short order, but it also locked the paper into a mold, which would catch up with the press in the '90s as older readers were not replaced by new ones. In the immediate term however finances were starting to look more healthy, aided by the newly active Friends who had independently raised £1,500 for a roof fund, subsidised the centenary issue with £2,000 and subsidised an expansion of the bookshop as well as a shortlived disto effort. The anarchist bookfair too became a driver for income, drawing more than 2,000 people to Conway Hall that October. In an editorial for the event, *Freedom* noted outright that it felt itself to be the intellectual voice of the movement:

> The differences between the various propaganda 'spider webs' may be seen, without too much oversimplification, as differences in the target audiences for propaganda. Freedom, to quote one of our contemporaries, 'appeals mainly to those who like to think of themselves as intellectuals'. Our contemporaries appeal to those who like to think of themselves as sturdy working class, those who like to think of themselves as oppressed outcasts, and so on. With the possible exception of those who like to think of themselves as guardians of anarchist orthodoxy, and damage the movement by excommunicating comrades, we are all working to the same end. The divisions are divisions of labour.

The Raven

Alongside the reordering of *Freedom* consideration was given to the idea of a new journal, following on from the original *Anarchy* and this was eventually founded in August 1987, though issues would end up being edited by a number of different people including Sylvie Edwards and as group. Once again, graphic design wasn't considered the priority as David Goodway recalls:

> When Peter Marshall and I were negotiating with Richards in the late '80s about a quarterly successor to *Anarchy* – our working title was Transformation – insisting on the need for good design, we were told very firmly that it didn't matter how tatty the production was since it was the words alone which were important. Peter and I were not involved with the resulting *Raven*, the first seven numbers of which were edited with considerable distinction by Heiner Becker and Nicolas Walter. Heiner was to tell me with great bitterness, though, that he and Nicolas had received no word of praise or even thanks from Vero Richards.

Intended as a quarterly (though not always precisely on time in its early stages) *The Raven* ran for 43 issues from 1987-2003 focusing on a different subject each issue and intending to build a new reservoir of contemporary research and writing from an anarchist perspective on social issues ranging from food production to international affairs and genetic engineering.

The magazine was hit and miss at times, but as with *Freedom* carried some excellent historical research in particular by Becker and Walter, and strong writing on ecology by the likes of Brian Morris and Murray Bookchin, later collated in *deep ecology and anarchism*. Colin Ward, Denis Pym and Geoffrey Ostergaard were among the *Freedom* stalwarts who contributed articles and a memorable piece on Haiti by Noam Chomsky can be found in issue 28.

With many of its writers leaving or in some case having passed away the journal lost momentum and was closed by Toby Crow in 2003 on the grounds it was uneconomical.

By the end of the year David Peers had retired from the editorial role (though remained a writer), leaving Charlie Crute, Francis Wright and Donald Rooum as de facto main editors under Vero's watchful eye. With this trio *Freedom* settled into more of a routine with occasional standout articles, such as some good reporting on homelessness and a piece on Earth First! in October 1989 which pre-empted that movement's formal leap across the pond by two years:

We — this generation of humans — are at our most important juncture since we came out of the trees six million years ago. It is our decision, ours, today, whether earth continues to be the marvellously living, diverse oasis in the blackness of space which it now is, or whether the 'charismatic megafauna' of the future will consist of Norway rats and cockroaches.

Earth First! is not an organisation but a movement. There are no 'members' of Earth First!, only Earth First!ers. It is a belief in biocentrism (Deep Ecology) and a practice of putting Earth first that I makes one an EF!er.

Because Earth First! is a movement, instead of a specific group, Earth First!ers can be active as Earth First!ers or as members of other environmental groups. Regardless, we promote a philosophy of deep ecology, an uncompromising defence of natural diversity, and visionary wilderness proposals.

Because Earth First! is not an organisation, there are no formal officers, nor any hierarchy. Earth First! was not formed to encompass the entire environmental movement, nor even all students of deep ecology or all militant environmentalists. The green fist and monkey-wrench were consciously chosen as our symbols, as was the name Earth First! — always with the exclamation mark!

We represent a specific point of view, a certain style, a particular vigour — and we don't plan to change. We never envisioned Earth First! as being a huge mass movement. While there is a broad diversity within Earth First! there is a general comfortableness with both this diversity and with the 'hardass' militant style of Earth First!

If you find yourself uncomfortable with it, don't try to change it — we've been through that a thousand times before. Either decide you can handle the militancy or find your environment group elsewhere. Everyone has to find their own tribe.

Issue Zero

The EF! article appeared in the last issue of the monthly version of *Freedom*, which was accompanied by a dummy for a new fortnightly paper, named as Issue Zero by Vero. The look once again moved backward to the older style of tabloid format, albeit with two "splash" pages, unfolded for street selling, folded for shops. Behind closed doors Vero had denounced the editorial team as incompetent, pushing out Francis Wright, while Donald retired from editorial duties as a fortnightly "seemed like too much work". Few punches were pulled in the editorial for the new offering:

> The early 1980s were the second worst period in Freedom's hundred-year history (the worst being the early 1930s when publication stopped altogether). There were frequent changes of editorship, many of them intended as rescues when a previous editorial collective had broken up or lapsed for a time, anyone who happened to be there could make editorial decisions. Style and content changed as often as editors. When the present editors took over in 1987, what Freedom needed most was stability. It had been a fortnightly newspaper in the 1970s (and one of us had been an editor), but what we took on was a monthly magazine so we stayed with that, though we did cut costs and bring the price down, and increase the proportion of news content.
>
> After three years of consolidation, the foundation is laid for another change, not of the ill-considered, almost random kind that occurred a few years ago, but a carefully planned improvement, albeit a bold one. Two of the three present editors will resign at the end of the year leaving the way clear for the new team, but we will continue as contributors and supporters.
>
> The "reprographic revolution" of the 1970s cut printing costs and made possible the profusion of small-circulation 'zines and papers which is the present strength of the English-speaking anarchist movement. But the movement also needs a widely circulated, regularly published propaganda newspaper like those of the French and Italian movements. That is what *Freedom* was, and what we intend it to be again. Support it, comrades. It will be worth supporting.
>
> ~ *The retiring* Freedom *collective*

Entering the '90s then, it would be an uncredited Charlie Crute, along with Vero and two new "section editors" Andrew Hedgecock (science) and Tom Carlile (industrial)* running the show, alongside the odd reliable columnist — most notably Colin Ward, who would write a regular Anarchist Notebook column for the next ten years. While the section editors idea dropped off from 1992, and Vero from 1995, Crute would see out the decade both as supporting editor and in the main role, making this period largely his era.

The '90s, or more specifically the technological changes wrought through it, effectively spelled the end for *Freedom* in terms of what had arguably been its most important function, acting as one of the few sources of information about contact points and actions around the movement. Pre-internet, regularity had made both *Freedom* and *Peace News* important reading for anyone wanting to keep up with events. With the founding of activist freesheet *Schnews* in 1994, which took advantage of both the digital revolution and the rise of home and office printing to put out a regular double-sided A4 freesheet, they were increasingly upstaged by weekly content that could be found easily online. Within a decade it would be daily as *Indymedia* came to the fore. *Freedom* would make some steps towards moving with the times, but mostly Crute's tenure would be one of continuity and an effort to keep the paper running in the shape Vero had fashioned it to, supported by Donald doing the books upon the retirement of Harold Sculthorpe.

This is not to say that there were no Crute scoops. At the start of 1990 *Freedom* reported on the first new anarchist group to emerge in the collapsing USSR, and would be one of the few outlets which covered its activities as Boris Yeltsin dismantled the bloc in the name of liberty. Correspondent Will Firth had been present at the forming of KAS in 1989 during a "boom year in anarchist activity" with publications reaching around 30,000 people and 300 activists in member groups concentrated in European cities Leningrad, Gorky and Kharkov, and some support in Siberia. Outside of Russia proper their reach was sparse. The grouping was very young, with most members in their 20s, and mostly consisted of young men due to "the strongly patriarchal nature of Russian society". KAS would last less than three years, splitting towards the end of 1992 after its leaders got sucked into State organisations, before being banned entirely by the Yeltsin government as it crushed internal dissent on its way to becoming the "free" society we see today.

---

* Tom was an old hand and pacifist from the Peace Pledge Union, who had been hidden by the Whiteway community when he refused to register in 1940 before eventually being caught and jailed for six months — he worked as a miner for a while and did talks with North East London Anarchist Group after the war.

Closer to home, 'Johnny Yen' reported consistently on the Poll Tax from an anarchist perspective and some of Yen's best reports take Brighton as a case study detailing ways in which groups had been refusing and undermining the tax — though Brighton's 31% refusal rate was dwarfed by Lambeth with 61%.

Freedom largely took a position of non-compliance over direct conflict in the anti-Poll Tax campaign, and was mildly critical of the spikier direct action tactics favoured by much of the rest of the movement, particularly *Class War*, though it supported the Poll Tax Riot Support Group in its fundraising efforts for people jailed at flareups such as Trafalgar Square. David Luton's article on the riot itself in the May 5th issue however gives an idea of the elation being felt in the anarchist camp about a genuine drubbing for Thatcher's forces:

The theme running through the so-called "Battle of Trafalgar" anti-poll tax demonstration riot and aftermath was that those claiming to have had some kind of strategy were not prepared to admit that by and large it had completely failed.

The classic example were the police. It is as much out of habit, as out of previous planning, that the police attack demonstrations and marches. They thought they could simply pick an easy target (as there's always some group that either stop and chant or else sit down outside Downing Street) and wade in. A number of arrests are usually enough to justify strong-arm policing and to discredit campaigns. But they didn't bargain for the mood of the 200,000-plus demonstrators unwilling to have mounted and riot-clad police as well as vans indiscriminately charging into them, making random arrests and dishing out beatings to whoever happened to be in the way. The police quickly lost control of a situation of their own making. People fought back and in a great many cases won.

Afterwards, despite the admission by one policewoman that "we lost it", senior police officers were careful to blame everyone except themselves; to pretend that they were in full control; and then claim that the riot was plotted by a tiny minority. Come Thursday and the tune was quietly changed. They were forced to admit there was no evidence of a plot. What they couldn't bring themselves to admit was that it was a spontaneous response to a police attack, in the context of years of attacks, the poll tax being only the latest The Tories were even more pathetic.

They were taken aback by the size and scope of the demonstration and clung to any explanation they could muster — anything to divert attention away from their hated tax. To try and blame Kinnock for the riot on the tenuous link between a handful of MPs breaking the law by not paying, and demonstrators breaking the law by resisting police violence is not only wrong, it is gross incompetence even by this government's pathetic standards. Thatcher has yet to realise that Kinnock has been one of her biggest allies on the subject of non-payment. His message is the same as hers — pay it!

Instead of stepping aside from the accusation and then smashing it and the government's policies, Labour did what it always does — grovel before the Tories, the police, the courts and the media. Deputy Labour leader Roy Hattersley blamed the SWP and anarchists and called for exemplary sentences for those arrested by the police. No doubt the anarchists warned that they would be arrested for the violent crime of carrying a black flag are included in this! The so-called left of the Labour Party — Militant — couldn't be distinguished from the right on this occasion. A witch-hunt of the Anti-Poll Tax Federation (APTF) was promised, along with a call to expel *Class War*. They revealed their true colours when some members said they were prepared to offer their services as police informants. How ironic after they themselves were witch-hunted in the Labour Party!

Anarchists have always been aware that [Labour Party left group] Militant might capitulate at some stage of the campaign but it nevertheless sticks in the throat. Many members of the APTF are left wondering just what mandate there people have from a grassroots campaign to go around launching attacks on other groups and to condemn those prepared to defend the march.

Eventually the media found their scapegoat Class War and a number of other (sometimes non-existent) anarchist groups were said to have organised a quarter of a million demonstrators to riot. How absurd! No group was even capable of planning and organising such a huge response.

The simple fact is that the advocates and apologists for the poll tax cannot politically admit the reality that stares them in the eyeballs — that people were angry and willing to fight over this tax and are not prepared to allow their action against it to be broken up by the police.

The size and feeling of the demonstration illustrates the potential that exists to defeat the Poll Tax. The strategy of non-registration and non-payment is important, but alone they will not defeat this tax. Neither too, will any pretence that some kind of insurrection on a heavily fortified Downing Street will sweep it away.

Non-payment must be used as a way to encourage non-implementation. Local council and other related workforces (DSS, Post Office, etc.) must be urged to take action against implementation of a tax which is against their class interests as workers, by boycotting poll tax work. Council offices must be picketed. Any worker victimised or sacked over the poll tax (and this includes Class War's Andy Murphy, suspended by Hackney Council for his comments to the media) must receive our backing. Strike action must be taken in support — something it is no use calling for the TUC to do — we must do it ourselves as a class.

Less well reported was street fighting simultaneously taking place between far-right boot boys and anti-fascists, which had been intensifying through the 1980s and would reach its height in the '90s, Whitechapel being one of the key flashpoints. This has historically been a difficult topic for the likes of *Freedom*, as having a physical open shop can make radical groups a target, and it seems likely the editorial choice was to try and avoid making too many waves. Actions such as the major anti-fascist victory at Waterloo in 1992 are therefore conspicuously absent from the paper, leaving something of a hole in the coverage of what was happening at the time. Sadly, this would do little to protect the Press when the thugs got going. On March 27th Freedom was raided by neo-nazi paramilitary wannabes Combat 18, causing up to £5,000 of damage. In the following issue (April 3rd) Crute writes:

Shortly after the bookshop was opened the building was invaded by five young men dressed in balaclava helmets and carrying long wooden truncheons, one with a spike. Two stayed on the ground floor. The others came up the the first floor to attack the bookshop and the Freedom Press office.

They smashed everything smashable: the typesetting computer, the photocopier, the telephones. They knocked over the bookshelves. One display case fell on a customer in the shop, pinning her to the floor. Other people were pushed over,but no-one was hurt.

Before they left, the attackers sprayed 'C18' in large letters on the wall above the office door. They left behind a bottle of petrol, which fortunately they made no attempt to explode. It was clear the attackers knew what they were doing. The operation was carried out with military precision.

Jayne was in the building at the time and recounts:

Frank Prebble was on the press downstairs and he ran up saying the fascists were coming, and I saw them out of the window so I went into the Aldgate Press office, dialled 999 and while I was on hold a man with a mask came in, smashed the phone, computer etc, dragged me down the stairs. Arthur Moyse was in the shop that day. I remember seeing them run off and then nothing seemed to happen with the police.

The incident brought sympathy, donations and media attention (e.g from news show *World in Action)*. The Anarchist Communist Federation (from 1999 the Anarchist Federation), *Class War*, AK Press, DAM (refounded as the Solidarity Federation in 1994), *Jewish Socialist* and many other groups rallied round, with fellow-travellers such as Mushroom Bookshop in Nottingham offering donations. Despite no formal appeal being made many people gave over the course of the next month, raising around £1,200 to help get the Press back on its feet.

Damage from the June 4th fire

This was not the end of the story. A follow-up break-in on May 7th robbed the shop of most of its replacement equipment. Most difficult of all however was an arson on June 4th, which saw the northernmost ground floor window broken after hours and petrol poured through the gap, then lit. Piles of paper next to the window caught almost immediately, and it was sheer luck that a passer-by saw the smoke. One of the printers, having a drink in the local pub (likely the White Hart) walked out onto the street to find fire engines on the scene and Angel Alley ablaze.

The damage was extensive, mostly to the Aldgate Press industrial printing machinery, with the guillotine, paper stocks and printed jobs all left as write-offs, wiring melted down and the offices on the first floor, as well as the loo, were all scorched. The cost, mostly to Aldgate Press, ran to around £40,000 in machinery, stocks and lost wages, mostly recouped by insurance. No-one ever came forward to formally claim responsibility, but arson attacks were targeted at soft anti-fascist targets across London, with Brixton's 121 Anarchist Centre and even the Cable Street mural similarly treated.

It was the second time that fascists had attempted to burn Freedom Press. Unlike the bombs of 1944 however they failed to destroy either books or archives, only managing to temporarily delay the next issue of the paper. Metal guards have since been installed on windows and doors, intended to ward against any further violence. In fact rather than hurt the press, a year after the event an editorial in the paper suggested that the solidarity on show may even have helped financially, as two longstanding supporters, Art Bartell and Hans Deichmann were inspired to give generously and a third, Fred Yates, left substantial funding in his will.

Controversially, the June 26th issue decided to offer space for whoever had attempted the arson to have their say, arguing:

Anarchists have always defended the right of minorities to express their opinions however disgusting for the obvious reason that we anarchists are also expressing minority views. How can we demand the right to express out ideas if we at the same time join a chorus to deny it to other minorities? Obviously if other minorities — and C18 and the British National Party are minorities — resort to violence not against the Establishment but against minorities such as anarchists, they must be warned that if they continue with their violence they must expect retaliation.

This led to a complaint from the ACF that perhaps anarchists shouldn't be encouraging the promotion of fascism, even in the cause of moral victories. Fascist attacks against the anarchists were common throughout this period, as the Direct Action Movement took an active part in suppressing the far-right street fighting movement of the time. Another victim of these tactics was the London Anarchist Forum, which was pushed out of its digs at the Mary Ward centre by fascist threats.

Despite these exciting events, the paper's readership remained relatively static or in decline over time, with fewer new readers replacing those lost, and old financial backers starting to die off. In replying to the initial returns from the readers survey in *Freedom*'s January 23rd issue, the editors also identified what was to become a killer moment for the radical left press as retailers started to move away from stocking so many full-size magazines.

The problem, booksellers such as W H Smiths said, was that magazines were an inefficient use of shop space. Large, high-effort and needing to be faced outwards to have any impact, even with its folded A4 front *Freedom*, along with similar publications like *Tribune* were finding it difficult to get stocked. The solution, editors suggested, needed to be a movement one of creating its own distribution networks for papers such as *Freedom*. While anarchist distributors such as A Distro and, from 1988, Active Distribution and AK Press did exist, what they couldn't do was direct sales of the sort which had taken place regularly in the 1940s but fell out of favour in the 1960s.

Survey Two

The second *Freedom* reader survey acts as a useful companion to the one of 1960 in terms of pinpointing changes. The version sent out by the editors of 30 years previous saw 358 responses to 1,863 forms sent, while the 1993 questionnaire pulled in 209 from 1,100 forms. The 1960s audience was younger, with just 10% over-60 compared to the 1993 figure of 23% and, rather than declaring for a particular type of anarchism such as communist or individualist, simply declared themselves "anarchist". Presciently, a 1994 comparison from Tony Gibson suggested that unless the situation was turned around, "when most of these oldies die off, as they must do in a decade or so, the paper will have a considerably reduced readership". Such a turnaround wasn't achieved by the turn of the Millennium.

Though the categories don't map particularly well (people wrote in with individual jobs in the 1960 survey) there is also a notable shift in work category, with a whopping 87% of the 1993 survey respondents being either a professional or retired (as opposed to working a manual trade). There was a clear divide in the type of readership by age, with working-class readers tending to be older. And rather than the biggest complaint being a lack of clear policy, as in 1960, this time around the lead complaint, particularly from younger readers, was that there was "too much of the gentlemanly, middle-aged, middle-class, white male perspective".

This impression probably wasn't helped a great deal by a related note in the March 6th issue of Angel Alley reporting a poor response to *Raven* 21, 'Women and Anarchism' which went on to complain about Mary Quintana's suggestion for a regular women's page "because we cannot accept that women comrades and readers are discriminated against in the pages of *Freedom*". The *Raven* issue in question, though at least edited by a woman (Sylvie Edwards) suffered from a lack of contributions from women and had thus run with just three, alongside a bundle of historical pieces and seven articles from men, including a particular gem decrying the "rigid dogma" of feminism titled 'Men are Human Beings Too!' — as though women have ever said otherwise.

But by 1994, with the exception of longer-length writing, *Freedom* had largely run out of road as a news vehicle that could inspire people to hawk it around at demos and actions. Email had reached a point where information, if it was available, could travel to thousands in a day rather than waiting two weeks and paying a pretty penny. *Freedom*'s circulation was in short order dwarfed by the direct action-led and entertaining fare of a new collective, *SchNEWS*. At its height that young crew would be mailing its frontline missives out to 11,000 people and mailing another 2,000, all for free. The Brighton-based freesheet would become the effective news hub for an entire generation of activism. As models went it was no contest, though *Freedom* did make some effort to engage with the future by involving itself in the founding of newswire A-infos.

Freedom wasn't left entirely unable to contribute by such epochal change, and showcased some of what its larger format could still do later in the year as a promotional and organisational tool for

Anarchy in the UK. The ten-day festival of anarchist ideas, from October 21st-30th was a high point of the London Anarchist Bookfair's run and demonstrated just how big the activist movement was becoming. Talks from every major group took place on everything from football to Earth Day Rainbow Gatherings across more than 30 venues.

Freedom was once again able to call on its physical presence as one of only a handful of outright anarchist venues in the capital, by far the most central, and it functioned mainly as a hub for directing people to everything that was going on. In its exceedingly upbeat report on the event, the paper noted a whopping £2,000 take on top of extra bookshop sales. *Freedom* reported afterwards:

> Ian Bone is to be credited with the idea of turning the week of the Anarchist Bookfair and the London Greenpeace Fayre into an anarchist festival, but much of the credit for its success is due to a few hard-working comrades meeting at the 121 Centre in Brixton, especially those who organised a squat near Conway Hall to accommodate hundreds of overseas visitors. Good timing. The Criminal Justice Bill will now make squatting illegal, after 650 years.
>
> Freedom Press's contribution was to keep the shop open for a welcome stream of visitors and to answer constant telephone enquiries about the whereabouts of events, some of which were moved and others which did not even take place (see below). The week of the Anarchist Bookfair and the London Greenpeace Fayre is always the busiest week of the year for Freedom Press, and this year we also had an advertisement in the *New Statesman* inviting people to write in for a short subscription to *Freedom*. So we did not have time to do much else, or even to attend many of the events.
>
> However two of us, Donald and Silvia, were invited to make the speeches of welcome at the opening ceremony on Friday October 21st. Donald represented the veteran anarchists (notice being too short to find a proper veteran) and Sylvie represented women. We shared the platform with the comedian Mr Social Control, the singer Steve Cope, and Roz who impersonated the Queen.
>
> The Anarchist Bookfair on October 22nd was the best ever, with not a policeman in sight and every table doing well. The welcome volume of sales indicated an enormous number of visitors. The associated meetings were a great success as well, especially the one addressed by Colin

Ward on "Fundamentalism". The launch of *Visions of Poesy*, with readings by poets including Bernard Kops, Christopher Logue, Adrian Mitchell and Monica Sjoo (with vocal interruptions from a dog) was very enjoyable once it got started. Clifford Harper was there selling the book and packs of his portrait cards. The Festival of Smut organised by members of Feminists Against Censorship was enjoyable, no less so for being presented by amateurs, and the debate on pornography and censorship was excellent.

This was to be the last bookfair of Vero's long career as proprietor of Freedom Press. While he would continue to produce the odd published work, finishing with a series of photobooks in 1998, his hand would at last relinquish its grip on the wheel. He continued to send in letters with suggestions for the group, and carrying out his wishes fell mainly to four comrades, Donald Rooum, Sylvie Edwards, Charles Crute and bookshop manager Kevin McFaul (the latter two now being paid a stipend).

The post-Vero collective would remain in place until around the 2001-2003 period, and while it was a period of some slow-going, important writers continued to engage within the newspaper's pages, including Ward and author China Meiville. The subscriber base had by this time declined into the hundreds, but there was a larger number of more casual readers, and a great deal of affection remained for the longest-running anarchist organisation in British history.

In its function as a paper of record for the anarchists, *Freedom* remained important. It is worth noting that even well-produced outlets such as *SchNEWS*, the *Earth First! Bulletin* and *Do or Die* which far more effectively reported the activist movement's extraordinary activities from the mid-'90s onwards are now available relatively sporadically.

The *SchNEWS* website for example is available only via archive. org, and its freesheets are collated only in a series of increasingly rare annual yearbooks. Later mainstay indymedia.org.uk remains online as an archive only for as long as people keep paying the hosting bill. *Freedom*, with its extensive hardcopy archives kept at multiple sites, picks out at least some of the key events that were occupying anarchists at the time.

One of these was the passage of the Criminal Justice Bill. Chris Platts, a *Raven* contributor, warned in *Freedom*'s March 5th 1994 issue that the implications of the forthcoming legislation were dire, as it aimed to essentially shut down avenues for protest. The Act is most infamous for its anti-rave provision which banned "repetitive beats" but Platts warned that it could also target squatters and noted:

There are wider implications, especially regarding the clause affecting hunt saboteurs. Remember the clause suggests it will be a criminal offence to trespass on another's land and prevent a lawful activity, This could be and would be used to cover a wide range of scenarios from pickets to public demonstrations and actions. In effect it will add to the enormous range of laws already suffocating freedom of speech, assembly and choice, as well as uphold the authority of those in power and its servants, the police and legal system.

Platts was not wrong about the intent of the State, as its subsequent efforts to shut down the animal rights, new age traveller and green direct action movements entered high gear over the next few years. Protests over the Bill kicked off with a massive 50,000-strong rally in Trafalgar Square attended by *Freedom* sellers amid the banners of the Anarchist Communist Federation. Silvia Edward reported:

Some of the crowd were complaining the speakers could not be heard above the sound of revelry. The way I saw it was that the sound of people enjoying life was the main thrust of the protest, It underlined the fact that events like these could be numbered if the Bill passes through Parliament uncontested.

That said, a more general lack of coverage for both the Bill and Operation Washington's raids against green and animal rights work (followed in 1995 by the GANDALF trial) were a direct inspiration for the creation of *SchNEWS*, which filled a gap in focused coverage for direct action activism.

The final years of the Millennium were some of the most active of any in the latter half of the 20th century. The Newbury bypass camp, M41 road shutdown, and innumerable smaller clashes between the green direct action movement and heavy industry. Most of this however didn't get heavy coverage in *Freedom*, which ploughed a relatively lonely furrow discussing arcane aspects of anarchist theory and commenting on broader social issues. Every so often reports would come in from demos and particularly the larger conferences, such as the 1998 revival of an anarchist Mayday by the 1-in-12 Club in Bradford.

Ex-members of Class War working out of the club made the splash for the paper's May 23rd issue, having run the Bradford conference, one of only a few genuinely successful cross-movement gatherings to have emerged in recent years bringing together a wide variety of different political strands in relative harmony. *Freedom* writers were impressed enough to fill a quarter of the paper with reports on both the conference and the attendant Reclaim Mayday rally, part of a revival of the Mayday tradition which had largely died off in anarchist circles thanks to its hijacking by Stalin banner-wielding authoritarians.Hundreds of anarchists turned out for the marches, which went on for several years before dying back again.

In the ascension of Tony Blair to Prime Minister in 1997 the anarchist movement, and *Freedom*, found a near-perfect example to use of the tendency of Parliaments to produce the same outcomes regardless of who was in charge. His reactionary politics came through early with the implementation of the New Deal, introducing forms of conditionality to welfare which *Freedom* extensively criticised from the first moment. The September 5th issue led with New Labour's introduction of the New Deal. Criticised in the paper from a historical perspective by HS, it was compared to the labour camps of the 1930s and 1970s, used to "harden the work shy":

No suggestion this time of labour camps, at least so far, because circumstances have changed and the landed gentry are less economically important and have less political clout. Now the government needs to appease a new aristocracy. So it is the multinationals and the Sainsbury's and the Tesco's who can use the cheap labour. Stacking shelves replaces digging holes. Television advertising attempts to persuade young people that this is their golden opportunity to acquire the skills needed for economic survival. But it is the employers that get the cash, up to £60 a week for each wage slave they accept, plus a Training Grant for joining the scheme. Even schools are now invited to apply, and as a *Guardian* editorial suggests (August 24th 1998) "the presence of the unemployed in the classroom might offer students a useful glimpse of their own future", for after three months most young people will be back at the Job Centre although of course the unemployment statistics will look a little better.

Unfortunately for Labour's third New Deal a new factor is threatening the government's desire to keep unemployment down. This is a gradual realisation by government, something the Conservatives knew instinctively, that there are certain essentials if the capitalist system is not to self destruct. Financial stability is important and this, as measured by inflation indices, requires a permanent pool of cheap labour which in turn depends on a pool of unemployed, which for Britain is calculated to be around two million. So we can expect a double act — one exhorting the unemployed to try harder to get a job, however low the pay, whilst the other tries to ensure that not too many of them succeed — Oh Happy Life.

What the editors didn't know at this stage was the secondary effect such measures would have, in conjunction with the housing crisis that was on the way. As the sanctions regime started to bite and was eventually joined by the decentralised new labour camp system known as Workfare, it crashed into the voluntarism which had thus far characterised Freedom's work.

Though many of Freedom's stalwarts had maintained other jobs while working on the paper or in the shop, others had been able to subsist on dole money while volunteering, as had been the case for many charitable organisations. As the Dole (later JSA) became more and more difficult to stay on without going through punitive measures however being an activist on welfare in the '90s became less financially viable, while rising rents alongside the later banning of squatting in the 2010s it would force many people out of the city centre altogether.

The impacts of this compound problem have been extraordinarily widespread, far beyond the political scene, contributing to a crisis in charity independence and informal social support structures.

As we end this chapter, with *Freedom* back in a pattern of ponderous survival, It would be wrong to miss out the paper's coverage of the last great activist event before the Millennium — the Carnival Against Capitalism. Also known as J18, the carnival took place on June 18th 1999 and represents the high point of anarchist street presence through this period in Britain. Part of an international day of protest against the German G8 summit that year, around 6,000 people took to the streets of London in the main rally, while multiple other overtly anti-capitalist events took place across the city. *Freedom* ran three pages of long reports in its next issue which represent probably its most interesting direct action reporting of the decade. 'J' focused primarily on the blanket media coverage which took place in the aftermath of the event, while Prometheus and Richard gave more direct impressions. Richard took part in the earlier part of the march, describing the atmosphere:

Just before 2pm the crowd moves. There is nothing more inspiring than feeling in control. The roads, the space belongs to us. As you move away from Liverpool Street towards the NatWest Tower you cross a wide road — London Wall — which marks the northern limit of the City. Emptied of traffic you get a feeling for how beautiful this could all really be. You feel the space, the air. Not hemmed onto a metre-wide pavement you can notice the buildings. Some ugly, some not. We walk past the NatWest the tallest building in the City, earlier leafleted in an attempt to explain the purpose of the day to the workers inside.

Just past the Tower a Mercedes drives down the road towards us. Amazingly rather than reversing the driver tries to carry on through a sea of six thousand people! He seems to believe we would move out of his way, after all that is how it is meant to work. He drives a big expensive car — we get out of his way. But not today! He soon realises the error of his way and backs, safely, away. Next stop the Bank of England. The Bank looks exactly like what it is built as: a fortress. Its doors are slammed shut. A few plastic bottles are thrown but there's no way into the Bank.

The "march" moves on past Mansion House and down by Cannon Street station where I started my day. At the side of Cannon Street we stop. Every Reclaim the Street action I have been on RTS (or someone) has managed to get in a sound system and despite the police road blocks they managed it again today, (they also always seem to get the weather right as well).

Upper Thames Street is blocked. The sound system starts and the party began. A fire hydrant explodes into life shooting water high into the air and down on to the protesters bringing some relief from the heat. CCTV cameras are covered with bin bags. Someone has made a huge Monopoly board and they play the game in the road. A volley ball net is spread across the road along with banners. One says 'No Solution but Revolution'. People dance to the techno or to a punk band who play in the small green space between College Street and Cloak Lane. As Emma Goldman said "if I cannot dance it's not my revolution". For half a mile around the railway station roads are closed, space reclaimed. The carnival is in full swing. City workers join in. As one person put it, "it was great just to show those people in the buildings, in their insular lives, that there is another world, that they can get off the conveyor belt".

Of course if you read the papers on the following days you would have read none of this or about the various other actions that were happening across Britain and forty other countries in protest against the effects of global capitalism. The Guardian's headline on Saturday was "The day the City turned into a battleground". I had actually moved on before the violence kicked off and so do not know what triggered it. Reports from people I spoke to later varied. City workers provoking people by waving their Gold American Express cards or fifty pound notes. The police over-reacting or unable to deal with the situation. The worst injuries certainly seem to have been experienced by protesters including one woman ran over by a police van (graphically filmed and shown on the news). The Observer said the violence "appeared to come from nowhere". While others claimed it was prearranged. Certainly it was the violence, which included the setting fire of a bank, trashing of a Mercedes car shop and storming of the LIFFE (futures) floor, which grabbed the headlines but, as the distributed spoof version of the Evening Standard called Evading Standards said, "a single nonrevolutionary weekend is infinitely more violent than a month of total revolution". Later people moved on to Trafalgar and Leicester Square and, surrounded by riot police, partied on into the evening partly in protest against the latest royal wedding.

The following Monday I got off my train and walked to work as normal. Except things did not seem normal. The City seemed different. On June 18th it became for the most of the day a place for people not profit. There was a glimpse of a possible future.

Prometheus Rex was more focused on the latter part of the day, picking up where Richard left off:

The action started at noon with a lively party of thousands of revellers in and around Liverpool Street station (the nearest thing to the expectations of the crowds that occurred all day). Following this carnival processions fanned out through the streets of London. It was then that things started to go badly. Police in dozens of vans (included some already kitted out in riot gear) began to slowly close in on the crowds. Many streets were blocked by advancing armoured police vans as the processions were herded in some unknown direction. At this point the threatening claustrophobic atmosphere caused the crowd to react and split at many points, to exercise a non-violent counter action. Their apparent aim to create space by advancing into the police barriers. Thus forcing them into retreat by sheer weight of numbers, slowly reversing back along London Wall the way they came. The sight of police being pushed out of the city encouraged a more enthusiastic response as vehicles were hit by water guns and a few soft cans and other objects. Others climbed onto vans that stupidly stopped, daubing some in graffiti. At one stage humiliated police piled out of vans and apparently tried to baton-charge the crowd causing brief panic, but seemed to think better of it. secured their vehicles and retreated further. Scenes like this were repeated at various locations while other demonstrators blocked traffic junctions.

Later we heard reports of various stunts throughout the City, including one in which phony bank notes were showered down on the crowd by 'construction workers'.

At this stage tensions were still relatively low and some City workers began to join in the fun.

What happened after this is not clear, but the crowd seemed dispersed throughout the City, confused and uncoordinated. The carnivalesque atmosphere began to die out due to the scarcity of any musicians and performers, and the complete absence of any sound systems (the latter being blocked by police perhaps). At previous RTS-type events the presence of these had always put the crowd into a positive mood, but now people were getting bored, and angrier with police tactics. Despite some enthusiastic attempts by the sparse few to get a carnival atmosphere going the main entertainment was increasingly found in drinking and playing cat-and-mouse games with the police, who now began to reassert themselves. Increased numbers of riot police began to move into the area at this stage as demonstrators roamed from place to place. The crowd got angrier and City workers began panicking and reacting against the crowd.

The key event seems to have occurred after a police van ran over a woman demonstrator, who had allegedly attempted to climb on the vehicle. According to witnesses the van accelerated, dislodged her, and ran over her legs. Speeding away the van did not bother to stop and it was left for demonstrators to call for an ambulance and clear a passage for it to get to the scene (with minimal police help).

This potentially lethal act may have been the last straw that triggered the most violent events of the day.

In localised small scale actions buildings were targeted and serious damage occurred. A branch of McDonald's was devastated and the Futures Exchange was attacked by an angry mob. In the latter case a water main was burst outside the building, creating a street fountain, and soon after masked activists smashed they way into the building and briefly occupied it. Later it appears the building partly caught fire.

Sporadic acts of violence (some of which were quite mindless) began to break out throughout the City as tempers flared.

Police allege the violence was organised and premeditated. Perhaps some individuals, with their own agenda, had planned small-scale direct actions, while many more seemed well equipped to defend themselves from the later police aggression, but most of the mass activity I saw seemed driven by anger against the police, with people taking out their aggression on whatever became a focal point of attack. In scenes perhaps unseen in the City since Wat Tyler came to town.

The riot squad then moved in to secure the attacked buildings (to hails of bottles) and increasingly violent skirmishes broke out at various locations between police units and demonstrators.

Ironically at the same time crowds began to party as small sound systems were set up and the carnival livened up at various locations. At one point mini riots were occurring at one end of streets while street parties were underway at the other.

Prometheus Rex followed up that report in the December 11th issue reporting on the N30 protests in London, timed to coincide with a meeting of the World Trade Organisation in Seattle. That gathering would mark a sea-changing moment for the anti-globalisation campaigning that had been building through the course of the decade, and the Battle of Seattle would gain legendary status for years to come as a moment when the activist movement shook the complacency of world leaders.

Already in London however the police force, which had been surprised and outmatched by the events of J18, had sharpened up with tactics that would be refined in the years to come into a highly-effective strategy of control.

The whole area had become a temporary police state. Roads and pavements were blocked, free movement curtailed and demonstrator and Joe Public alike stopped and turned back at road junctions. Interestingly this had the effect of raising much apparent support for the demonstrators and against the police. A few even began quietly encouraging the roving bands of protesters.

Passing through back streets we arrived at Kings Cross where some demonstrators were regrouping. While some senior officers seemed to be going out of their way to discipline and restrain their troops at times, there were still some outrageous acts of individual brutality — one of the worst in which an invalid left behind by departing demonstrators was battered with a police shield for "not getting off the street quick enough".

The reporting was relatively fulsome for *Freedom*, but also showcased the way it was being left behind by new technology. Livestreaming and blogging were by now at a stage where most of the march was covered in real time,* and even video was being brought out in short order — the premier of a 30-minute news documentary on the protests was shown by the Undercurrents video collective well before *Freedom*'s report hit the streets. This new media focus was to grow over the course of the next year into the *Indymedia UK* group, which along with *SchNEWS* as a printed outlet (and later website) would be the go-to sources for a new wave of summit confrontations in the 2000s.

---

* Activist livestreaming has since fallen out of favour in some quarters as it was being used by the State to identify activists to harrass, though is still used in some cases, primarily on social media.

Top to bottom, the London Anarchist Bookfair in 2008 and 2012, copies of *Freedom* with the 2003 Clifford Harper design and the Freedom Press Bookshop in mid-2018

2001-2018
Third Millennium

In beginning the new century, I shall mostly cease mentioning the great events which have gone on and *Freedom*'s coverage of them, as I have been directly involved through much of this period and I'm not quite self-indulgent enough to start referencing and analysing myself. So I'll stick with telling the story of Angel Alley and let the future pass judgment on whatever scribblings my contemporaries and I might have produced.

A brief overview of the 2000s as a whole however would show an astonishing breadth of activity which went on, from the establishment of the No Borders Network in 2000 beginning decades of support through similar groups against Fortresses Europe and Britain, the WOMBLES, the shortlived Anarchist Youth Network and multiple new media groups, particularly *Indymedia UK* and *libcom*.org, though this was paralleled by a wave of radical bookshop closures.

Class War temporarily collapsed, replaced by the Whitechapel Anarchist Group, while summit hopping and confrontations with the likes of G8, G20 and the WTO went global, matched by the brief but vibrant series of World and European Social Forums set up in direct counterpoint.

From 2006 to 2010 the survivors of the green fluffies, looking for a way forward in a difficult environment, ran the Camps for Climate Action, while groups tired of seeing friends sent to jail turned into the Legal Defence and Monitoring Group and Green and Black Cross. The student fees protests in 2010, riots in 2011, the anti-squat laws in 2012 and the biggest-ever London bookfair in 2015, along with its collapse in 2017, as well as the horrifying revelations of the spycop investigations exposed by activists, would all rank high on the list of events and social campaigns where anarchists have been active and influential.

Much of this activity has died away since the centre of political gravity on the left shifted back towards a social democratic approach, but the movement still has a surprising level of infrastructure, which in many ways has actually strengthened over the last few years with more venues opening, expanding archives and libraries being available, and a seeming pragmatic approach making some progress under the surface froth of everyday political argument. I remain an optimist.

Abhor the vacuum

The death of Vernon Richards left Freedom Press in fairly dire straits. Speaking in a 2016 interview, Donald Rooum recalled:

> Vero Richards was magnificent, but when he retired he left a mess. After Vero's death we carried on and I was not too happy with the attitude of the comrades who were running the thing, because Vero had quarreled with Albert Meltzer who had managed to get most of the London anarchists on his side and opposed to Freedom Press. Vero had counteracted that in 1996 with an article about Meltzer's death titled 'Instead of an Obituary' which was very rude, and I wrote an article about Albert's funeral which was rejected on the grounds it presented him as having too many followers.
>
> I would have liked to make overtures to the rest of the movement after [Vero passed] but Charlie especially was very much anti the rest of the movement, which I thought was inappropriate. So we were just plodding along ...

Later that year a major upheaval occurred following the entry of a new volunteer, Toby Crowe. A large, energetic young man who had recently jumped ship from the Socialist Party of Great Britain, Crowe "just walked in with no invitation at all" to a group consisting of two paid members, Charlie as editor and Kevin as bookshop manager, barely enough volunteers to function and a rapidly draining bank account. Readership was pegged at around 600 at this point, though with many being free subscriptions to prisoners and old friends of the paper. Working almost full time he immediately set about making major changes leading to the resignation of first Kevin, then Charlie. Hailing from a class-struggle oriented background as a former activist with the SPGB, Crowe intended to invite in the movement's anarchist-communist and anarcho-syndicalist currents, upsetting supporters who well remembered the bitter arguments of the past. He and Jayne also commissioned and implemented, towards the end of his tenure, a redesign of the paper by Clifford Harper in 2003, producing the masthead which is still in use today.

There was a certain amount of grumbling but Rooum, the length of whose association with Freedom had by now surpassed even Lilian Wolfe's, running from the late 1940s through to 2017, backed Crowe's view that the Press, which had accrued a reputation for sectarianism, needed to reach out beyond its established base and embrace co-operation with other anarchist groups. Once Toby was installed Donald took a step back from work at the Press recalling:

> I retired (apart from Wildcat and some writing) in April 2003. I had taken over running the shop on Saturdays from Arthur Moyse, whose idea of running the shop was to close it, leaving a note on the door telling customers "We're in the White Hart. Join us". I was also keeping the subscriptions and other correspondence up to date, which I could fit in easily, supposing Saturday to be a slow day in the shop (I was wrong. It was the biggest selling day of the week). I finished doing the subs on April 20th 2003 (my 75th birthday) and went into the shop to find a lot of balloons, and comrades who took me off to the Aladdin restaurant in Brick Lane for a party. Unexpectedly called on to make a speech, I recited Bonar Thompson's joke peroration: "Consider the struggles of our forefathers and our five-fathers, our stepfathers and our stairfathers, our grandfathers and our shabby-fathers ... I declare this stone well and truly laid, and pronounce you man and superman".

With Donald gone, Toby was the main organiser left in the building. His tenure didn't last much longer however, and he subsequently left to become a Church of England priest, shortly after I arrived for my first shifts at the paper.

A reluctant new editor

When I walked through the door in late 2003 Freedom's long-term decline was already very obvious. Aldgate Press having cleared out to a Gunthorpe Street workshops unit across the yard, the ground floor room had instead been filled with unsold stock from the 1990s and was stacked almost to the ceiling with boxes, so high in fact that it was difficult to see what they all were even when the lights were on. I vividly remember spending hours upon hours shuffling around boxes to create some sort of order to the madness of years of "put-it-wherever". To get to the back wall you had to climb over piles of unsold *Ravens,* past colourful stacks of *Wildcat* and books with anarchist takes on social struggles which were years or decades out of date. At the right-hand corner of the room was a doorway leading into a lean-to, which was totally full of rubbish — this had previously been a dark room for developing photos, but now stank of damp and mouse excrement.

The walk to the first floor was revolting, up stairs covered in a carpet which could not have been cleaned in years, and stuck to the feet (I pulled this up early on). On the first floor there was an ill-defined "Hacklab" comprising one rickety computer terminal, and in the other room the shop, where the lino was black in the corners from lack of washing, worn down to the wood near the desk and dust-covered windows let just a little light into a dingy space stuffed with books, which deadened the sounds of life outside to a distant wheeze. Further up the stairs, a half-finished paint-stripping project had left raw wood paneling and banisters splotched with a patina of bright red and dysentery yellow paint from the previous decorations.

As now, the floorboards were grey from dust, unloved and uncared for.

The second floor, where an editorial office and the (usually empty) Autonomy Club were set, was a little better with the latter having been recently done up by volunteers, while on the top floor was a small, locked office where A Distribution kept their stock and an attic space, in which thousands upon thousands of copies of the paper sat, unsold and undistributed. The place was a wreck.

I don't describe this to give an impression of ineptitude. If I were to sum up the situation then as I saw it, the word would probably be exhausted. With the exception of Jayne as sub-editor/administrator and the bookshop worker, whose roles were self defined and limited, no-one was considering it a main job, and as such no-one was taking responsibility. This was a feature throughout the first few years of my time at the Press.

I had, similarly to Dave Peers decades before, heard about *Freedom* as being The Anarchist Newspaper and a place to start when learning the ropes, so had offered my services as a newly-qualified journalist and been invited to come along to an editorial production Sunday at the office.

It turned out this was one of the last production Sundays before Toby Crowe moved on. I was introduced to him, the sub-editor Jayne, two young Londoners, John and Jim, who had gotten involved a little earlier off the back of their experiences with the Anarchist Youth Network (AYN), and their American housemate. Beyond them, there was the young man in the bookshop, who was significantly more keen on getting the hacklab going than selling books, Scott who looked after mailing books out to our distributors, and not much else.

From around December to February the four editors, all in our early twenties and I think I can say without offence, almost entirely clueless, put out the fortnightly with Jayne doing the design and keeping an eye on mailout. The entire situation was ludicrous, and only got more so when John and his US friend quit, the former to become more involved in news, forum and archive project enrager. net (now libcom.org). By the end of 2004 all the other editors were gone from what they saw as a bad job, leaving me in charge of filling the paper every fortnight. I was 23, had read *Anarchy in Action* and a bit of Kropotkin, and at that point knew precisely sod-all.*

It was probably Andy Meinke, later to run the bookshop, who summed up the situation best as far as the anarchists were concerned — after Vero's death Freedom Press was there on a plate for anyone who might want it, and the movement didn't notice (or if they did, thought better of taking on the stress). So instead I found myself committing to filling an eight-page A3 fortnightly as sole editor of the oldest anarchist newspaper in the English language, given no-one else seemed to want the job — and then had to spend much of the following 15 years trying to get other people to do it instead. What an idiot. The arrogance of youth I suppose.

At the time I thought I was lucky to have gotten at least some handover via the last few weeks of Toby's tenure and the three-ish months working with the AYN kids, but in retrospect the 2000s Freedom crash was likely one of the worst. With the death of Vero an awful lot of background information, financial support and contacts had passed, while Toby had given virtually no clues as to how he was running things when he did his disappearing act. Most of the old readership had either stopped engaging or in many cases had died, and virtually all of the Charlie Crute-era contacts were alienated either by Toby or by our youthful foolery with badly photoshopped front pages of Rupert Murdoch with the body of a flea, Saddam Hussein in a Santa outfit.

I was mostly running *Freedom* as a side project, largely because I had a romantic notion that the anarchist movement should have at least one regular paper, while living and working 80 miles or so away in Suffolk. My actual interests lay more in trying to organise a local group and working on an activist news project for the East Anglian Social Forum (a wannabe offshoot of the European Social Forums, now long defunct). In the day I would work as a sub-

---

* Days before I first started at the Press I was handing out SolFed leaflets I'd been given at a punk event in the Steamboat pub, Ipswich, when a guy commented 'ah you're a syndicalist then?' I had to shamefacedly admit I had no idea what they were talking about.

editor for a local newspaper and write articles or attend a meeting in the evening, then every other Sunday I would take the train to London and work in the building, which included turfing out boxes upon boxes of old unsold papers from previous months and doing little bits of bodged DIY here and there. Because of my schedule I was only able to work one week in two, so this dissertation-length monstrosity had a seven day turnaround.

All of which sounds very active, but was entirely foolish and the main lesson I've taken from that experience is try and do one thing well, rather than a dozen things badly. Freedom has always been a place of enormous potential with a building in the heart of London, free newspaper printing from Aldgate Press and a great deal of international goodwill for English anarchism's grand old lady. With more people specifically dedicated to the place a great deal could likely have been achieved.

Physical distance was also making life difficult in further recruitment, as a London-based paper really needs a London-based staff. People could come in and ask about helping, and it might be another month before I would be down in London to talk to them. Thus the only regular correspondents the paper picked up were by necessity well-acquainted with the internet, again excluding older readers.

As a result to start with we had very few writers, and of these a couple dropped off when John left. Among the best stalwarts were Iain Mackay, Mark Barnsley, Svartfrosk, Louis Further and Richard Griffin, while my brother took on international news.

Toby was, although I didn't know it at the time, a fanatically organised person. He had an entire file full of correspondence, he replied to everything. His system was highly individual, and months later I was still finding files of things which would have been useful — but which I had no idea even existed until far too late. Correspondence went missing, unanswered, features were lost, former disagreements and feuds went unnoticed, only to resurface months down the line as the group struggled to cope with his departure.

In terms of other parts of the Press, I wasn't heavily involved. Scott ran the book mailout service, 'S' mostly ran the shop, alongside a few other volunteers who I didn't meet as I wasn't in that often. Other than Jayne, who made sure administration was done and the paper was laid out, and a small daily stipend for shop workers, no-one got paid.

Operating purely on volunteer labour the bookshop's take was low (on the order of £13,000 per annum), while the paper was continually losing money.

The building was kept open during this period largely through a series of bequests in the wills of former supporters, but there was little energy in the collective and amid a mid-2000s decline in the movement, rising business rates, ongoing wage costs not matched by income and a series of large-scale print runs which failed to sell, this money slowly drained. In 2006 the Press was in an enormous mess, losing £14,000 in a year as it vastly overprinted books which it then didn't sell, spent far more than it could afford in the long term on the paper, and ran a bookshop which, if it made any money, got nowhere near paying the rates.

Largely ignorant of this broader malaise, I managed about two years as editor with regular missives near-enough begging for new people to come in, before bowing to the inevitable reality that I couldn't manage the job alongside everything else in life. In October 2006 I wrote an article, 'I'm on Strike', with my only demand being that someone take the paper off my hands for one issue in every two. Amazingly there was a serious reply, and from November 2006 I shared the task with Matt B, making it essentially a monthly job and much more manageable.* This situation lasted reasonably stably for me until my employer went through yet another round of layoffs and as a union father of the chapel, my suggestion of threatening strike action did not go down well. Both Matt and I would drop out from editorial duties at this point.

We were replaced first by first Dean Talent from 2009-2012, whose workrate was excellent and oversaw the sensible decision to take the paper monthly, Matt Black (2012-13) and finally the paper's last regular print editor, Charlotte Dingle (2013-14).

At the bookshop meanwhile there was a major transformation when in 2007 first Mo Mosely and then Andy Meinke, both experienced book sellers, took over the co-ordinator role.

Mo and Andy's arrival made a great deal of difference to the building, alongside the decision to allow other groups to start using office space and paying in towards the rates. The Advisory Service for Squatters moved into the old archive space while the London Coalition Against Poverty took over the first floor office in 2008. Corporate Watch moved in on the second floor, the Autonomy Club

---

* Being more than slightly a sucker, I promptly made life more difficult again by agreeing in 2007 to help produce a bi-annual issue of *Black Flag* with Iain McKay and Ade Dimmick as the existing collective had collapsed. This de facto buried the hatchet, as I could hardly have much of a feud with myself and my fellow editors were fine people. We lasted until 2015 putting *Flag* out as an in-depth journal.

was cleared up, and the collective grew to consist of around nine people. Most impressively, the downstairs store room was cleared out, with some of the giant piles of unsellable old Ravens being junked, and the space was instead filled by the bookshop, finally placed somewhere more accessible after 40 years of being hidden away upstairs.

Andy's ambitious plan was to take what was a whopping £15,000 annual loss by this point with outgoings of £54,000 in running costs including £13,000 for the paper, £31,000 for shop, distro and rates, £10,000 publishing, and try to break even by 2011.

That never happened as distribution didn't sustain at the higher levels of the 2000s, meaning the large print-run books that were put out mostly sat in storage while money ran down. Shop income didn't bump quite high enough to make up the difference, and the paper continued to drain cash with sales failing to pick up in the absence of a solid distribution or sales network. Difficult rows in 2012 saw Dean Talent leave, followed by other burnt out volunteers, and a £4,000 bill was levied by a photographer for pictures used in Freedom Press title *Beating the Fascists,* plunging the collective back into trouble.

In 2013 the money ran dry and ironically, it would be the third major attempt to burn the Freedom building down that got the Press out of this latest jam.

Fire and the future

On Friday February 1st 2013, at about 5am in the morning, an arsonist took advantage of lax security at Freedom Press, which meant that the metal shutters hadn't been pulled down, to smash through a ground floor window, pour lighter fluid into the gap and set fire to it.

Thanks to the quick reactions of a neighbour and a speedy showing by the fire brigade working out of Whitechapel Fire Station, Freedom was spared the worst of the possible damage. The shop's walls and ceiling were charred and blackened, electrics were seriously damaged, hundreds of books ruined and worst of all, the beautifully bound archives of *Freedom* stretching back all the way to the beginning were charred and burned, though thankfully not destroyed.

This timing was almost disastrous as just the week before the fire insurance had run out, leaving the near-bankrupt Press with cleanup bills potentially running into five figures, but what

happened next was remarkable. After a *Twitter* callout and a post on *libcom.org*, at first friendly journalists started appearing to ask about the situation and then major media, asking what had occured. Stories appeared about the situation everywhere from the *Morning Star* and *Vice Magazine* to the BBC, with the general view being that once again fascists had attacked the building — though nothing ever came of the police investigation.

With the story going out worldwide Freedom received an outpouring of support. Well over a hundred people turned out at short notice for a clean-up day, leaving us entirely unsure what to do with them all (the shop doesn't really have room for that many people at once) but in double-quick time scrubbing down the walls, repainting, sorting salvageable books and clearing the shop space of rubbish. Thousands of pounds poured into the bank account, more in fact than we needed to fix the place back up, and at one point we started turning money down from anti-fascist groups in countries blighted by far more violence than London can usually manage.

While the more complicated works were underway Freedom was even able to keep a (reduced) bookshop going out of the second floor common room while the electrics were being sorted, nicknamed the rainbow shop because a volunteer had arranged all the stock by colour.

But while donors' money would keep the place going, panic over Freedom's financial direction remained, and a year later the decision was made to cease regular publication of the paper, also temporarily stopping publishing until money became available. The notice to readers from Andy Meinke was as follows:

> In the Anarchist Bookfair 2009 edition of *Freedom*, the then-editors set out a strategy for the future of the paper. The core of this was having *Freedom* as a non-sectarian organ distributed by all the national federations and by independent local and campaigning groups. In parallel, *Black Flag* was put forward as a pan-movement theoretical magazine — the hope being that selling these at stalls and demos could be combined with local freesheets. To sum up, the editorial said: "For *Freedom* to achieve its aims, the Anarchist Movement needs to distribute and sell the paper outside its own scene."
>
> With all praise to the few individuals who carried on selling the paper to the very end, this proved impossible. Leaving aside the practical problems of a newspaper that was never new (a consequence of the printing/folding process more than shortage of good contributors) very few people wanted to distribute it. Anecdotally those comrades who subscribed were doing it largely because they felt they were "supporting" the paper — which was losing money at a rate of around £7,000 a year. Moving to a monthly in 2010 cut this to around £3,000 but this was a retrograde step to stave off the inevitable. Towards the end of 2012 it was clear that the paper couldn't continue bar a miracle and we paid redundancy to our layout/admin person before we ran out of money. Then we got firebombed! The Fash to the rescue! We were inundated by donations and offers of help and though it was a great strain we kept the paper coming out because it would come over as an obvious defeat if the far right could claim they had shut it down. However there was one thing that people wouldn't help with after the fire: selling the paper. What's more people on the Freedom Collective didn't want to sell the paper. Meantime *Freedom* was forced to publicly advertise for an editor having been unable to find anyone through inquiries in the movement. Although many people applied, only one turned out to be an anarchist! Short

of becoming a radical media magazine and apply for arts council funding we decided to wrap up the print version and go online.

When the Freedom Collective decided to stop the print version of the paper many of us thought it would cause a shitstorm in our already troubled movement. We were considering a big meeting at the Bookfair to explain why we had give up on the last regular for sale anarchist newspaper in Britain and foregone £10,000 a year's worth of free printing, courtesy of Aldgate Press.

However, the silence was deafening. Roughly 30 out of 225 paid up subscribers replied and one person came to a monthly Freedom Collective meeting to find out why. The movement had voted with its feet, and it was not by shuffling them along to the nearest demo to sell a paper.

The following few years have been hectic, with a building survey undertaken by the Friends causing a hullabaloo when it turned up a £40,000 estimate for fixing up 84b to a reasonable standard, the relaunch of *freedomnews.org.uk* as a daily anarchist newswire, the re-establishment of the journal as a free bi-annual and last year, the launch of the Freedom Newspaper Archive, which now contains more than 1,300 digitised papers. Andy has left, replaced by new co-ordinators and volunteers, and in 2018 we've seen the first tranche of repairs completed after a successful fundraising drive for initial works, alongside our most ambitious year of publishing for some time.

Given the anarchist movement's position at the tail end of the 2010s, squeezed between the shifting promises of Corbynism and the overwhelming damage of austerity, Freedom's relative health today is cause for a cautious celebration. London is a beautiful but rancid place, and Angel Alley sits just metres away from bloated glass and steel pustules which have risen high into the air, evidence of the financial disease poisoning the city, pushing working people ever further away. The centre is a hostile environment for anyone without money to burn. Yet we survive, and small pools of libertarian socialism continue to exist across the capital in the face of this aggressive destroyer. We quietly dream, and plan for the next wave.

This tiny little argumentative press, with a historic readership frequently bested by small town dailies even at its height but a story and philosophy so colourful it can fill tomes, has survived 132 years of revolution, war, repression, recession, failure, violence and fire. For all its many faults and foolish notions, it has represented a voice and a vision that will always terrify those who control our lives, where the circumstances of your birth truly *don't* matter, and the chains which bind us all into relentless, self-destructive competition over the crumbs from great endeavours have fallen to dust.

Freedom began its journey with a statement of intent, and it seems fitting to finish with another, slightly updated, from issue one, October 1886:

> The spirit of revolt has been the saving grace of humanity. The whole story of our species is full of the resistance of the mass of people to the anti-social spirit of domination of certain individuals — the strongest, subtlest and least scrupulous. Without such resistance to the authority usurped by one over another, human society must have withered away, and human beings become as unsocial as hawks and tigers
>
> ...
>
> From a consideration of the wrongs and the courage, the failures and the triumph of our brethren throughout the world we may each and all, derive inspiration, warning and encouragement, and learn to feel that each petty action, each effort apparently isolated and fruitess, is in reality part of the universal war against oppression in all its forms, in which, consciously or unconsciously, we must all take our share, and fight for human freedom or against it.

Fire damaged *Freedom*, 2013

PEOPLE

The biographies in this section expand upon a selection originally published in centenary book *Freedom / A Hundred Years*, primarily written by Heiner Becker and Nicolas Walter. Additional articles are taken from Nick Heath's libcom.org biographies series, obituaries published in the paper, or are bespoke. Given the sheer number of people who have passed through Freedom Press this list is not comprehensive and relatively famed contributors, or those with existing memoirs and biographies in circulation, are mostly eschewed here in favour of lesser-known names. I considered writing one specifically for Vernon Richards, but much of what I would have said is contained within the main body of the book, and a biography has recently been written by David Goodway as part of a foreword for the forthcoming PM edition of *Lessons of the Spanish Revolution.*

Marie Louise Berneri (1918-1949)

Berneri was a leading member of the Freedom Group during the Spanish Civil War, the Second World War, and until her early death. British anarchism in the 1930s was far from being an active or even lively movement, despite the appearance of the *Freedom Bulletin, Journal* and the later incarnation of the paper. This changed only in the second half of the decade after, as Albert Meltzer once quite rightly pointed out, "Vernon Richards ... started *Spain and the World* on his own, and with only very meagre support in the following years, made it the focal point for the revival of Freedom Press and the propagandist activity well known to ... readers of *Freedom*". Of that meagre support the most important contribution came from Marie Louise Berneri.

Maria Luisa Berneri was born on March 1st 1918 in Arezzo near Florence, the elder daughter of Camillo and Giovanna Berneri. Her father, originally a socialist, became an anarchist in the early 1920s, and was soon one of the best-known (and at times most controversial) intellectuals in the Italian anarchist movement. He was a teacher who after Mussolini's seizure of power in 1922 refused to accept the demands laid upon the teaching profession by the fascists, and in 1926 he went into exile in France. In Paris his — and his family's — home soon became a centre of anti-fascist activities, and his two daughters grew up in a highly politicised environment.

Adopting the French version of her name, Marie Louise obtained her baccalaureat and in the mid-1930s started to study psychology at the Sorbonne. She soon became involved in the anarchist movement and participated in the production of the short-lived paper *Revision* (with Luis Mercier Vega, alias S Parane, alias Ridel). At the outbreak of the Spanish Civil War her father went to Spain and, after a short period of active fighting on the Aragon front, eventually took up residence in Barcelona in order to edit the Italian- language paper *Guerra di Classe*, perhaps the most clear-sighted revolutionary anarchist paper to come out of the Spanish Revolution.

Marie Louise went twice to Barcelona, the second time after her father's assassination by Communists in May 1937; subsequently she came to England, where she joined her companion Vernon Richards and spent the rest of her life. (They married to give her the protection of British nationality). Her sister Giliane remained in France where she studied psychology and in the years after the War also became active in the anarchist movement. Their mother Giovanna, who during the 1920s and 1930s had become more and more involved in anti-fascist activities and eventually the anarchist movement, was during the War arrested in France, interned for a while in the South of France, and then eventually handed over to the Italian authorities; she was imprisoned in Italy till the end of the War, and then after the liberation became one of the most prominent and active anarchists in Italy.

From 1936 until her death 12 years later, every activity undertaken by Freedom Press was infused by Marie Louise Berneri's personality. Already in Paris she had been closely involved (with her father and Tom Keell) in the preparatory discussions and collecting of funds for *Spain and the World*, which Vernon Richards started in December 1936. After coming to England in 1937 she took an active part in the production of the paper; and between February and June 1939 she took part in the attempt to provide some formal link for the anarchist movement by the production of *Revolt!*, the successor of *Spain and the World* (with Vernon Richards, Albert Meltzer, Tom Brown, Mr and Mrs Leach, and Sturgess).

She also was one of the small group which started *War Commentary* in November 1939. Already knowing Italian, French and Spanish, she quickly mastered English and became one of the main editorial writers, specialising in international affairs. She was an effective public speaker, paper-seller, and meeting organiser. But above all she was the emotional and intellectual centre of the group.

At the end of the Spanish Civil War she was active in organising relief for Spanish orphans and refugees. Her wide contacts in and knowledge of the international movement gave her great authority among anarchists, but her libertarian principles and personal modesty prevented her from misusing it.

In April 1945 she was one of the four editors of *War Commentary* who were tried for incitement to disaffection, but she was acquitted on a legal technicality (a wife cannot conspire with her husband), and when her three comrades were imprisoned she took the main responsibility for continuing the paper into the postwar period. She maintained her interest in psychology, and she was one of the first people in Britain who discussed the work of Wilhelm Reich, in an article 'Sexuality and Freedom' in George Woodcock's *Now 5* (August 1945).

At the end of 1948 she gave birth to a stillborn child, and on April 13th 1949 she herself unexpectedly died from a virus infection. She was a highly intelligent and deeply committed revolutionary anarchist; and a widely loved personality. Her sudden death at the age of only 31 was a tragedy not only for her friends and comrades but for the whole anarchist movement.

Apart from her many contributions to the Freedom Press periodicals, she added an interesting postscript to *Vote — What For?* (1942), a new version of Malatesta's anti-election pamphlet of 1890, and she wrote a substantial part of the Freedom pamphlet *The Russian Myth* (1941), partly reproduced in her *Workers in Stalin's Russia* (1944), a detailed and influential booklet describing the real situation in the Soviet Union.

After her death the Marie Louise Berneri Memorial Committee produced *Neither East Nor West* (1952), an anthology of her editorial articles from 1939 to 1948. Another posthumous publication was *Journey Through Utopia* (1950), a survey of utopian ideas which was originally published by Routledge and is still available from the Freedom Press (and which, with Vernon Richards' *Lessons of the Spanish Revolution*, was the most widely translated publication of Freedom Press after the war).

Much valuable material about her appeared in *Freedom* and other anarchist periodicals after her death, and the Marie Louise Berneri Memorial Committee produced *Marie Louise Berneri, 1918-1949: A Tribute* (1949).

An article about her by Philip Sansom was published (in a mutilated form) in *Zero 1* (June 1977), and a recollection by George Woodcock in *Open Road 6* (Spring 1978).

~ Nicolas Walter & Heiner Becker

Tom Brown (1900-1974)

Born close to Tyneside's shipyards, Brown grew up in earshot of the noise and ceaseless activity of the gunsmiths and armour platers that built the first British naval ships of the 20th century. He came from a rebel family (his grandfather had met Garibaldi during the nine hours strike of 1871) and started early as a union man — he participated in the 1911 school children's strike, downing his exercise book in September for the kids' demands of a weekly half-holiday, Friday payments of a half-penny and the abolition of caning.

As he entered his teens he joined the crews, signing up for an engineering apprenticeship as the First World War ground onwards, and began working on war munitions as a teenager. Reminiscing in *Direct Action* in 1969, he wrote:

"My first inside view of the factory was of rows of 60-pounder and 18—pounder field guns, anti-aircraft and mountain guns, tanks and anti-sub artillery, then lines of machines turning gun barrels or milling breech blocks ...

"There was one foreman who claimed he remembered the days when his like were allowed to strike apprentices. One day he found six of his boys warming themselves in the smithy. Taking a hazel rod from a pickle tank, the proverbial 'rod in pickle'. he crept "up behind the boys and lashed out at them. Although taken by surprise, they quickly recovered and four of them held him down while two lashed him with the hazels, to the sound of his yells and the laughter of the smiths.

"I soon realised that the new life I had entered was a kind of social war, the scene suitably furnished by the ever-present artillery. On the one side were the overseers, the lowest agents of the invisible but powerful enemy, the informers, the anti-unionists, the few who hankered after being scabs and who whispered, 'Don't trust unions and suchlike, keep your nose clean and you'll get on', and the management. Facing them, bold and contemptuous, were our people. l was learning sociology without books".

Brown was swiftly drawn into the union ideal, drinking in the history that, "almost within living memory" had seen men and women die on the scaffold to defend their union and as the war drew to a close, he came upon "two new terms, syndicalism and revolutionary industrial unionism," which he saw spread rapidly throughout Tyneside and the Mersey.

In his factory, hitherto a morass of interconnected and competing union groups, factory committees of syndicalist form were created and, according to Brown, briefly exercised the sort of influence that worries governments before falling back.

He would not initially become an anarchist from these experiences however, fired as many young people were with enthusiasm for the Russian Revolution. Initially joining the Socialist Labour Party, he moved over to become an early member of the Communist Party and, for a time, became its industrial organiser for the North-East.

The source of his increasing radicalism was a very direct and simple one — he saw the top-down unions capitulate to the State during the war, and saw them to be "as much a part of the war machine as were the Brigade of Guards or the Royal Navy. With a stroke of the pen, all the rights won by a century of hard fighting were signed away".

But the double-dealing of the Communists and reports of repression in the USSR brought disillusion and he left the party.

Brown moved to work in Coventry and then in 1926, when the General Strike ended, he lost his job and tried to move north, but was slowed by ongoing chaos with the railways and settled in the mining town of Birtley, built originally as a temporary haven for Belgian refugees in 1914. There he took part in the brutal miners' struggle against the national lock-out of May 21st 1926, a period covered in an article he wrote for *Direct Action* in July 1963.

"There were village fiestas, without the feasting. A procession led by at least one excellent brass band, a meeting, a sports day with athletic events for children and adults (first prize, a bar of chocolate) and, in the evening, an open-air dance or a concert. There were ladies' football matches and comic football matches between teams of boisterous clowns and comic boxing shows – at times everything comic. But frequent meetings were important too, for they served the part of a Press."

Brown moved again to work in the West Midlands motor industry during the Depression, where he likely was attracted to anarchist ideas, beginning a lifetime of libertarian activism as he became involved in the movement while spending his life as a militant stop steward on the factory floor.

He also got involved in physical anti-fascism, including confrontations in Gateshead in May 1934. He recalled the first appearance of the British Union of Fascists there in a 1964 interview with *World Labour News*:

"I was near the labour exchange on Windmill Hills. A few small groups of men were chatting or waiting for their time to sign on and a few, less than a dozen, were listening to an ILP speaker. Suddenly the sound of men's voices singing the Italian fascist song were heard. Then a party of Mosley's fascists wearing black shirts rounded the corner; giving the Mussolini salute and chanting M-O-S-L-E-Y, M-O-S-L-E-Y. In quick march with threatening voices they strode to the ILP platform.

"Then came a rash of men as the groups and the dole queue broke up to run and defend the platform. In a few minutes the fascists were scattered. The fallen ones were begging for mercy until they were rescued by some active members of Gateshead Labour Party.

"After a few weeks a small party of Blackshirts came in peace and were not molested. But some workers realised that a much stronger fascist party would not be so peaceful and a band of them formed the Anti Fascist League in Newcastle and Tyneside. Good open air and indoor meetings were held and new members recruited. Marches showed that the older men remembered their military life in World War I.

"The ancient hall of the Smiths Guild in Newcastle was hired and the people who lived nearby kept an eye on the premises at night. Many of these good people were street sellers and offered their barrows and carts to form quick barricades to keep the fascists in if they attacked. Some of them, such as the newspaper sellers who worked in and around the Central Station, were able to keep us informed of fascist visitors to the area.

"Our meetings, especially in the Newcastle Big Market and on the Town Moor, were well attended and applauded. The Newcastle police were courteous to us, even though our support was almost exclusively working class with 50 per cent of that out of work.

"The Labour Party said "Don't do anything about it, just leave them to the police to deal with". The Communist Party said "Just ridicule them — shout Mickey Mouse at them." This deadly weapon had been suggested by the national leadership of the CP: it referred to the fascist rank-and-file uniform of black shirt and light gray flannel trousers. Only two prominent members of the Labour Party supported us — they were both full time officials of the Transport and General Workers Union.

"Our members singly, or in pairs, interviewed fascist recruits and in most cases persuaded them to pack it in. The trade union movement, the Labour Party and the middle-class liberals returned to their slumbers. Only when Mosley put up New Party candidates against the Labour Party were trade unionists, for a short time, roused to anger. To oppose fascism was never popular in such circles."

In the early to mid 1930s he drifted south to work on aircraft in London with his wife Lily and their daughters, Ruth and Grace, continuing to be active against the blackshirts, particularly in Soho where Italian fascism was in control. There he became involved with the Anarcho Syndicalist Union, where he gained a reputation as a strong and lucid speaker and would remain until the organisation collapsed in 1944.

He also became a member of the grouping around *Spain and the World* in the mid-1930s, speaking at meetings supporting their struggle, several times sharing the platform with Emma Goldman.

Brown, with his fellow ASU member Ralph Sturgess, got involved with what would become the core of the new Freedom Group in 1939 after the end of the Spanish Civil War, working on *Revolt!* with Vernon Richards and Marie Louise Berneri, where his first writings appear. He would continue the collaboration as *Revolt!* Became *War Commentary*, also joining the Anarchist Federation of Britain when it was set up in 1944.

During the war he produced his first two pamphlets, *Trade Unionism or Syndicalism* and *The British General Strike*, both of which had wide sales.

The promising situation would fall apart in 1945 however, as a rift developed between the vision of the syndicalists for the future of *Freedom* and the other editors. That year saw Vernon Richards cement his position as editor of the paper, while Brown was forced out and the AFB stripped of its influence. Embittered, he warned that the intellectuals would abandon their anarchism when they had made their name as writers.

The AFB fell apart as a result, and from its ashes, he would go on to be a founder member of a new AFB. He also established a new paper, *Direct Action*, in 1945 which would last, on and off, into the early 2000s. Saddened by the failure of an attempt to form an International of Anarchist Federations in the late

1940s, he supported the AFB's decision to change its name to Syndicalist Workers' Federation (SWF) in 1950 and affiliate to the International Working Men's Association (now the International Workers Association). This group eventually became the Direct Action Movement, and is now the Solidarity Federation.

The SWF maintained friendly contacts with the IWW in the States and Tom visited them

when he and Lily crossed the Atlantic to see their daughters, who had both married GIs in London and later emigrated. He also went to see the veteran anarcho-syndicalist Rudolf Rocker in a libertarian colony near New York.

Tom and Lily returned to London after a year where he resumed his SWF activity and Brown would remain a driving force of the group into the 1960s, involving himself in two important dockworkers' strikes. Recalling the time, former comrade Dave Coull notes:

> I remember Tom Brown from attending Syndicalist Workers Federation meetings in London, which if I remember right (my memory is hazy, for reasons which will become obvious) were held in The Prospect of Whitby pub near Kings Cross. One of the things about meeting in a pub was, I usually had a pint, or sometimes half-a-dozen. Tom was already regarded as something of an elder of the SWF back then, but as well as holding "meetings", the SWF did sometimes also hold "socials" (at which it was okay to sing and you were expected to have a drink or a few) and I was surprised when Tom did his party piece, singing quite a bawdy song.

Brown was also active in community struggles and this latter activism was, tragically, to nearly kill him. He served as spokesperson for a residents' protest group in London that opposed the opening of mob-run brothels in their area. On his way home from working a nightshift he was beaten with iron clubs so badly that it left him unable to work.

He and Lily, who was then in poor health, returned to Tyneside in the late 1960s and his continued activity there included several lively contributions, on libertarian subjects, on local radio. He was also a member of the North East Labour History Society up to his death.

Belatedly, another tragic event struck when, retired and almost disabled, he wrote his memoirs by hand. A university student offered to type them up if she could use parts for her thesis but Tom died before she completed the job and, when the time came to hand them back, Lily reputedly told her to keep them. Both the memoirs and the thesis are currently missing..

~ *Rob Ray*
Hat tip to Mo Mosely for his piece in Tom Brown's Syndicalism

Tom Cantwell (1864-1906)

Tom Cantwell was born on the Pentonville Road in London on December 14th 1864, the son of a map-mounter's clerk. He worked first as a basket-maker and then as a compositor. It was while he was working as a basket-maker that he probably joined the Socialist League in 1886. It was there that he learned the basics of the compositor's trade. He signed a notice of the North London branch and served on the committee to organise the Whit Monday outing. At this time he was living in Holloway. In February 1887 he served on the committee to prepare for the commemoration of the Paris Commune. He became a lecture secretary, served on the SL executive, and worked hard as a lecturer and propagandist. He had become an anarchist by at least 1887 which is indicated by a lecture he gave entitled "No Master". That year he spoke with John Turner, Sam Mainwaring and H.B. Samuels at an anti-Jubilee meeting in Hyde Park. He played the part of the foreman of the jury in William Morris's play The Tables Turned put on in the SL hall in 1887. He lectured at the Berner Street Club in the East End in 1888 on sweated basket-makers and was particularly critical of the Parcel Post department's behaviour in its contracts for basket-making.

On the evening of May 1st 1891 he was a speaker on the Mile End Waste alongside David Nicoll, Yanovsky, Charles Mowbray and Arnold. The large crowds were mainly made up of dockers and other riverside workers. In attendance was a large force of police, both foot and mounted.

With the repression brought down on the movement by the Walsall affair in 1892 the Commonweal offices were raided. According to David Nicoll the Special Branch officers were told by Cantwell in jest that "We have been expecting you for some time, and do you think we should be fools as to keep anything here likely to get men into trouble". This was contradicted by W C Hart in his highly sensational book *Confessions of An Anarchist* who says that a book — *The Emancipator* — which was an explosives manual being prepared by the provocateur Coulon had its type already made up. According to Hart Cantwell " accidentally" dropped the formes of type during the raid. However this is contradicted by Inspector Melville, one of the police officers supervising the raid who was to construe Cantwell's sarcastic comment as an admission of guilt but fails to mention the dropping of type formes.

Cantwell was one of the speakers who spoke at the protest meeting on Sunday April 24th at Hyde Park. A large crowd were amused by his imitation of the Scotland Yard inspectors Littlechild and Melville who had told him that they were anarchists.

He was one of those who restarted the Commonweal in May 1893 alongside John Turner, Carl Quinn, Ernest Young, Joseph Presburg and H.B. Samuels. On December 5th of the same year he wrote to the Chief Commissioner of Police on behalf of the *Commonweal* Anarchist Group Publicity Committee giving notice of a meeting to be held in Trafalgar Square "for the purpose of obtaining a condemnation of your actions in suppressing anarchist opinions and misrepresenting anarchist principles". He had received no intimation on the expected conduct of the police and wanted to know "if you adhere to the claptrap in which you indulged about a fortnight ago". The letter was minuted as to be ignored and that no meeting would be allowed subject to a decision by the Secretary of State. Cantwell was described as a militant anarchist who had been connected with The *Commonweal* for some time. In 1893 Cantwell produced the last issues of the original series of The Commonweal as well as the new series during 1893-4 — with only the six month break when he was imprisoned. He started printing it from May 27th 1893 at 4 Sidmouth Mews. On 29th June he and Ernest Young were arrested for flyposting a poster about the wedding of the Duke of York. The poster advertised an indignation meeting to be held in Hyde Park on 2nd July to protest against the "waste of wealth" expended on "these Royal Vermin". Apparently Cantwell was behind the idea of the poster and of meetings around the theme. The case was finally dismissed, both Cantwell and Young remaining in prison until the trial, though the owner of the hoarding fined them both.

In 1894 Cantwell published an edition of Mikhail Bakunin's God and the State with a postscript from Max Nettlau.

On June 29th 1894 he and Carl Quinn addressed a meeting at the new Tower Bridge which was to be opened the following day by members of the royal family and politicians. They wanted to appeal to the workers who had built it and Cantwell had printed a placard which read : "Fellow workers, you have expended life, energy and skill in building this bridge. Now comes the royal vermin and rascally officials in pomp and splendour to claim the credit. You are taken to the workhouse and a pauper's grave to glorify these lazy swine who live upon our labour". The reaction to the two anarchists speech was violent.

There were many professional anti-socialist hecklers around this speaking pitch, many of them retired soldiers. A mob of 400-500 attacked the anarchists, surrounding Cantwell and shouting "lynch him", whilst others attempted to strike him with large pieces of wood. For this the police arrested Cantwell for disorderly conduct! As John Quail says " being pursued by people who were trying to hit him with large pieces of wood obviously amounted to disorderly conduct".

Quinn managed to escape but was arrested the following day when he went to the police station "to see fair play for Cantwell". They were kept in prison for a month during various court appearances. Their subsequent trial was something of a travesty. The meeting had been like many previous ones, with no charges brought by the police but this time the charges were incitement to murder members of the royal family, seditious libel on the royal family, and two other incitements to terrorism, all rather flimsy. The judge showed much bias towards the defence. The police were doing what they could to get Cantwell and Quinn sent down, part of the ongoing State campaign against anarchism that had began with the attacks on free speech in Manchester in 1893. Despite many defence witnesses — including William Morris who declared as a character witness that Cantwell was "a good-natured man, perhaps rather rash" — the two anarchists received six months imprisonment with hard labour.

In the period after his release he was also involved in the publication of the anarchist paper *The Torch* which was set up by the well brought up young ladies Olivia and Helen Rossetti and their brother William. However Cantwell's habits and character became sources of irritation for the rest of the group. The Rossetti sisters in their fictionalised account of the London anarchist movement of the time, *A Girl Among the Anarchists*, were to write in a derogatory fashion about Cantwell (disguised as Short in the novel). Geoffrey Byrne, another member of the group was to state that the Rossettis were driven away from the movement because of Cantwell's behaviour, although there may well have been other reasons for their departure (see Oliver p.124).

In spring 1895 Cantwell was invited by Alfred Marsh to join the Freedom Group together with John Turner and Joseph Presburg to "reinforce" the ranks and to relieve William Wess who was seeking other employment. With occasional interruptions, when other people were available, Cantwell was in charge of the *Freedom* printing office from 1895-1902. Harry Kelly, an American anarchist who had moved to England, wrote that "Cantwell and I were the only simon-pure workingmen in the group". However Cantwell had become difficult. It may be speculated that his imprisonment had affected both his physical and mental health. Harry Kelly was to remark that "he had never quite recovered from the six months hard labour". He threatened the Italian anarchists Pietro Gori and Edoardo Milano with a gun and appears to have tried to dictate editorial policy to Marsh.

In April 1895 the printing of *Freedom* was re-started at Judd Street in Kings Cross, in a small building described as a "glass house".

In April 1896 Cantwell moved with all the print type to 127 Ossulston Street in Somerstown. The printshop there was known as the Cosmopolitan Printery until 1902. In the next year all other anarchist papers closed down. From September 1898 A Belgian, F Henneghien was able to replace Cantwell and this was a relief to many as he tended to fall out with comrades on a regular basis and was seen as very unreliable rarely producing anything on time. As regards *Freedom* George Cores noted that Cantwell " had, as acting editor, a peculiar habit of censoring all contributions, making everything which appeared conform to the gospel according to Cantwell. This did not suit the comrades". Marsh himself was to write in 1897 to Nettlau that " you cannot imagine what a time I had. 2 ½ years with Cantwell is enough to kill anyone" (Cantwell had left Freedom in November, at least temporarily). He was again responsible for the printing of *Freedom* after Henneghien left in 1900.

Cantwell had a heart complaint from at least 1894 and he was soon to have a stroke.

Tcherkesoff found him on Christmas Day 1902 with his head lying in the "ashes of the fireplace all but dead. He recovered and lived several years after but was never able to work and was never again the same man". Apparently he had continuing heart trouble after the stroke. *Freedom* published an appeal for him in 1903 saying that he was "overtaken by a long and trying illness". He died on December 29th 1906.

He was buried at Edmonton Cemetery on January 3rd 1907, his funeral being attended by William Wess, Tom Keell, and Frank Kitz, among others.

~ Nick Heath

Mary Canipa (1920s?-1999) and Jack Robinson (1921-1983)

We are sorry to hear of the death of Mary Canipa last month. She was diminutive and self-effacing and was one of those people who would automatically undertake a dozen routine jobs in the work of Freedom Press in the 1950s and '60s; minding the bookshop, folding, addressing and stamping the paper, selling it at meetings and setting out and running a bookstall at fairs and summer schools, as well as making overseas visitors welcome.

Together with her equally small but far more assertive partner, Jack Robinson, she would set out on demonstrations like the Aldermaston marches, and would never dream of complaining about being soaked, nor about dragging around a satchel-full of unsold papers.

In the 1950s she and Jack settled in Fulham and in the 1970s moved to Boxford in Suffolk, where they became a local institution and where her typewriter was seldom out of use, whether producing copy for *Freedom* or earning an income to pay the rent. After Jack's death she moved back to her birthplace, the Isle of Man, and was cared for there in her last years by her sister Margaret.

~Freedom *obituary, November 11th 1998*

Born in Birmingham, Jack Robinson trained as a nurse and was one of the many conscientious objectors drawn towards anarchism during World War II. During the war he worked in an epileptic colony and clinical volunteer in a Vitamin C deficiency study, living on a diet which caused scurvy.

Touring the country after the war he earned money as a book trader before moving to London in 1953 and moving in with Donald Rooum in 1954 while he worked with Lilian Wolfe in the Freedom Press bookshop.

Robinson later settled down with his companion Mary Canipa at Rumbold Road in Walham Green, London and moved out to Boxford on their retirement. A teetotaler and vegetarian, he was a regular contributor to *Freedom* from the early 1960s, often anonymously — his most regular alias was as Jon Quixote, under which he wrote the Out of This World column tracking activity in anarchist movements worldwide. He also wrote essays in *Anarchy* for Colin Ward.

Robinson and Canipa were both regular volunteers at the Press's Fulham bookshop through the 1960s, and worked alongside Rooum in the Colne and Nelson Anarchist Group.

~ Rob Ray

George Cores (1867-1949)

George Cores was born in St Georges in the East End of London on September 20th 1867. His father, John Henry Christopher Kors, was born in Hanover, Germany.Illiterate, he worked in a sugar refinery in the East End until he died of lung and heart disease at the age of 38. George grew up in dire poverty.

He came in contact with socialist ideas in 1883 when he saw Justice, paper of the Social Democratic Federation, in newsagents in Globe Road in East London. He appears to have become involved in the activities of the Labour Emancipation League, affiliated to the SDF, where he met Joseph Lane.

By 1887, he was secretary of the Hackney branch of the Socialist League which also included William Wess and Joe Lane. He served as its librarian in 1899. He spoke throughout 1899 at Clerkenwell Green, outside Hoxton church, on Gibraltar Walk and outside the Salmon and Ball in east London. He became a specifically anarchist propagandist in late 1889 and 1890. In September 1899 he incurred a month's imprisonment as a result of free speech agitation in Yarmouth.

He spoke regularly in 1890 on the Mile End waste and at Union Street off Commercial Road. The Commonweal reported him as speaking at very successful meetings in Victoria Park on Sunday afternoons where many copies of the paper as well as pamphlets were sold. He was also one of the many speakers at the May Day rally in Hyde Park organised by the Socialist League. He addressed three large meetings in Braintree, Essex that year and together with Johanna Lahr started a speaking pitch at Stratford. This was soon shut down by the police however.

In the summer months he spoke in Leicester, Sheffield and Nottingham where he ended a large meeting by rendering a revolutionary song. He attended the Socialist League conference at the Autonomie Club in Fitzrovia, London in August 1890.He was active throughout autumn and winter of that year and into the next addressing meetings and distributing propaganda in Leeds. He was one of the Leeds speakers listing themselves available to speak, giving his own specialities as The Coming Change in Society, The Fraud of Politics, Why Pay Rent, Trades' Unionism and Socialism,Socialism, its Aims and Methods. In August of 1891 he addressed a large meeting in Hull.

He took part in discussions with the recently-created Freedom Group. He moved to Leicester in 1892 where he combined his brief stay as a laster in Leicester with his activities as occasional editor of the *Commonweal* after editor when David Nichol , its previous editor, was arrested for incitement to murder) He then moved to Walsall where he co-ordinated support of the imprisoned Walsall anarchists. He mysteriously left the Commonweal, probably after a quarrel with the politically suspect H. B. Samuels.

In January 1893, Cores and Billy Macqueen responded to the cry of "Hurrah for Anarchy" from the Birmingham gasworker Christopher Davies at his trial in Birmingham. They were severely beaten by the police, arrested and charged with disturbing the proceedings of the court and released with a caution.

In February 1893, he got work again in Leicester and was active in the unofficial strikes in the boot and shoe trade. He was a member of the Leicester branch executive of the National Union of Boot and Shoe Operatives (NUBSO) where he and T F Richards fought against the domination of William Inskip. He took an active part in the unofficial shoemakers' strikes. Cores was to propose to No 1 Branch of NUBSO the resolution that: "Hundreds of unemployed who are able and willing to work are in such a state of starvation that they will be compelled and entitled to take the means of subsistence by illegal methods unless help is speedily forthcoming". There was uproar within the crowded meeting but Cores won the motion.

He was a delegate to the Trades Council and was secretary of the organising committee of Leicester's first May Day demonstration in 1893. The Trades Council took over the organisation of these events from then on. He was also involved in the establishment of the Leicester Labour Club in May 1893.

In 1911 he began contributing to the Notes on the front page of *Freedom* with the encouragement of Alfred Marsh.

He clashed with Tom Keell over the latter's editorship of Freedom in 1915 and an on-off dispute continued between them into the 1930s. He was unhappy that Keell eventually took *Freedom* away from London to the Whiteway Colony in Gloucestershire, where it dwindled in size and regularity. As a result he decided to bring out *Freedom* himself along with John Humphrey (see the biography of Humphrey here at libcom for more details of this venture). It then continued to publish as an eight page paper until August 1936. It appears that Cores and Humphrey did not always get along, according to a letter from Mat Kavanagh to Tom Keell.

Cores helped set up the London Freedom Group which met at 144 High Holborn as well as holding open-air meetings in Hyde Park. Its members included William Wess, Albert Meltzer, George Stenzleit, Harry H. Jones, Jack White and Alf Rosenbaum.

Cores was against the merger of *Freedom* with *Spain and The World* in 1936, whilst the remainder of the group were in favour. He continued his activities of the Freedom Group as more or less a one-man operation with weekly lectures until its demise in winter 1939. Cores was out of step with the majority of the British anarchist movement over WW2 and his attitude to it was considered dubious. As a result he found himself estranged from the movement.

After WW2 Cores made contact with Anarchist Federation (later the Syndicalist Workers Federation) of Ken Hawkes and Tom Brown and remained in contact with them. He died on September 20th 1949 in Willesden, having recently completed his *Personal Recollections of the Anarchist Past*. Donald Rooum remembers coming down to London from Yorkshire where he was met by Cores who put him in contact with the anarchist movement there. He recalls him as being well turned out in a bowler hat and bright blue suit.

~ *Nick Heath*

Leah Feldman (1899-1993)

The last living link to the era of Kropotkin, Leah Feldman was an undimmed presence in the anarchist movement post-war, cutting across all arguments. As such, I include two articles on her life here, the first being the Freedom *obituary written by Donald Rooum and the second written by Albert Meltzer, who along with the Black Flag group became very close to her in the final years of her life.*

Our comrade Leah Feldman died on 3rd January 1993, aged 94 years. She was forthright in her opinions and given to quarrelling, but will be remembered with affection for her freedom from spite or vindictiveness. She would criticise anyone to their face, but would tolerate no criticism of friends or comrades who woe not there to defend themselves. Many an argument started, indeed, with a fierce debate of some figure from the anarchist past whose perfection had been questioned.

Amusing anecdotes are told of her refusal to compromise and her fluent but idiosyncratic English. One story she told about herself was how she stormed out of a job when PAYE was introduced and she found income tax deducted from her wage packet Her employer was the Co-operative Wholesale Society, which she thought should have made a stand against the order to collect taxes from the workers. "This is none a workers' society," she told the manager, "It is become a directors' and managers' society. Would the Rochdale

Pioneers be alive today, they would turn in their grave".

Leah was born to a Yiddish-speaking family in a part of Poland at that time part of Russia. She remembered at the time of the 1905 risings asking her father to explain why God permitted such suffering. Before long she was an atheist and an anarchist, and fled to London where she trained as a furrier, and was a trade union activist and a member of the famous Jubilee Street anarchist club.

She returned to Russia in 1919 to support the revolution. A cutpurse in Moscow stole her shoulder bag containing everything she owned, and she was forced to turn to the police for financial assistance. Leah was impressed by the kindness of the Communist police, but unlike some Western anarchists of the time, she did not make the compromise of supporting the Marxist dictatorship as a lesser evil than capitalism. Seeing that the revolution had failed, she returned to London via jobs in Berlin and Paris, and acquired a British passport through marriage to her lover Philip Downes.

In 1936 she participated in the decision of the old Freedom Group, at that time almost defunct, to use the remaining assets in support of *Spain and the World* (now reverted to the old name *Freedom*). Always a keen, though vociferously critical supporter of Freedom Press, in the 1950s she was one of the two regular *Freedom* sellers (with Lilian Wolfe) at Hyde Park speakers' corner. The police on duty often engaged newspaper sellers in peaceful conversation, but if they approached Leah she always amused them by saying "Will you please move. You are wasting mine time". Her eyes were injured in a bomb blast during the war, and the injury compounded by an accident in emergency surgery. From then on she was registered blind, but refused to compromise with her disability by canying a white stick or anything of that kind. Late in her life she did not often go out after dark, but eagerly attended anarchist events which took place in daylight. We will remember her at the Anarchist Bookfairs, sitting at the Freedom Press counter talking to friends all day.

Sprightly, outgoing and argumentative to the end, she will be missed by London anarchists old and young.

~ *Donald Rooum*

***

Leah (Leila) Feldman, who was cremated at East London in the presence of some fifty comrades from DAM, ABC, Black Flag and the feminist movement, on January 7th 1993, was a history lesson in herself. She merits more than an obituary.

She was born (she always said) in Warsaw around 1899. Her British passport says she was born in Odessa, but in view of her problems through life, she must have had many occasions to "change" birthdays, names, birthplaces and nationalities. The problems faced by a woman just in travelling independently in the old days were immense, apart from her anarchist activities. While she was still a schoolgirl she become interested in anarchism (her mother used to hide her shoes so that she could not attend meetings, then illegal). Finally she ran away to her sister in London to earn her own living at the sewing machine.

Working in the sweatshops of the East End, she become active in the Yiddish-speaking anarchist movement that flourished at the time and vanished. She was possibly the last survivor of that Jewish workers' movement. When the Russian Revolution was thought to have come about and the army was in rebellion the overwhelming majority of Russian Jewish male anarchists, who had resisted conscription up to then, joined up to return to Russia. The women Anarchists had a more difficult problem — many with husbands or companions who were able to go back, arranged to follow later but that was the last they heard of their menfolk, overtaken by the triumph of Bolshevism. This Jewish (in the sense they used, neither racial nor religious but language) anarchist movement, gradually dwindled away over the years. A few remaining males survived until the early fifties, and the women, often married into English dockers' families, ended with Leah so far as this country is concerned.

Leah, however, independently made her own way back, a tremendous task. Viewing Russia from the train, a comrade jestingly remarked she was like Madame Butterfly watching for her lover (we played 'One Fine Day' at her funeral, and also Paul Robeson singing the equally appropriate 'Joe Hill'). Unfortunately it was no fine day and Leah, as a working woman, was one of the first to see what would be the effects of Bolshevism, something one [none] of the intellectuals who visited could see.

She attended Kropotkin's funeral, the last permitted anarchist demonstration before the long dark night (they stole the flowers from Lenin's tribute in the House of the People, but all those paroled from prison for the day returned to jail).

Leah left Moscow to join Makhno's army in the Ukraine (perhaps that was when she decided she was born in Odessa), which fought into the last against Tsarism, Bolshevism, the Social Democratic oppression and foreign intervention. She was one of a number of Jewish Anarchists who were living testimony to the lie started by the Soviet historian Yaroslavsky and accepted by academics universally (including many encyclopaedists copying each other) about Makhno's pogroms. Though she did not actually fight, as a few women (who could ride horseback) did, she joined the train that followed the army and prepared clothes and food for the orphans and strays they picked up everywhere. For the rest of her life she was to follow the pattern of behind-the-lines support for revolutionary action.

When the army was defeated, Leah took advantage of one "privilege" offered to women — she changed nationality by a formal marriage to a German anarchist, and left the country. They did not meet again. She made her way to Paris and then back to London. She still wanted to travel and was involved with the Anarchist movement in many countries. She was however tied by her German "marriage" once she had left Russia, but was later free to contract another formal marriage to a British ex-serviceman, named Downes. In a deprecating obituary in *Freedom*, which takes into account only her selling of *Freedom* during and a few years after the war, it is said he was her lover. This is rubbish. He was a derelict, like many wounded old soldiers after 1918, found for her by Charles Lahr and paid £10 for his services, lent by the Workers' Friend group and repaid by Leah over a period. (Typically, Charlie joked that to find a real husband would cost a lot more). They never met again until Leah found by official communication her 'husband" was in a geriatric hospital and she used to visit with presents of tobacco. When she was abroad, Polly Witcop (sister of Milly Rocker and Rose Witcop) undertook the visits for her.

Leah visited both Poland and mandated Palestine once she was a British citizen, working her way to both places. In Palestine she organised a federation of anarchists, mostly old friends from the old country. One surprise was her old friend Paula Green, who had been pressurised into marriage in Russia, so had decided on an atheistic Socialist-Zionist with whom she was in love. Forced into exile he had obviously chosen (Ottoman) Palestine. Paula knew he was into active Socialist politics but thought it as impossible he would ever be in government as he thought her ideas impossible. Green changed his name to Ben Gurion, and after 1945 become Prime Minister. His wife did not leave him but did not take part in any public activities, and the whisper in Socialist-Zionist circles was that she was mad and could not be taken on an official platform. ('Because he becomes the baker do you have to be the baker's wife?" Leah asked her back in 1935, ten years before Paula faced the final humiliation as Premier's wife though a still believing if passive anarchist, getting the reply, with a shrug, "So what do I get but the smell of the bakery?").

Eventually Leah decided there was nothing she could do in Palestine and returned to London at the end of 1935 when I met her for the first time. She helped raise finance for the German sailors who organised a resistance group in the thirties, and took a tremendous part in activities for the Spanish movement when the civil war broke out. I used to go to her flat in Lordship Park (Stoke Newington) and hump great parcels of food and clothing which she had collected from her fellow fur machinists. She could never understand why I could "only raise pennies among my friends when she raised pounds" and never appreciated I was still at school, which for some obscure reason I was somewhat abashed at mentioning in then mostly ageing anarchist circles.

She took part in the selling of *Freedom* after the war and still thought of it as Kropotkin's paper until her death, but a lot of people made that mistake. She could never understand in later years why they persistently ignored her except when she gave them money, and never visited her when she was ill, but the truth was they resented her criticism that Kropotkin intended it for the anarchist movement not for a few cronies of one man who had seized control. When *Black Flag* come along she supported it equally always saying to me, "How is it that the people in this group are so different from the Freedom Group?" — I always answered "Because they're anarchists" but I fear she didn't want to hear that.

Leah was associated with Spanish women anarchists in a joint working collective of different Anarchist women in Holborn (London) with Marie Goldberg, Suceso Portales and others, ever since 1939. How, with the confusion of tongues, broken English, Yiddish, Polish, bits of French, Spanish and Catalan, Indian-English of one and broad Scots of another, plus the total lack of verbal communication of two Cypriot women, one Greek and the other Turkish, they could ever have understood each other was a mystery to many, but they made up for it in volume, and maybe that's how new languages are born. (The postman once said to me on the stairs, "I can never work out what nationality those ladies are — they told me they come from somewhere in anarchy but Christ knows where that is.") Leah had to give up work when her eyesight went after an operation (she was blind in one eye thereafter and increasingly so in the other).

She wanted to give aid to the Spanish Resistance in spite of all, and during the turbulent sixties, with the International First of May Movement, helped in taking care of the armoury, even taking it with her luggage into Spain. She was known affectionately by Catalans, always prone to giving nicknames, as "la yaya (granny) Makhnowista".

In her seventies she revisited Warsaw in a vain attempt to find her relatives. A Polish journalist took her round as she refused to believe everything and everybody in the ghetto had vanished. "Maybe the neighbours know something," she said and they had to show her visual proof that the neighbourhood had been flattened, the Polish inhabitants dispersed and scarcely one of the Jewish residents remaining anywhere in Poland other than those who had come in after the war. Presumably this episode appeared on local TV or radio as the journalist took enormous trouble in convincing her of the reality.

Her last years were sad. Not only were all her family and early friends dead, there was nobody left to whom she could even talk in her own language. She still supported anarchist meetings and went on holiday independently but in the last years of her life accompanied by Margaret, Jessica, Peter, Terry from *Black Flag*. One of us used to take her to the annual Anarchist Bookfair whenever her health permitted — she always sat at the Freedom Press stall in the hope of meeting some of the people she knew in Freedom who only appeared on the scene that day of the year, if at all, stubbornly refusing to admit it was now quite a different ball game.

As she got increasingly deaf and almost totally blind, she had to surrender some of her cherished independence and allow people to do things for her. She became paranoiac, argumentative and even aggressive in her nineties, after a series of horrendous street accidents, feeling her best friends were trying to kill her by driving cars or motorbikes straight at her, The fact that these dedicated young people still persevered week after week looking after her, being fond of her, and remembering all she had done in the past, says a lot for them especially, in addition to those already named, the feminists Ann and Cathy, and DAM people like Ken and Helen.

George Cores said that "most of the work that was done (in building the anarchist movement) was due to the activities of working men and women, most of whom did not appear as orators or writers in printed papers", Cathy and Margaret, and our late comrade Leo Rosser, obtained in a series of interviews, and a video, notes of her life which have been transcribed but are voluminous though chronologically jumbled. We hope that these can be edited into a coherent volume, which will be well worth publishing, far more so than the oft-repeated hagiographies of the "secular saints" of the movement in the past.

~ *Albert Meltzer*

John Hewetson (1913-1990)

Born to wealth, John Hewetson went into the medical profession and became involved with pacifistic anarchism during World War II, joining the Forward Movement via a group of militant pacifists who broke away the Peace Pledge Union and becoming involved with Freedom *during the second world war. He worked from early on in the field of birth control "because anxiety about getting pregnant was tremendously common ... it was an enormous factor in preventing working-class women from enjoying their love-making, and this was especially true in those who most believed they were likely to fall pregnant if they had an orgasm, and who used to try and inhibit their orgasms."*

After the war he settled into new work at a practice in Elephant and Castle, and for many years he and his colleagues were the visiting medical officers for the Camberwell Reception Centre helping homeless single people in South London, known as The Spike. Below is a slightly shortened version of Philip Sansom's obituary, published in the January 12th 1991 issue of Freedom.

Ironically, the very morning I intended to get my head together and get down to writing this tribute to John Hewetson, the early morning news programmes on the radio were crackling with the story of a new report on the relationship between poverty and ill health. Ironic, because among my early collaborations with John was to design the cover for his booklet *Health, Poverty and the State*, published by Freedom Press in 1946. This was a brilliant and damning indictment of capitalist and authoritarian society, packed with facts and quotations from medically impeccable sources, going back to the early years of this century — and beyond.

...

Colin Ward says "John spent a lifetime in quiet propaganda", which is, I think, slightly an understatement He was certainly not a street-fightin' man, not even an outdoor orator, but he could be deadly in debate and most incisive in the many articles and editorials he wrote for *War Commentary* and *Freedom* over more than 12 years, he went to prison twice — once as a conscientious objector and again as the "disaffecter of the Forces". He lost his job at St Mary's Hospital, Paddington, as a result of our imprisonment in 1945 but both managed to avoid further harassment and to lead constructive lives.

For John this meant building the unique practice that Colin has described. But certain things can be touched upon today that had to be dealt with tactfully at the time. It was a well-kept secret that a small "workshop" — for want of a better word — was set up in London in the 1950s for the purpose of getting birth control materials into France, where De Gaulle's authoritarian rule and Mother Church forbade such sinful things.

The supplies were requested by French women (and, I shouldn't be surprised, a few men) and by various means including voluntary working by men and women here in London, guided by John, both goods and expertise were exported to Gaullist France. It was not until the early '70s that the French law was relaxed.

Hewetson was a pioneer among male doctors both for freely available birth control and abortion on demand. Here in Britain abortion was available legally, after the famous Bourne case of 1936 — but under such carefully hedged-in conditions that it was virtually only the moneyed classes for whom it was possible legally and safely.

It was necessary for the woman to get a statement of certificate from a general practitioner, a psychiatrist and a qualified gynaecologist before the latter could legally and privately (i.e. not on the National Health) terminate a pregnancy. For those with a few hundred guineas in their pockets it was virtually abortion on demand, as long as the proper certificates showed that their health, or that of the foetus, was endangered by a continued pregnancy.

Because of John's known advocacy of abortion on demand over many years (the first such article ever read anywhere appeared in *War Commentary* in 1943] he had come into contact with others in the medical professions who, like him, were very careful not to step outside the law — for that could lead to being struck off and banned from practice forever — but were quite prepared to work within the limits of the law to their own judgement and to their own reduced scale of fees, for worthy or desperate cases.

Among Colin's "many elderly women readers" (do we have many?) there must also be a few whose lives were not only transformed by liberation, but also escaped the occasional consequences of careless love! There must be hundreds of thousands more for whom the changes in the law on abortion in 1968 have saved months of anxiety, panic and pain. There are many doctors who have opposed these changes but many more who have supported them, thanks to the continuous work over the decades by John Hewetson and his partner John MacEwan, who is now also retired from the "very remarkable practice at the Elephant and Castle" to which Colin refers. MacEwan now has a chair as consultant in birth control at Kings College in London. Indeed, I heard his voice on BBC Radio 4 only a few weeks ago protesting about the government's plan to close down a number of birth control clinics. So he has now developed as an authority to be listened to.

...

My years of friendship with John Hewetson began in 1943, when I discovered the anarchist movement in London — having done three years work on the land in Kent. I was immediately impressed (although 27 years old, I was a political innocent) by the integrity and knowledge of world affairs expressed by this small group of people only a little older than myself. Hewetson was outstanding for his clarity of thought, firmness of conviction, and, no doubt, for an East End secondary school product like myself, his educated speech. My first collaboration with him was in drawing a cartoon which appeared with an indignant article of his on famine in India where, during the war, the British masters had manoeuvred even the 'pacifist' Congress leaders into supporting Britain in the war against Japan by promise of independence after the war. Part of the bargain had been (though perhaps not...) that Britain could use India as a source of food for Britain itself — which meant great shortage for the Indians. It was still "Imperial India" remember. But still things haven't changed a lot have they? Food is still a political weapon.

Within two years, John and Vernon Richards and I were in jail together on charges of disaffection of the Forces, a very serious offence carrying a penalty of 14 years! I won't go into details of the trial, which lasted four days—but it was most illuminating. At one point John's counsel, a Mr John Maud who later became Recorder in Exeter Assizes, referred to John as "that silver-haired surgeon, sitting in the most unhappy seat in England!"

Well, the unhappy seat was okay — it was the dock in number one court at the Old Bailey. But the "silver-haired surgeon" was a bit steep, since John wasn't a surgeon, and it was a family trait that Hewetsons all found their hair turning grey — white even — at a very early age! But it was good emotional stuff.

In spite of that, the jury found us guilty and we held our breath as the judge declared sentence: "I therefore sentence you all to nine..." (pause) "... calendar months". Collapse of stout parties in the Special Branch pew! While we had thought for a moment he was going to say nine years!

What John knew, however, and nobody else since he hadn't breathed a word to anybody else, was that the judge in our case, Mr Justice Birkett, had been, as Mr Norman Birkett KC, a leading defence lawyer in Birmingham at the same time as John's father had been Chief Gynaecologist at Birmingham s chief hospital —

and Messers Birkett and Hewetson senior had been great drinking chums in Birmingham's best clubs! Who says the old pals act can't work both ways?

~ *Philip Sansom*

Thomas Keell (1866-1938)

Thomas Keell was certainly one of the little-known and often misrepresented people who helped to keep *Freedom* going through its most eventful years. As Mat Kavanagh, also one of the lesser-known indefatigable militants, after some 50 years' activity in the movement wrote: 'I know of few men who did more quiet hard work, or were so completely indifferent to praise or blame, or yet so free of personal feeling.' Between 1903 and 1932 and then again from 1936 to 1938 it was his name or at least his neat handwriting that most of those who relied upon Freedom Press to supply them with Anarchist literature identified with the Press, and *Freedom*.

Thomas Henry Keell was born at Blackheath, London, on September 24th 1866, 'of good rural English stock'. Little is known of his early life. On November 8th 1881 he was apprenticed to letterpress printing for seven years, and in October 1887 was admitted to the London Society of Compositors, which became his early school of trade unionism. Apart from that his earliest political interests concerned the land reform movement, having seen 'at close quarters the evils of landlordism' during his favourite activity: long-distance walks (later on bicycle) mainly across the country on old footpaths, taking an active interest in their defence and preservation. But he soon became attracted by the broader aims of socialism, and in the mid-1890s he became a member of the Independent Labour Party and then the secretary of its Peckham branch. At about this time, in 1896, he also came into contact with the anarchist movement.

> My first introduction was as a compositor on *Alarm* in Judd Street. I was out of work at the time, and a fellow member of the ILP asked me if I would work on an anarchist paper. So I was introduced to Will Banham. I think it was number three of *Alarm* that I set. When I presented my bill (about 35/-) Banham took me along to 127 Ossulston Street to get my money. He gave me £1 on account. The rest is still owing. I little thought that 127 Ossulston Street would be my home for so many years when I entered it on that occasion.

He soon found regular work again, as compositor on the weekly paper *The Spectator*, from now on, however, he regularly attended anarchist meetings. "On all such occasions," as Max Nettlau later recalled, "one could see the tall bearded frame and face of the silent Keell from South London who would scarcely say a word, but if he did, very modestly, it was to the point, usually a useful suggestion. Thus we got used to him as a helpful element and he himself came to understand that the commonsense socialism which he advocated was identical with the opinions of all commonsense anarchists."

His first contact with the Freedom Group was in June 1898, when Walter Needs and W F Rean (at this time still an anarchist and editor of a little-known libertarian magazine, *The Harbinger*, where Louise Michel published the beginning of her memoirs) took him to the "private" gathering to bid farewell to Lilian Harman, the American anarchist and birth control activist. During a meeting in Trafalgar Square he got acquainted with Harry Kelly, the American Anarchist who had just come to England and soon joined the Freedom Group, and invited him to talk to the ILP Peckham branch on conditions in America.

> In that talk I spoke of Thoreau, who had thrilled me as he has countless others; later Keell told me that it was his reading of that most original of all American minds that changed his line of thinking and eventually brought him to our movement.

When Tom Cantwell had a stroke on Christmas Day, 1902, and became incapacitated, and the other compositor on *Freedom*, Mr Boyd, also proved inefficient for managing work, Alfred Marsh approached Keell (who had helped Cantwell on several occasions with the paper during the previous year) to ask if he would be interested in becoming the compositor and manager. Keell agreed and so in January 1903 became a regular feature of the Freedom office.

One of his first activities was to clear up the already legendary mess in the Ossulston Street Office, and from then on comrades came to meet there and it gained some sort of social value to the movement. For the first time in more than a decade orders were executed promptly, and the sale of literature (and the reprinting of pamphlets) speeded up considerably.

Having proved his reliability, he was asked in September 1903 to take over the business side also. From 1904 (and until the building was pulled down in 1928) he was the responsible tenant of the office. That year he also moved from Camberwell to Leyton to set up there a household with his wife (whose first name incidentally was also Lilian) and William Wess, which however lasted only some 18 months. Then Lilian Keell left with Wess; they were both instrumental in setting up, in February 1906, the new Workers' Friend club in Jubilee Street, and she tried to initiate an Anarchist Sunday School. (Some years later, as Lilian Evelyn, she ran one of the two Modern Schools in London, the Ferrer School in Charlotte Street.)

In the aftermath of the abortive Russian Revolution of 1905, the discussions soon centered on the value of direct action as an important means to bring about a social revolution, and the Freedom Group decided to publish a paper more or less entirely concentrating on industrial activities and especially agitation for all forms of direct action. A draft for a programme was prepared by Kropotkin, all practical preparations done by Alfred Marsh and Tom Keell, and a name soon found: *Voice of Labour*. A dummy of a first number was produced (and distributed in a few copies) in November 1906, but the paper started only on 18 January 1907. Since 1903 he had done all work on *Freedom* in his spare time; but now with two papers to set, to print and to manage he had to give up his job at the *Spectator*. The first eight numbers were edited by Alfred Marsh:

> He then withdrew and it was decided to stop the paper. Two days after some of the V of L group approached me & asked me to accept the editorship, if they would find the money to carry on. Reluctantly I agreed.

The principal contributors were John Turner, Guy Aldred (in his own name and also as 'Ajax junior'), Karl Walter, Harry Kelly, S Carlyle Potter and Jimmy Dick. Keell himself wrote only one article: "I had never written but one article in my life before. Perhaps that accounted for the death of the Voice!" The keynote of the paper was the futility of parliamentary action and the value of direct action. Altogether 36 issues were published.

In August 1907 Keell was, with Karl Walter, one of the English delegates to the International Anarchist Congress in Amsterdam. The following years saw a boom in publishing activities by the Freedom Press, and it was Keell who did most of the donkey-work, day in day out. But his role at Freedom was more than that of a mere compositor and manager paid wages. As Nettlau later recorded, 'he was also a thoroughly efficient member of the Group and if very many facts and impressions can be recalled in a few words, I should say that Keell's sober judgement greatly helped Marsh to preserve *Freedom* for years from well-meant, but one-sided influences of others, even of Marsh himself who might, alone, have given way to others. Keell was also a most useful member by reason of his real observation of economic life. We were sometimes very good at general conclusions and sweeping hypotheses or rather affirmations. Then we needed just a few hard facts which none of us could have produced. But Keell had read these things up and not a few very plausible theories had to take on a more modest aspect.

When after 1910 Marsh, due to growing health problems, withdrew more and more from the actual practical work involved in producing the paper, Keell had also to take over more and more editorial tasks. George Cores, later one of Keell's bitterest enemies, returned at this time to London and appeared regularly in the office, presumably to help, but Keell saw things just a little differently:

> There was always a coolness between us. He also ... had many meals at my expense at the office when he turned up again in 1912. He was a fearful bore ... usually turned up at teatime and talked incessantly on elementary anarchism. I had to tell him that the office was not a discussion forum and as I had to set type he must not hinder by talking. He evidently has never forgiven me.

In 1913 Keell became "acting editor" of *Freedom*, George Ballard ('Barrett') having refused to take part in that work as he felt the strong tradition of *Freedom* to be too much of a burden, and preferred to eventually start another paper (the *Glasgow Anarchist*). In controversial matters, however, Marsh retained the final decision.

From around 1911 a group of young anarchists developed independently from *Freedom* and the Freedom Group, calling themselves in 1913-1914 the Anarchist Education League. From mid-1913 they were loosely linked to the Freedom Press and especially to Tom Keell, and from November Freedom Press published for them *The Torch*, which after five issues from May 1st 1914 on became the *Voice of Labour*. The editor was in the beginning 'officially' George Barrett, who being very ill could however write only a few articles, while other editorial work was done mainly by Fred W Dunn. It was this group — Dunn, Mabel Hope (who having been for years a contributor to *Freedom* actually had brought about the initial contact), Elizabeth Archer, Tom

Sweetlove, W Fanner, and Lilian Wolfe — who supported Keell in his difficult stand against the supporters of the First World War in the Freedom Group, and who soon were to constitute the new one, after Kropotkin, Tcherkesoff and wife and their friends no longer took part in the production of *Freedom*.

The story of this rupture has been told elsewhere, and need not to be repeated; but it would be wrong not to stress how much courage Keell showed to oppose 'secular saints' like Kropotkin, whom he himself had admired so much: 'To work with them was indeed a pleasure and an inspiration, and my greatest regret was when the War...split our group asunder. One doubted the judgement of those members who supported the War, but one never doubted their sincerity." But "the other side" (with the exception of Kropotkin!) was never so generous, and from now on called the same Keell, who up till now had always been regarded by some as the paid servant, a ruthless dictator who had seized all the valuable *Freedom* assets.

However, at the next anarchist national conference at Hazel Grove (Stockport), in April 1915, all the accusations which George Cores ('the man selected by Tcherkesoff and Turner and others to denounce me as a thief) brought forward against Keell were repudiated and his "only crime" approved of unanimously: to have prevented "the paper joining the patriotic and pro-war crowd". The same group then started, in March 1915, Marsh House at 1 Mecklenburgh Street, which functioned until September 1916 as anarchist commune and meeting-place for the London anarchists and the Anti-Conscription League formed in May 1915. After the passing of the Military Service Act in January 1916 both *Freedom* and the *Voice of Labour* soon ran into trouble, first for an article 'Defying the Act' by "one of those outlawed on the Scottish Hills" (Fred Dunn), which was published in the April issue of the Voice and subsequently as a leaflet. This was enclosed with a letter from Lilian Wolfe to Malatesta which was intercepted by the police. The consequent raid on the *Freedom* office then brought to light another article just set up for *Freedom*, headed 'The Irish Rebellion' and worthy of a second charge.

On June 24th 1916 Tom Keell and Lilian Wolfe were tried at Clerkenwell Police Court under the Defence of the Realm Act (DORA). The charge arising from the second article was dismissed, but for the first article Keell was sentenced to a fine of £100 or three months imprisonment, and Wolfe to £25 or two months. Both refused to pay and were imprisoned.

The whole affair at least proved Freedom office to be quite a tempting place for the police, for it was raided three more times in the course of the next year. Despite all harassment Keell managed to keep Freedom going. The group so far responsible for the publication soon dissolved, the men hiding or going to the United States, and Mabel Hope and Elisabeth Archer also soon leaving for the States. From 1918 it was mainly Keell alone who did all the work, occasionally helped by Percy Meachem on the practical side, and then more and more by William Charles Owen, who eventually came to live with Tom and Lilian (and their son Tom junior) in their house in Willesden.

In the decade after the war Freedom's existence was a long struggle for survival, one appeal for help following the other. Except for a few comrades abroad, and W C Owen and Lilian Wolfe, nobody actually came to help. The price of *Freedom* was increased in May 1918 from Id to 2d; but the income in the mid-1920s was not more than that in 1914, when the printing costs were only about a third of those in 1925.

In December 1926 Keell officially retired as compositor to live off the superannuation income provided for by the Society of Compositors, and when in 1927 the London County Council gave notice to quit 127 Ossulston Street, as the whole quarter was to be pulled down, he issued a last desperate appeal, again to no avail. Finally, with the agreement of Lilian Wolfe and Owen, he decided to close down Freedom.

> I must be very sentimental as I do not mind telling you that a tear was hard to suppress when passing the final page proofs for the last time. *Freedom* has been a dear friend all these years and I could not part from it without feeling a wrench.

For others however the "death" of (this series of) *Freedom* proved to be quite a re-animating event, for though they had overlooked for years all statements of the desperate situation and all appeals for help, the fact that *Freedom* no longer turned up regularly in their letter-boxes eventually had more effect.

At a meeting arranged by Keell in February 1928, many faces that had been familiar before the war showed up again for the first time, and Keell...

> Was told that the enthusiasm of the movement would revive and *Freedom* could start again. The collapse of *Freedom*, I told them, was due to the collapse of the anarchist movement in this country and they should concentrate on a revival in London at least.

But still in August 1928 they had ...

> done nothing — absolutely nothing. Not one meeting have they held and not one pamphlet have they sold. They wrote a lot of letters, though, mainly to old comrades abroad, complaining about the dictatorship of a former servant.
>
> By what right do these people criticise Lilian and I and say we regard Freedom Office as our private property? For many years these people have never come near us to help and lift a finger — let alone their voice — in Anarchist propaganda. Lilian and I have stuck to our job here through thick and thin, and Owen has been a hard worker also, ever ready with his pen ... he has lent us money when we were in difficulties. Lilian has given at least £50 since 1914, and when my father died during the war and left me £160, at least £100 of it was swallowed up by *Freedom*.

Keell moved with the Freedom Press literature to Whiteway Colony (near Stroud), and published at irregular intervals a *Freedom Bulletin*. His old opponents from 1914 saw in this removal of the Freedom Press away from London only new fodder for their accusation of 'a dictatorship', and as a result of this altogether utterly unpleasant quarrel published from May 1930 on a paper called *Freedom (New Series)*, which however Keell (and other former members and friends of the Freedom Group, like Nettlau, Mabel Hope, Elizabeth Archer, Emma Goldman, Alexander Berkman, and others) did not recognise as a continuation of "the old *Freedom*". (The group itself it seems was soon dissatisfied with the poor standards of the new paper, and eventually Keell's old opponents dropped out, to be replaced by people sympathetic to him, like Victor Neuburg who became editor for a while in 1934, or even by his friends, like Oscar Swede and Harry Jones who became editors in November 1934.) Keell himself published 15 issues of the *Freedom Bulletin* between 1928 and 1932, and was from autumn 1928 secretary of the Whiteway Colony, but otherwise felt quite disillusioned.

> The event of 1930 had such a disheartening effect on me that I cannot get up any enthusiasm for anything that would mean co-operation with others. I do the work connected with Freedom Press because it is work I understand & does not call for any great effort, writing for the Bulletin is only an occasional effort and I also get some pleasure in knowing that I can help to spread our ideas.

With the labour movement as a whole he felt not happy either:

> They have concentrated on the economic side of the movement and never gave a thought to the libertarian side. Many years ago I heard a lecture by an old Fabian — I think his name was Leakey — on "The Morality of Socialism" in which he spoke of freedom and tolerance, saying that unless socialists gave more attention to the economic changes for which they were working would be of little value. But his voice was raised in vain. Everything has been put aside as Utopia. The "Scientific" Marxian philosophy, with its idea of an all-powerful State in which the individual would be number 232,855-B, has carried the day. "Freedom is a bourgeois idea," said Lenin, and all the Communists repeat it ad nauseam. We have been sliding down the slippery slope for years.

He found a consolation in working on the land, and most letters to friends contain references to sowing and the encouraging effect that seeing seeds grow has on the mind. In 1936 however he was again brought back to a more active role in the production and distribution of anarchist literature and papers, when he was approached by the son of an old Italian comrade to help with the distribution and eventually editing of *Italia Libera — Free Italy*; and he then helped with the production of the pamphlet *The Struggle for Liberty in Spain*, and, of course, with the new paper *Spain and the World*, which he eventually came to regard as the proper successor to the old *Freedom*. The success of *Spain and the World* cheered him up again a little at a time when

> We are even threatened with visits from officials who will measure us for gas masks. The gas mask seems to me the supreme symbol of the degradation of mankind. It is the lowest level I can imagine... when I think of the dreams of socialists and anarchists 30 or 40 years ago and the realities of the present day, it seems to me that those who died then cherishing their dreams are the last of that happy race. Today dreams are no longer possible. The world is faced with the herd instinct of fear.

He did not have to face this world much longer. He died some three weeks later, on June 26th 1938, at Whiteway, of heart failure. Tom Keell wrote no books or pamphlets, and only very few of his articles were signed; but he wrote most of the 'Notes' on the front page and the major part of the leaders of *Freedom* between 1914 and 1927.

Obituaries were published by Max Nettlau in *Spain and the World* (July 15th 1938; a corrected and expanded version was published shortly afterwards in the Yiddish *Freie Arbeiter Stimme* — the English manuscript of which survives in the Rocker collection in the International Institute of Social History, Amsterdam); by Harry Kelly and 'A Correspondent' (Dr Oscar Swede) in *MAN!* (September-October 1939). And Mat Kavanagh published a recollection in his series on *British Anarchists in Freedom* (18 January 1947).

~ *Heiner Becker*

Thomas Fauset MacDonald (1862-1910)

Born in Lanark to Thomas and Jane MacDonald, Fauset (he used this for his pen-name) grew up the son of a successful GP and followed his father into the profession, graduating in medicine and surgery from Glasgow University in 1882. He sailed to Australia and New Zealand in 1883, spending six years becoming a specialist in tropical diseases and contributing several reports to medical journals at the time. In 1889 he returned to Britain and began studying for a veterinary degree, which he achieved in 1892.

At this point, aged 30, there appears little to suggest that he was particularly politically active, having followed a vaguely interesting but not terribly noteworthy path through the medical profession and achieving much the same middle-class position as his parents before him. He seemingly hadn't made contact with the anarchists, as it was noted by David Nicoll (of whom more later) that Fauset only "came into the movement in the summer of 1893," spending money freely and "in favour of the most violent action." It is unclear exactly what sparked his conversion to the cause.

Fauset certainly made a splash in his first few months of activism, bringing funds, expertise and his travel bug to a movement that was constantly on its uppers. His apparent first ports of call were with middle-class socialist elements and Russian exiles, then moving on to correspondence with Peter Kropotkin and contact with the Commonweal and Freedom groups.

The Rossetti siblings paint a glowing portrait of the early involvement of Fauset in the socialist and anarchist sets in their book *A Girl Among the Anarchists*. As teenagers, the Rossettis published anarchist paper *The Torch* out of their father's basement, and Fauset appears to have contacted them at some point in 1893, shortly after they had acquired a printing press — his name began appearing as a contributor in June of that year. By 1894 he was the publisher.

While semi-fictional, the Rossetti's novel refers to numerous figures from around the time, and Fauset in particular gets a hefty role under the moniker "Dr Armitage." Writing of first meeting him, they describes attending a "small and stuffy" parlour room belonging to Nekrovitch (actually the Russian nihilist Sergey Stepnyak-Kravchinsky), mostly bare of furniture but full of well-connected and cosmopolitan people. Russian exiles, British liberals, socialists and Fabians mixed with "journalists and literary men whose political views were immaterial ... all manner of faddists, rising and impecunious musicians and artists—all were made welcome." Throughout the book, he is favourably compared with what they perceived to be a gruff and often lazy community of anarchists:

> Dr Armitage was one of the most noticeable figures in the English Anarchist movement, and it was with him that I first discussed Anarchist principles as opposed to those of legal Socialism
>
> ...
>
> Dr Armitage was a fanatic and an idealist, and two convictions were paramount in his mind at this time: the necessity and the justice of the "propaganda by force" doctrine preached by the more advanced Anarchists, and the absolute good faith and devotion to principle of the men with whom he was associated ... Not for a single instant had Armitage hesitated to throw open the doors of his Harley Street establishment to the Anarchists: to him the cause was everything, and interests, prudence, prospects, all had to give way before it.

It's easy to see why the politically-minded teenagers might have gotten on with Fauset in 1893. In among a variety of dilettante London worthies and heavily bearded international hardliners the handsome 31-year-old doctor, as thoroughly middle-class and mannered as they, appears to have been gregarious, enthusiastic and genuine, friends with eminent figures. He was especially connected with *Commonweal* by May 1st of that year, acting as its financial backer (with Max Nettlau) during the editorship of tailor Henry B Samuels.

The appointment of Samuels as acting editor had been controversial. Stridently anti-trade union, he was of the opinion that Englishmen — and only Englishmen — should be free to blackleg. Along with a strong position in favour of propaganda of the deed (ie. terror to "wake up the people"), which comrades of the time such as Max Nomad noted always seemed to involve action being taken "by others," he seemed an odd choice to follow publisher Charlie Mowbray and former editor David Nicoll, who had both been jailed for 12 months in connection to the Walsall bombing plot. He was however very much on Fauset's wavelength, and when Nicoll tried to regain his editorship in December 1893, he found Fauset blocking the way:

> Tom Cantwell acted as porter and excluded all 'possible disturbers'. The usual pretext was they were 'not members' of the 'Commonweal Group'. Most London anarchists were not, the Commonweal Group consisting of about a dozen members (...) If however a man's principles were alright, i.e. if he were a friend of Mr Samuels, they let him in. Besides the benefits of 'scientific packing', Mr Samuels had the advantage of the official support of the Freedom people. There were two delegates present – Agnes Henry and Dr Macdonald. Miss Henry was neutral, Dr Macdonald supported Samuels with enthusiasm (...) Seeing how everything had been 'arranged' I threw up the editorship.

Though there are suspicious elements to Samuels' time in the movement, Quail notes that no more than circumstantial proofs were ever offered that he was anything other than an anarchist. What is certainly true however is that Samuels ran a paper that was dedicated to a spectacular and insurrectionist approach, which inspired Fauset to keep his wallet open seemingly until shortly after Samuels was deposed in June 1894 under suspicion of being a police ringer. Funding dried up just a month later, and Commonweal closed that August.

The catalyst for Samuels' demise as editor was the Greenwich Observatory incident of 1894, in which Martial Bourdin blew off his own hand and killed himself while trying to plant a bomb. Bourdin died hours later, saying nothing about his accomplices, but Samuels was quickly put in the frame for having potentially provided the explosive materials.

The movement had come under intense pressure from the public in the aftermath, with an angry mob attempting to overturn Bourdin's hearse during the funeral march and anarchist events being attacked by reactionary elements, including direct action from police to disrupt anarchist organising, both covert and overt. May 1st saw police-led attacks against public anarchist meetings.

In this atmosphere, Samuels was busy bragging about his links to Bourdin. Then, at the end of May, David Nicoll (who was holding a grudge against Samuels over his ongoing editorship of Commonweal) reported a story where Samuels had come good on a boast that he could lay his hands on sulphuric acid to another tailor by handing him a small vial of the substance — the other man's house was raided two days later.

At a subsequent meeting, Nicoll relates, Samuels was confronted over his handing out of acids and his links to Bourdin, and admitted both, subsequently being expelled from Commonweal. In mounting his doomed defence however, Samuels noted that he had acquired most of his materiel from the stocks of his good friend Fauset MacDonald.

There is a direct parallel in the report of this confrontation by Nicoll and a scene in Rossetti's novel, in which she describes Armitage/Fauset as being shocked by Samuels' admission. Whether he actually spoke to her on the subject or not is unknown, but her characterisation is as follows:

> After some seconds' hesitation Armitage [Fauset] replied: "I do not desire or intend to go into any details here concerning my past conversations or relations with Jacob Myers [Samuels], neither do I consider myself in any way bound to discuss here the motives which prompted, or which I thought prompted his actions, and the requests he made of me. As Anarchists we have not the right to judge him, and all we can do is to refuse to associate ourselves any further with him, which I, for one, shall henceforth do. The knowledge of his own abominable meanness should be punishment enough for Myers.

Fauset could not entirely disassociate himself from the situation however, inasmuch as he had also found himself in Nicoll's line of fire. For Nicoll, Fauset was as much to blame for the Greenwich debacle and the subsequent police crackdown as Samuels and Bourdin, acting as a silent partner in providing the explosive chemicals, and he said as much when the doctor visited him in Sheffield a month later:

> I have stated that Dr Macdonald declined an inquiry into the case, though I told him plainly at Sheffield that I suspected

him. My readers will see that not only Dr Macdonald, but the "Freedom Group" have joined in the conspiracy of silence, and done their best to hush up the case.

Certainly it was true that *Freedom* hadn't backed Nicoll, much as it hadn't covered his activities since his release from prison, and it seems plausible that Fauset could have used his connections through *Freedom* to outmanouver Nicoll in the broader movement, as Nicoll was already by this point considered something of a crank by many senior voices, including Kropotkin and Max Nettlau. Fauset's willingness and ability to travel brought him a wealth of contacts across the country, allowing him to take on a tour of Dublin (April 1894), Sheffield (June/July 1894) Leicester (July 1894) and Manchester (late 1894). By August, Nicoll was being accused of having "spy mania" by John Turner and pressed to cease publishing screeds accusing Samuels and MacDonald.This was partially successful, as after his initial accusations Nicoll remained silent until 1897, by which time Fauset's anarchist boat had long since sailed.

Fauset seems to have left for Australia at some point between August and October of that year, to seek a new life omitting bombs and fractious British anarchism.

The White Supremacist Anarchist
It's possible that Fauset entertained some racist thinking before he began his long boat ride to the other side of the world — his good friend H B Samuels was certainly of the opinion that Englishmen were of superior stock and "racialism" was hardly uncommon at the time. He seemed to hold no particular grudge towards the Irish however, as he happily went to talk in Dublin in 1894, shortly before he left, at a time when anti-Irish prejudice was rampant. His attitude towards his hosts was approvingly cited in the local press:

He is a Scotsman, cool and shrewd in manner. Not once, even when closely "heckled," as they would say in his own country, did he show any sign of heat. His arguments may be put thus. He objects to any form of artificial government to begin with: but he would not remove our governors by the summary method of lifting them into the air in so many atoms. He desires to remove Parliament by a natural and constitutional process. To workingmen, he says, absorb the "blacklegs," form free associations, let those associations associate with other associations, and go on developing

in this manner until great international federations are
established ... the lecturer is a great believer in Darwin's
theory of evolution, and referred to this subject frequently to
enforce his arguments.

At this point in his life he appears to have been in favour of an
internationalist approach, but was also prone to looking at life
through the lens of evolutionary theory — sometimes a precursor to
the developing of a "social Darwinist" outlook and not unacquainted
with racism towards non-Europeans.

His interest in the supremacy of the white race however only
bloomed into full-fledged activism during his time in Australia,
opening the oddest chapter in Fauset's exceedingly strange political
journey — one which suggests he was never a mole, for what logic
would send a police undercover from the heart of anarchist London
to a Australian frontier town in order to found a racist class struggle
movement?

But this bizzare project would eventually drive Fauset's politics
in the latter years of his life, and while his two years in London
were hidden from the *British Medical Journal's* obituary writers,
who instead were fed (or made up) a cock-and-bull story about a
two year medical studying jaunt around Germany, America, Italy,
Egypt, China and Japan, his efforts to "pioneer the White Australia
movement" were officially documented.

He settled, initially, in Queensland, where he initially made
his name as a vet, dealing with a tick epidemic in 1895-6, but
seems to have also tried to immediately immerse himself in radical
circles around Sydney. Joining the Australasian Association for
the Advancement of Science (Aaas, now Anzaas) he wrote for
Sydney's *The Worker* in 1896 on "the social question" castigating
the iniquities of government, opining that "the laws of the universe
are anarchical" and expressing his admiration for the Surplus
Labor League.

The next year, he delivered a paper to the Aaas on Kropotkin's
approach to anarchism, and then moved around 2,300 miles north
as the crow flies to set up a cottage hospital at Geraldton (now
Innisfail) — Dr T F MacDonald's Bureau of Tropical Disease and
Cottage Hospital.

The outback village could not have been further away from the
electric, seething paranoid circles he had frequented in Britain.
Settled as a post office site just 25 years prior, Geraldton wouldn't
have its own paper until 1906 and even today contains just 9,000
people.

Due to a goldrush in the surrounding area, it did become a more multicultural place than most while Fauset lived there, with First Peoples and Anglo-Celtic settlers quickly being outnumbered by "Kanaka" South Sea Islanders. Aboriginal and Torres Strait workers, Chinese miners who developed the banana industry and retail businesses, French merchants, and German timber and sugar producers — though the most influential Italian influx wouldn't happen until Fauset had moved on.

It is possible that Geraldton was where he first developed the disdain for non-English peoples that would lead to his embrace of eugenics. He certainly had a difficult time at the colony, struggling to deal with a hookworm infestation which he found "deeply rooted and flourishing among the inhabitants of the Johnstone River District." Nine out of ten children were infected, and MacDonald recorded a trend for them eating dirt as an "irresistible craving," saying that such children became pale, disobedient, cunning, dishonest and immoral. Affected adults meanwhile he believed to have developed an extreme fondness for pickles, curry and alcohol and were lazy and aggressive. His requests for help to stamp out the infections in 1900 were ignored by the Queensland government as sensational nonsense.

Fauset refused to give up however, and the nearest larger town to Geraldton at that time was (and largely still is) Brisbane, so it was to the Brisbane Courier that he wrote in 1903, complaining again about the "earth-eating" disease. It appears that 1903 is the same year he was swayed to the cause of eugenics.

While she gets his place of birth wrong, Diana Wyndham's description in her thesis Striving For National Fitness of "Tom" F MacDonald, a Queensland doctor running a 30-bed hospital in a "north Queensland town" from 1896-1906 could hardly be anyone else, and she gives an insight into his movements in those years:

In January 1905 he wrote to Francis Galton at the Eugenics Record Office in the University of London to enquire about his Eugenics fellowship and to offer himself as an applicant. He explained that he had read about it in an Australian paper, which appears to be the first reference to eugenics in an Australian newspaper. His application included a reference to a paper (renamed "Evolution and Sociology") which he had read at congresses in 1903 and 1905.

Fauset noted to Galton that he would have to keep his interest off the written page, as he hoped to sell articles to the London press on the subject in due course, but his interest clearly extended to his organising and speaking activities, as he would would go on to flat out argue the case for Eugenics on the basis of increasing white control of labour in his 1907 book *Experiences of Ankylostomiasis in Australia*. In it he suggested that southern Europeans were particularly vulnerable to hookworm infection (ie. laziness and fighting), and noted approvingly that "South Sea Island, and other coloured labour generally, has been replaced by workers of our own people in fulfilment of the national ideals of 'White Australia' ... the Caucasian skin has been presented with an opportunity of proving its power to survive." He really was off the deep end by that point — not even kidding, he'd patented a diving suit in July 1906.

By the winter of 1906, Fauset had had enough. At some point between July and November he upped sticks and got on a boat headed East, to New Zealand, arriving in Wellington in time to be the guest speaker of the Socialist Party there at an event advertised, suitably, by their party paper — *Commonweal*:

> A visiting speaker from Australia, Dr T F McDonald, 'also referred to the US Governmental conspiracy which led to the judicial murder of Parsons and his comrades', before proceeding with his prepared speech on the philosophical inheritance of Kropotkin, Bakunin and others.

A noteable thing about the writeup is that Fauset clearly still felt himself to be in touch with the anarchist movement while he was pursuing his Rights for Whites campaign in Australia. In *Sewing Freedom: Philip Josephs, Transnationalism & Early New Zealand Anarchism*, Jared Davidson looks into this period of his life:

> When he arrived in New Zealand, the London ex-pat 'introduced himself to the then honorary secretary of the Wellington Branch of the Socialist Party as an anarchist communist,' and energetically engaged himself in the scene. Macdonald's 'clearness of vision' and 'honesty of purpose' was put to good use."
>
> "As well as lecturing on behalf of the Discharged Prisoners' Aid Society, he gave numerous talks on socialism and anarchism, published a number of medical pamphlets and regularly penned articles in the *Commonweal*, such as 'Humanist Interpretations of Crime'; 'The Prime Minister' (a satirical text mocking those in power); and 'Freedom and Union'—"the principles which provide the anarchist-

communistic ideal of a freely federated humanity.

In late 1906, he toured the country advocating for an Imperial Labour Conference in London, which was warmly approved of in a printed address to Macdonald delivered by "representatives of the labour movement, the Socialist Party, and others interested in the economic advances of the masses." The undersigned recognised "the enormous potentialities of a gathering of Labour representatives," and added, "we believe the seed you have sown amongst us will grow." His activity eventually caught the attention of conservative cartoonist William Blomfield, who put ink to paper in order to ridicule Macdonald's revolutionary politics.

But eugenics were never far from the surface for Fauset after 1903, and alongside keeping up a steady stream of racist writings. Davidson notes:

> Numerous press interviews, pamphlets, and letters to Nettlau [from the time] are rife with discriminate statements that betray his racism. The labour question in the antipodes, wrote Macdonald, faced "the element of cheap, coloured, absolutely servile alien labour... with the presence of Japanese, Chinese and other eastern peoples, the workers of Australia have had an extra battle to fight.

Indeed MacDonald, still friends with Peter Kropotkin, wasn't afraid to push his line internationally. In a quite extraordinary rant published first in *Freedom* and then in Emma Goldman's *Mother Earth* in 1907 he argued that:

> For some 30 years the work in tropical agriculture fell entirely into the hand sof cheap alien workers, who were in reality slaves, having neither social privileges extended to them, nor could they in their helpless ignorance form even the simplest institution of of self-defence. In the mines, Chinese labour had to be opposed.; in the pearl fisheries, the Japanese.

With some pride he goes on to argue that white Australian labour had successfully forced out this "hydra-headed enemy" before decrying its fall into parliamentarianism. It appears that *Mother Earth* made less fuss (this was a magazine that also carried adverts for the *American Journal of Eugenics* in the same edition) than the New Zealand Socialist Party, whose members slated him and called him out for lying about having acquired their official recommendation in the first place. He fell out of favour with the group and was officially declared persona non grata in July 1907, the same month in which he set up the White Race League, placing himself as president.

Fauset's presidency was shortlived however, and with the humiliation of yet another public rousting from erstwhile comrades looming, he once again took his heels to the other side of the globe — by September he was back in Liverpool, taking in a whirlwind tour of his old mates (including a visit to Kropotkin in Paris) before returning to Britain to bring the Good News of socialist eugenicism.

For the next two years he appears to have toured, spoken, and in 1909 he published a book of verse, *North Sea Lyrics*. In 1910 he took up a post with Compagnie de Kong in San Pedro, Ivory Coast, and worked there until his death from yellow fever on December 14th, aged 48.

~ Rob Ray

Alfred Marsh (1895-1914)

After Charlotte Wilson resign the editorship in January 1895 *Freedom* ceased publication for three months and was revived in May mainly through the efforts of Alfred Marsh, who for the next nearly 20 years ensured the survival of the paper.

Alfred Marsh was born in Clerkenwell on November 3rd 1858. His mother died early and his father, a close personal friend of George Jacob Holyoake, married Holyoake's daughter. Thereby young Alfred had, as he was to put it later, 'the good fortune to enter the good fortune to enter life with a secularity education' and had 'the advantage to read and hear hear discussed the principles of Free Thought from early childhood on.' 'It is great luck to start one's life with a mind free of theological dogmas and the fogs of superstition.' Not surprising in a secularist household of the tune, he was much influence by the writings of Robert Owen and even more by those of Dr Henry Travis.

In about 1883 he came across a copy of Bakunin's *God and the State*, which 'enormously impressed me by the dear, intrepid and convincing logic with which he dissected our political and social institutions'. Around this time he broke with his father who, convinced freethinker as he was, would not forgive his son marrying one of the girls from his brush factory. From then on till his father's death more than 20 years later Alfred Marsh had to live (and sometimes supported *Freedom* to a considerable extent) from his meagre earnings as a violinist (the fiddle has a long tradition in the Freedom Group). As John Turner (who certainly did not suffer the same deficiency) deplored later: 'He was just as modest about his musical talents as everything else. It was a pity he had not more confidence, for many with less ability secured popular favour and financial success where he remained obscure.'

He joined the Social Democratic Federation in 1886, but soon left again appalled by the intrigues of the different cliques and the personal ambitions of certain individuals in the SDF. Much impressed by the Haymarket affair and the speeches of the Haymarket defendants, he became a convinced anarchist-communist. When in February 1888, the first series of *Freedom* discussion meetings started, he was among the regular attendants, and in September read a paper on 'Work and Social Utility', subsequently his first (identifiable) article in *Freedom* (October 1888). He very soon became identified with the Freedom Group, and from then on contributed regularly to the paper, mostly anonymously (e.g. 'Anarchism and Organisation', March 1889), pseudonymously (e.g. as DIABOL., 'Anarchy, Communism, and Competition', July 1891), or signed M. (Individual or Common Property', October 1890), When *Freedom* ceased publication in January 1895, he took the initiative to get it re-started in May and on the advice of *Freedom's* compositor, William Wess, asked the former members of the Commonweal Group, John Turner, Tom Cantwell, and Joseph Pressburg to join the Freedom Group. It was mainly he who was responsible for the paper's survival in the following very difficult years for anarchism in Britain, especially during the Jingo reaction of 1899-1902, the time of the Boer Wars.

In 1907 he edited the first eight numbers of the syndicalist paper published by Freedom Press, the *Voice of Labour*. He believed strongly in the efficiency of cheap literature, and when after the death of his father he inherited some money, he ensured the publication of the first complete edition of Bakunin's *God and the State*, and provided the means for reprinting the whole range of Freedom Pamphlets, not to mention a whole series of propaganda leaflets, in 1909. Parly in 1910, already in very poor health, he made with his wife his only journey abroad, to Paris and the South of France and to visit Kropotkin in Rapallo, finding him surrounded by rich sycophants and melancholically squeezing out a few minutes to see anarchist friends from England. In 1912 he resigned the task of acting editor to Thomas Keell, though he retained the final decision in matters of controversy.

His health now gave way rapidly and he rarely would be in London, living most of the time in Hastings. In September 1914 he was operated upon, only to confirm that he had an inoperable cancer, and he died on October 13th 1914, in his fifty-sixth year. All tributes paid to him mention his extreme modesty and absolute sincerity, while stressing how much the movement was indebted to him. As Thomas Keell summarised it, Freedom's existence to 1914 'is almost solely due to his courage and his faith in anarchism. His pen and his purse were always at its service, and on several occasions his last half-sovereign ensured the publication of the paper ... As a writer he was simple and clear ... to him, the Social Revolution meant a revolution in ideas and a clean sweep of the mass of superstition — economic, religious, and sexual — which clogs the minds of the people'.

Alfred Marsh wrote no books or pamphlets; most of his articles were published anonymously ot signed only with his initials, and nearly only in *Freedom*. The most concise summary of his ideas is his article 'Anarchist Communism: Its Aims and Principles (signed freedom Group, London) in in *The Reformers' Year Book: 1902* (London & New York), also published as a Freedom leaflet.

~ *Heiner Becker*

Rita Milton (1924–2011)

Born in the middle class district of Kelvinside in Glasgow on May 31st 1924, Rita was the daughter of Alexander Inglis Milton, a left Scots nationalist who was curator of Annan Burgh museum and editor of the New Scot (1945-1959) one of the Scottish 'reconstruction' journals that emerged after the Second World War. one of her three older brothers fought in Spain in 1936.

She became a shop assistant at the age of 17, before being conscripted into the Women's Land Army during World War Two.

In 1945 she started working with her father in Glasgow at the New Scot, journal of the Scottish Reconstruction Committee. Its offices were located above the Cockburn pub, in Campbell Street and here she met the anarchist Eddie Shaw and was impressed by his oratory. She began to attend meetings of the Glasgow Anarchists where she acted as chairperson. These meetings took place on Sunday evenings and attracted hundreds of people (the pubs were closed on Sunday in Scotland and there was no television then). Here she heard speeches by the likes of Jimmy Raeside, Jimmy Dick, Frank Leech and Eddie Shaw:

I came to London in 1946 to attend what I believe was the first post-war Anarchist Summer School ... I stayed at Burgess Hill School with Tony and Betty Gibson ... Here I met Philip Sansom who later introduced me to the Freedom Press Group ...

I was the first anarchist to speak to millions on television. I got a lot of letters and it was a bit of fun, but we knew that any immediate propaganda value would be lost when the next programme was switched on.

The television appearance Rita refers to here was a debate in 1952 with the Marriage Guidance Council, where she used her wit and sarcasm to defeat these puritanical bigots.

Rita established a relationship with Philip Sansom, another of the speakers at Hyde Park. Philip was then an editor of *War Commentary* which soon changed its name to *Freedom*. She worked with him at Express Printers which was owned by Freedom Press. She worked for two of Express Printers customers, as editor of *Sewing Machine Times* and as production editor of *The Journal of Sex Education*.

As a redoubtable orator Rita spoke at the Hyde Park and Tower Hill pitches. She was one of the leading lights in the returning confidence of British anarchism in reaching out and spreading anarchist ideas as for example at the May 1st public meeting put on by the London Anarchist Group in 1951 at Holborn Town Hall on Internationalism and War where she spoke alongside Jack Rubin, Mat Kavanagh and Philip Sansom. She was also one of those who drew up a list of debating societies in London and arranged debates on anarchism with them.

She was one of the founders of the Malatesta Club in 1954. Here she met another anarchist, Hew Warburg, son of Fredric Warburg of the publishers Secker and Warburg. For some time the three shared a house, until Philip moved out in an amicable arrangement. When the son of Rita and Hew, John, reached the age of 15, they married so that Rita could receive the benefits of a legally married widow, Hew had been unwell for some time and died in 1983.

Later Rita's own health took a turn for the worse, though she continued to subscribe to *Freedom* and to support it financially. Towards the end of her life she had a stroke which deprived her of the ability to read. She decided to end her life by refusing food and died on December 17th 2011.

~ *Nick Heath*

Max Nettlau (1865-1944)

Nettlau is best known as the 'Herodotus of Anarchy' — that is, as its first and greatest historian — and less as an anarchist militant. Yet he was one of the most assiduous contributors to *Freedom*, if not the most assiduous, for over 40 years.

Max Nettlau was born on April 30th 1865 in Neuwaldegg near Vienna (and all his life regretted missing the First of May so narrowly). His father — a Prussian — was court gardener to Prince Schwarzenberg. His parents (and especially his father, as he always stressed) gave him a liberal and secularist education, and he spent most of his childhood playing on his own in and exploring the great garden, an experience that influenced him deeply and had some bearing on his understanding of anarchism as the most natural form of life. He came to socialism when still a student, between 1878 and 1880, and while a number of his schoolmates were social democrats (and were later to play leading roles in Austrian and German social democracy), Nettlau soon regarded himself as an anarchist-communist (and a very 'revolutionary' one — more than 45 years later he was quite embarrassed to be reminded that around 1883 he had even drawn up a kind of 'murder list': who and in what order was to be eliminated during a revolution).

From Autumn 1882 on he studied philology, soon specialising in the Celtic languages, and he received his doctorate for a thesis 'Contributions to the Cymric Grammar' (Spring 1887). While working on his thesis, he came to London in October 1885 and immediately joined the Socialist League (the only organisation he was ever to join, and to him always the 'ideal' political organisation with its concentration on education and the building up of political consciousness).

Living just off Tottenham Court Road at the time, he joined the Bloomsbury branch, the centre of Marxist intrigues against the anti-parliamentarian policy of the League, and he claimed later that this 'workshop in practical Marxism' facilitated his understanding of the Marxist intrigues in the First International. The *Commonweal* published also his first political articles, the very first one actually being one on Marx on the fifth anniversary of his death (March 10th 1888, signed Y Y). In July 1889 he attended the International Socialist Congress in Paris (the Founding Congress of the Second International) as delegate of the Norwich branch of the Socialist League; and from May to September 1890 he served on the council of the League. Between May and August 1890 he edited and financed The *Anarchist Labour Leaf*, four numbers of which were published and distributed gratis and which consisted entirely of articles by Nettlau and Henry Davis, who had been one of the most active anarchist-communists in the Socialist League — mostly in the East End. Davis was shortly later to change colours and declared himself an individualist, which prompted Nettlau's first contribution to *Freedom* ('Communism and Anarchy', May 1891; signed N). In these years he wrote also his first longer and more substantial historical articles — 'Joseph Dejacque — a predecessor of communist Anarchism' (published in Johann Most's *Freiheit*, January-February 1890), and 'The Historical Development of Anarchism' (*Freiheit*, April-May 1890, reprinted as a pamphlet), the nucleus of his later historical works, and the first results of his studies of Bakunin, 'Notes for a Biography of Bakunin' (*Freiheit*, January-April 1891).

In March 1892 his father died and left him a small fortune, enabling him from now on to devote all his time 'to study, to travel and to collect' material for the biography of Bakunin and on the history of anarchism and socialism in general. In 1893/94 he was active in the Commonweal Group (the continuation of the London Socialist League) and wrote for the group 'Why we arc Anarchists' (published anonymously in 1893 as a series in the *Commonweal*, and reprinted as a pamphlet in 1894). At the request of a number of comrades, he wrote *An Anarchist Manifesto* issued by the London Anarchist Communist Alliance (London, May 1895), approved of and slightly 'corrected' by Kropotkin. After the merging of the Commonweal and Freedom Groups in April/May 1895, he eventually joined the Freedom Group, and after the closing down of *The Torch* provided (with another German, Bernhard Kampffmeyer) the means to acquire the press and printing equipment of the *Torch* and rent its premises at 127 Ossulston Street, for *Freedom* and 'the movement' (Spring 1896).

With Joseph Pressburg ('Perry') he did the work to prepare the anarchist meetings in connection with the International Socialist Congress in London, July 1896. He and Pressburg actually were also the 'Spanish Atrocity Committee' in 1897, Nettlau doing all necessary translations and writing nearly all articles on the subject for *Freedom*, the *Labour Leader*, and other papers. (He was also the author of the committee's pamphlet *The Revival of the Inquisition*, 1897.)

Between 1896 and 1900 he wrote and 'autocopied' in 50 copies his huge biography of Bakunin, and in 1897 also published his *Bibliographie de l'Anarchie*, still the standard work on the subject up to that date.

After the mid-1890s Nettlau's own anarchism changed, and from being a rather dogmatic anarchist-communist he developed his own variety of anarchism without labels, stressing more and more the need for mutual toleration especially among anarchists — this being a fruit both of his historical studies and of his personal experiences with all sorts of religious wars in the movement. One of the earliest published results of this development was a lecture (one of only four lectures he gave in his life) which he gave to the *Freedom* discussion group on December 5th 1899, and which always remained one of his pet productions — 'Responsibility and Solidarity in the Labour Struggle', published in *Freedom* (January-April 1900) and reprinted as a Freedom Pamphlet. (The Freedom Group also sent it as a report to the International Anarchist Congress in Paris, Summer 1900.)

He continued his work on Bakunin in these years, summarising his findings in four unpublished volumes of supplements to the biography; and from around 1900 he started collecting more books as a form of sport, spending most of the year on the Quais in Paris and around Farringdon Road and Charing Cross Road in London, usually getting very nervous when in October/November he still had not reached the magic figure of 1,000 for the yearly additions to his collection.

He nevertheless continued some research (mainly on Buonarroti and the Secret Societies) and of course his regular contributions to *Freedom*, most of which are either unsigned, or published with initials (N, MN, or X, XX — in *Spain and the World* XXX — XYZ, **).

Between 1896 and 1913 he contributed to *Freedom* most of the International Notes, all the 'Reviews of the Year' (usually published in the January number), historical and general articles, obituaries, and many reviews. He always enjoyed being provocative, opposing 'Esperanto from an Anarchist Point of View' (December 1906, and debate in following numbers), on the small nationalities and their movements for 'independence' (the Balkans), being here the most fervent opponent of Kropotkin (January 1909; January 1913), or on 'Anarchism: Communist or Individualist? Both' (March, May 1914).

He prepared for Freedom Press the revised and augmented edition of Bakunin's *God and the State* (1909-10), thus fulfilling what he had proposed in his Postscript to Tom Cantwell's 1894 edition.

He spent the First World War in Vienna, and in letters and discussions with friends supported Austria-Hungary, thereby continuing his opposition to Kropotkin in the question of national politics (though his own stand was much more ambiguous than

Kropotkin's support of the Allies). In the post-war inflation he lost all his money, and for some years thereafter lived on the edge of starvation, until Tom Keell and other friends started to send regular food parcels, to the joy not only of the post office employees and their families, but eventually also of Nettlau. From now on he had to live as 'a slave of his pen', first thanking the American Society of Friends not only for their food parcels but also for 'the pleasant experience of contact with people who try — despite all religious narrow-mindedness — to uphold their human dignity'.

For a while he wrote regularly for the *Christian Science Monitor* (though that must have caused him, a life-long freethinker, some problems), then subsequently he made a very meagre living by writing for a number of anarchist publications who could afford to pay occasionally for contributions, especially the *Freie Arbeiter Stimme* of New York, *La Protesta* of Buenos Aires, *La Revista Blanca* of Barcelona, and the anarcho-syndicalists in Germany and Sweden.

From 1919 on he also resumed writing for *Freedom* (unpaid, as *Freedom* itself had to fight for survival). His last contribution in 1914 had been on 'The Literature of Anarchism' (September). The first one after the war was 'The Tragedy of German-Austria: An Appeal from Vienna' (September 1919), 'from an Austrian comrade, well known in the anarchist movement both here and on the continent, but who does not desire his name to be published'. All his further articles in 1919-1920 then concern 'The present situation in Austria', until in September 1920, at the suggestion of Tom Keell, he published in *Freedom* the first of a series of biographies of Malatesta (each one enlarged and corrected). This was the first of the major historical works which were to occupy him for the next 15 years. The most important ones are: several articles on Kropotkin; a biography of Bakunin (4 volumes, unpublished except the first few chapters); two biographies of Reclus (1928 in German; revised and enlarged edition in Spanish 1929-30, 2 volumes); three volumes on *The International, Bakunin and the Alliance in Spain* (published 1929, 1930 and 1969); a study of Bakunin and the International in Italy (1928); and most important of all his huge *History of Anarchist Ideas*, of which only three volumes were published in his lifetime.

All these (and innumerable articles as well) had to be written under difficult circumstances, since although Nettlau had the most comprehensive collection on anarchism in existence, and had collected before the war all sorts of information from and about people in the movement, most of this was stored away in depositories in France and England which were inaccessible to him.

In all these years he continued to write first for *Freedom*, then the *Freedom Bulletin*. In 1936 he wrote the major part of the pamphlet *The struggle for Liberty in Spain 1840-1936* at the request of Vernon Richards, and also the first leading article for *Spain and the World*, July-November 1936 in Spain, signed XXX.

He continued to write for *Spain and the World*, including many other articles on Spain, a long and very critical review of E H Carr's biography of Bakunin, and a series on the early history of anarchist ideas in England.

He eventually broke with *Spain and the World* over the attitude its editors took towards the CNT involvement in the government and the criticism of Federica Montseny in particular, whom Nettlau, very untypically, supported absolutely uncritically.

In 1935 he sold his collection to the International Institute of Social History in Amsterdam, and here in 1938, for the first time in his life, he saw all parts of his collection 'united'. He lived in Amsterdam from that year on, writing a version of his memoirs, classifying materials from his collection, and then seeing a major part of his (and other) collections seized by the Germans in 1940. Between 1940 and 1944 he wrote the last version of his memoirs, some 6,000 pages of 'Reminiscences and Impressions' of a 'libertarian socialist without a public sphere of activity, known to small circles as student of historical socialist materials, collector of such documents and printed matter ... and also as an exponent of some from-the-routine-departing opinions ...'

Max Nettlau died in Amsterdam on July 23rd 1944. His work and his collection, the most important source for the history of anarchism and anti-authoritarian thought in general, arc not forgotten; many of his writings are reprinted again and again. Nevertheless they are rarely properly used by those who write about anarchist history. Is this just to avoid the depressing experience that, whatever field one might enter, one would have to acknowledge that somebody else has been there several decades before?

~ Heiner Becker

William Charles Owen (1854-1929)

W C Owen played an important part in *Freedom* after the First World War. He was also one of the very few English anarchists who played an important part in politics outside Britain: the first 32 years of his life in radical movements were nearly all spent in the United States.

Owen was born on February 16th 1854 at Dinapore in Bengal Province (now Danapur in Bihar State), India — one of the centres of the Indian Mutiny of 1857. Born into a military and medical family, he was the posthumous son of Dr William Charles Owen, an assistant surgeon in the medical department of the Bengal Army; his mother was Adelaide Anne Owen.

The child was soon brought to England; little is known of his childhood and youth because, though he was often asked to write his memoirs and even eventually agreed to do so, he apparently never wrote them. Occasionally in an article or letter he said that his 'memory goes back to boyish days when we collected money desperately for the Lancashire cotton spinners who were starving by the tens of thousands owing to the American civil war which had brought the production of cotton to a standstill'. He was educated at Wellington College, and studied law, but never qualified. He married against the wishes of his family, and left with his wife for the United States in 1882; there he stayed for a while in New York, until in 1884 he moved westwards to San Francisco, working as a teacher and journalist. On the West Coast of America he became a socialist ...

> not from books, or any reading about economic determinism, the class struggle, or all that exceedingly dubious philosophy with which we fret our brains, but from the poverty of a great city that stank beneath my nose. When I had money I found myself exceedingly unhappy and melancholy at the constant thought that I was living, a useless parasite, by levying tribute. When I ceased to have money I was, at least, equally unhappy over the perpetual tribute levied on me. It did not take any profound reasoning or erudite scholarship to convince me that, fix the thing which way I would, there was no genuine happiness under existing conditions.

He came to know Burnette G Haskell, the Californian radical, and joined the International Workingmen's Association (the 'Red International', as opposed to the 'Black International', the International Working People's Association of John Most and other anarchists and social revolutionaries); in 1885 he was secretary of its central committee. He contributed to Haskell's paper *Truth*, and eventually became the editor of the *Nationalist*, a socialist paper published in Los Angeles and then San Francisco. So far he had been influenced in his 'socialism' mainly by the writings of Herbert Spencer and especially Henry George; now he began to read Kropotkin, and 'his writings revolutionised my own life and convinced me of the necessity of universal revolution; he ... showed me the sternness of the economic struggle and the power of the allied privileges that mass themselves under the shelter of the State ... He made me, in a word, a rebel, inspired me with those prodigious hopes which, as he himself so clearly shows, are the mothers of revolutions.' He translated and published, 'as best I could, everything by Kropotkin on which I could lay my hands'. Thus he produced the first English translation of Kropotkin's *Words of a Rebel* in various American labour papers (especially the *Avant-Courier* of Portland, Oregon).

Regarding himself now as an anarchist, he got in touch with the socialist movement in England and soon wrote articles mainly about labour subjects in the United States for the *Commonweal*, the paper of the Socialist League. In 1890 he moved back to New York and was instrumental in setting up a New York Socialist League; he got acquainted with Saverio Merlino, a member of the original Freedom Group, who had just moved to the United States and in 1892 started to publish in New York Solidarity, to which Owen contributed. In November 1892 he returned for a while to England and in December of that year he was expelled from the NY Socialist League for 'deserting his young wife who will soon become a mother'. At the beginning of 1893 he lectured at a number of occasions in London, mainly to the Autonomic Club in Windmill Street; one talk was on 'The New American Revolution', which then formed his first contribution to *Freedom* (June 1893).

After a few months he returned to the United States. In 1894 he proposed to produce a regular American page in *Freedom*, but nothing came of the idea. Then his anarchism underwent a substantial change: he became influenced by Benjamin Tucker, and "his cold logic saved me from what threatened to become chronic Kropotkin hysteria". Owen found himself 'steadily drifting away from communism, just as I had been compelled to drift away from State socialism'.

Following the discovery of gold at Klondike in 1896 he tried his luck there for two winters, 'but gained nothing but experience'. He eventually returned to California, worked again as journalist and especially as court-police reporter (which eventually led to a book on crime and criminals), and contributed regularly to the anarchist press (for example *Free Society* and Emma Goldman's *Mother Earth*).

From now on he concentrated with particular energy on the land question; and he soon felt himself vindicated when he got drawn into the agitation around the Mexican Revolution: 'My own experience is that if you attempt to discuss politics with the Mexican proletarian he shows no interest, but that the moment you mention the word "land" he becomes alert'. His involvement in the Mexican struggle between 1910 and 1916 was his most active time in the working-class movement. 'Of all the heart-breaking experiences that propaganda work has brought me, none begins to equal that through which I find myself passing in connection with the Mexican revolution ... The Mexican Revolution... is literally a titanic struggle, for it is against the money power of the world'. From the beginning he regarded the Mexican Revolution not 'as a subject on which the various camps of the international revolutionary movement should take sides, and never have I felt myself called on to endorse the particular creed of the Magons or other Mexican agitators.

From the first I have regarded it as a struggle by many millions of the disinherited to win hack their heritage; as a battle for the right to live ... A second French Revolution is being fought out in Mexico: a stand-up fight between the proletariat and the money power ... this may prove more important in its ultimate results than did the great French Revolution, precisely because it comes at a much more delicately critical moment in history.' From 1911 to 1916 he was editor of the English section of *Regeneration*, the organ of the Mexican revolutionists published in Los Angeles; at the same he provided a great number of labour papers with a Free Press Service issued in connection with the Mexican Revolution, and in addition a weekly syndicated letter on general political matters.

He also resumed his collaboration with *Freedom*, and between 1911-1914 contributed a number of articles and translations, mainly on the Mexican Revolution. From May 1914 until June 1915 he also edited and published his own paper, *Land and Liberty*, the title aptly reflecting not only the standard slogan of the Mexican revolutionaries but also what from the 1890s had been his own driving motives. During the First World War he sided almost immediately with the Allies (and Kropotkin) 'against Prussian militarism and chauvinism', thereby alienating himself from virtually the whole English-speaking anarchist movement. On February 18th 1916 the Magon brothers, as editors of *Regeneration*, were arrested on the little co-operative ranch near Los Angeles that had served for some time as their headquarters and editorial office and imprisoned. Owen, whom the authorities shortly afterwards wanted to add to their impressive collection of imprisoned radicals, was warned in time and went into hiding for about six months, until he finally left the United States for ever and returned to England in late 1916.

He lived for a while in Plymouth, earning his living as a professional writer and journalist, writing for example for the *Commercial Review* and the *Middleton Guardian* (whose founder and editor, John Bagot, incidentally had been a correspondent and occasional contributor to *Freedom* for years before the War). When Thomas Keell found out that Owen was in England, he wrote to him asking to write for *Freedom*. 'Owen replied saying that he was an individualist and he did not think his writings would please the readers of an anarchist-communist paper; but on being told we were anarchists first and foremost, he consented.' So from 1919 on Owen wrote more and more for *Freedom*, and in later years sometimes provided two-thirds of the material printed.

'His knowledge of languages was a great help to an editor who knew hardly any, and he translated many letters and articles received from foreign correspondents.'

But the land question remained his pet subject, and to support the agitation against land monopoly he joined the Commonwealth League (later the Commonwealth Land Party) and wrote regularly for its organ, the *Commonweal* (as W.C.O., or as X., or anonymously). At least twice a week he addressed open-air meetings, most discussions centring on the land question, expropriation, or the role played by Labour politicians. He never ceased to regard himself as an anarchist, and he had often to challenge the interference of editors who has 'a little difficulty over the seeming approval of "force"'; in anarchist papers and private letters his opinion on this was unwaveringly clear: 'I hold that unjust institutions upheld by force can only be overthrown by force.' He summarised his line of thinking over many years in a comment on the editor's tampering with an article of his, headed 'Imperialism on Trial' (*Commonweal*, March 12th 1927):

> The passages objected to stated simply, & in moderate language, that the stage has been set for a long, & probably bitter & bloody struggle, & that in opposition to Imperialism we shall find the opportunity of establishing a world-wide 'solidarity' of thought & thereby presenting a 'united front', hitherto impossible ... I ... want to drag the Commonwealth Land Party in the general revolutionary movement.

Around 1920 he had lived for a couple of years with Tom Keell and Lilian Wolfe and their little son in their house in Willesden: 'Many were the long talks we had at midnight, and sometimes long after, over innumerable cups of tea and cigarettes.' From 1926 on he lived at 'The Sanctuary' near Storrington, on the Sussex Downs, a little community started by a Miss Vera Pragnell, who invested part of her inheritance in buying land and giving it away in plots to anyone who cared to live there; after several operations which he had to undergo in the winter of 1928-29, he died of cancer in a nursing home at Worthing on July 9th 1929. In an obituary, Tom Keell summarised his own experience with Owen:

> To know him was a liberal education. His knowledge of books and men was tremendous and his memory wonderful. As a writer for *Freedom* and the *Bulletin* he was always willing, and there was never anything slipshod about his work.

Apart from two books, *The Economics of Herbert Spencer* (New York, 1891) and *Crime and Criminals* (Los Angeles, 1910; published by the Prison Reform League without mention of the author), Owen wrote a great number of pamphlets and leaflets, under his name, pseudonymously or anonymously — *Anarchism versus Socialism* (London, Freedom Pamphlet, 1922; the revised version of a pamphlet originally published in New York); *The Mexican Revolution: Its Progress, Causes, Purpose and Probable Results* (Los Angeles 1912); *Set My People Free!* (London, Commonwealth Land Party, n.d. = 1926); *England Monopolised or England Free?* by SENEX (London, Freedom Pamphlet, 1920); *The Chancellor's Dream by X* (London, Commonwealth Land Party, n.d. = 1924); *What is the Commonwealth Land Party?* by X (London, Commonwealth Land Party, n.d. = 1926).

His articles appeared in numerous periodicals, a few of which have been mentioned above; for *Freedom* he wrote a few articles in the early 1890s, then quite a number mainly on Mexico between 1911 and 1913, and from 1919 until his death he wrote with Tom Keell the major part of the paper.

Obituaries were published in *Freedom Bulletin* (September 1929), *The Commonweal* (July 20 1929; by J W Graham Peace and Victor Neuburg), *Middleton Guardian* (29 July 1929; by Tom Keell and Victor Neuburg). Further information is to be found in an article in the *New York Times*, December 2nd 1892 ('Too Bad for Socialists'); and in histories of American anarchism and the labour movement in California — for example Ira B Cross, *A History of the Labor Movement in California* (Berkeley, California, 1935); and in memoirs like Emma Goldman's *Living My Life*, or Frank Roney's *An Autobiography* edited by Ira B Cross (Berkeley, California, 1911).

~ *Heiner Becker*

Philip Sansom (1916-1999)

Our comrade Philip Sansom died on October 24th, at the age of 83. No obituary can convey the likeability of the man, his creativity, his energy, his enthusiasm for anarchism, his joy in life or his generosity.

During the 1950s and 1960s, on sunny Sundays, people would gather on the grass near Hyde Park Speakers' Corner, sunbathing, picnicking, keeping a vague eye on the successive speakers for the London Anarchist Group, until Philip got| up to speak. Then they would swarm towards the platform, sometimes adding three or four hundred to the audience. They came to be entertained by his eloquence, and his quickwitted but always courteous response to questioners and hecklers. Of his generation, only the methodist Donald Soper could match him as an open-air speaker. Many middle-aged anarchists today testify that it was Philip in Hyde Park, or on the platform at Manette Street or Tower Hill, who first convinced them of the anarchist case.

At the Malatesta Club, his talents were used for simple entertainment. He once announced that he had composed a calypso about an 'underground movement', which turned out to be the London Underground railway: "Cosmopolitan, Vicious Circle, Daffodilly-doo, We're all going to change at Double Cross to ride the Shakerloo". At home, he was a splendid cook, with a magnificent collection of jazz records.

Philip was born in Hackney, the son of a lathe operator, on September 19th 1916. After elementary school, he attended art school, and in the 1930s worked as a commercial artist. He was an amateur boxer of some local standing in the sport.

In 1939 he was in trouble with the authorities as a conscientious objector to conscription. In 1943, he became a member of the then Anarchist Federation, and almost immediately was invited to join the editorial board of *War Commentary*. By his own account, his chief value to Freedom Press at the time was that he had a flat, and could accommodate the *War Commentary* cartoonist John Olday.

In 1944, John Olday was arrested in the street, on suspicion of stealing a typewriter which he had borrowed. The owner of the typewriter confirmed that he had borrowed it, but Olday was identified as A W Oldag, a German national and deserter from the Royal Pioneer Corps, and imprisoned. To conceal the connection with *War Commentary*, it was necessary for Olday's unsigned strip cartoon of three soldiers to be 'ghosted'. Philip, who had already illustrated some articles for the paper, undertook this work, and later replaced John Olday as political cartoonist, a function which he retained when *War Commentary* changed its name to *Freedom*. He signed his work 'philip' when the idea was his own, and 'Skitz' when the idea for the cartoon was supplied by someone else.

The many articles he wrote were sometimes anonymous, sometimes signed 'PS', and sometimes signed 'Justin', because they had arrived just in time for publication.

In late 1944 the Anarchist Federation split. One faction called itself the Anarchist Federation of Britain, later the Syndicalist Workers Federation. The group which held on to *War Commentary* and Freedom Press called itself the Freedom Press Group. Shortly after the split, Freedom Press was raided by Special Branch and all its files and typewriters seized.

In April 1945, as the war in Europe ended, four members of the Freedom Press Group — Philip, Vernon Richards, John Hewetson and Marie Louise Berneri were charged with Conspiracy to contravene Defence Regulation 39A, which was about inciting members of His Majesty's Forces to disaffection. This was the only prosecution under that particular regulation. The three men were leach sentenced to 12 months in prison (Bemeri was acquitted on a technicality). Philip was already in prison, serving a short sentence for possession of an army greatcoat, which he had bought from a market stall.

After his release, Philip was "the nearest thing *War Commentary* had to an industrial editor", the cartoonist, and the manager of Express Printers, which Freedom Press had taken over in 1942. In the latter capacity he came to know trade suppliers of typesetting, bookbinding and other services, and was later able to earn his living as a printer with no plant of his own, buying all services through the trade.

Besides *War Commentary*, which changed its name to *Freedom*, Philip had a hand in many other publications. In the 1940s, Dr Norman Haire hired Express Printers to print *The Journal of Sex Education*, and Philip was proud to be production editor.

About the same time a group called the Anarcho-Syndicalist Committee, consisting of Philip, his companion Rita Milton (another able orator), Albert Grace and Albert Meltzer, launched a paper called *The Syndicalist*. Philip, already the author of a well-received Freedom Press pamphlet, *Syndicalism the Workers' Next Step*, was editor and political cartoonist. It lasted about a year.

Among other short-lived publications were a surrealist magazine, a near-anarchist journal called *Wildcat*, and a paper called *Zero* which proclaimed itself 'anarchist-feminist'. Philip quit after, without telling him, they ran a front-page article demanding the re-imprisonment of a soldier, convicted of indecent assault, whose sentence had been reduced by the Appeal Court. Philip was also employed as editor of *Sewing Machine Times* and *Loading Machine Times* (a loading machine is a device for loading industrial sewing machines; "Believe it or not", Philip said, "we get genuine letters to the editor of *Loading Machine Times*"), and after his retirement continued as a freelance photographer for these papers.

In March 1952, some members of the (then illegal) Spanish CNT were sentenced to death in Barcelona, and Freedom Press organised a big meeting in their defence, of celebrities like Michael Foot, Fenner Brockway and Jacob Bronowski. The sentences were commuted.

In 1953, Philip was asked by two comrades for help in campaigning for the abolition of the death penalty. Using the contacts he had made in meetings defending the Spanish CNT members, Philip organised two big meetings addressed by famous people against the death penalty in Britain.

The first meeting was called in the name of London Anarchist Group, the second in the name of 'The League Against Capital Punishment'. This was the foundation of the National Campaign for the Abolition of Capital Punishment, which went on to success.

In 1964, Philip organised a series of meetings in support of Stuart Christie, a young anarchist arrested in Spain and accused of importing explosives. Out of these meetings arose the Christie-Carballo Defence Committee, in which Philip and others continued campaigning, lobbying Parliament and so on, until Christie's release. Christie was a member of the Syndicalist Workers Federation. After his release he seems to have been persuaded that the campaign had been organised, not by Philip and friends, but by a group including the late Albert Meltzer who had in fact refused to join the campaign, on the grounds that it had no chance of success.

Philip was 'prime mover' in the foundation of the Malatesta Club, an anarchist club with its own premises, open almost every evening from May 1954 until sometime in 1958.

In his sixties, he entertained as the bingo-caller at the local old people's club in Camden Town. About this time, he quietly married at least one refugee, to give her a British passport. Towards the end of his life he retired somewhat, while remaining the genial, delightful entertainer in private. He leaves two children now in their thirties, from his time with Frances Sokolov, and a lot of anarchists who took him as a role model.

He was once described in a letter to an East End local newspaper as "the anarchist leader", a description which he was quick to deny. But if 'leader' is taken to mean, not a boss of any sort, but an originator of activities in which others enthusiastically join, anarchist leader is a good description of Philip Sansom.

~ *Donald Rooum*

Jack Stevenson (19??-2018)

An electrician by trade, and a keen gardener of vegetables on his allotment, Jack was prominent among London anarchists and in the 1960s. Among other achievements, he was the founder, treasurer, and an inconspicuous donor to the Sit-Down-Or-Pay-Up fund, which subsidised legal expenses and fines of supporters of the Committee of One Hundred anti-bomb campaign, mostly charged with obstructing traffic. By political inclination he was an anarcho-syndicalist, though one often frustrated with the attitude of other syndicalist activists. His partner was Mary Stevenson. Below is an article he wrote in 1963, describing his personal conversion to anarchism.

I became an anarchist on a Sunday afternoon in 1956. It was the Sunday afternoon of the Labour Party demonstration against the Suez "armed conflict". I was already well on the way and as 'I heard the speakers one after another saying: "No Industrial Action" felt any feeling I ever had for parliamentary socialism die.

Though I never had been a young socialist or young communist, I had paid lip service to both organisations at different times. I have always believed "That the world should be owned and run by the people who are living in it", as I once said to one of my teachers when I was about twelve.

I stood in the square that afternoon and I sang the "Red Flag" and felt that the Labour Movement would do something to stop the war and the killing of the Egyptians. Well, as we all know, how silly that was, but I did not go on being silly (at least not in the same way) for I became an anarchist.

In my eyes an anarchist differs from a socialist in one main respect. He thinks of people as people. Not something that can be moulded by an organisation, dragged along by some self-elected vanguard. An anarchist cannot believe in an anarchist or free society that has people like the people who live under capitalism. The anarchist is not interested in power. He is trying to sell an idea, that is all, just an idea. The socialist wants to force a dogma on the people for their own good. An anarchist has a different attitude and he also has a different language. How many of us have met 'Trots' or other politicos who bore us to death with their talk of parties, groups and splits?

We cannot overthrow the state at the moment, and even if we could it wouldn't do anarchism any good. For anarchism to work it needs anarchists. Revolutionaries are not enough, if they are the kind of people who call "fascist" at someone who does not quite see it their way.

So having become an anarchist what did I do? Why, I read books about it of course. I had already got some out of the local library and now I began to buy them. One of these books was *Fields Factories and Workshops*. I read this book and about the workers around Paris in Kropotkin's day. Then I decided to try to grow my own food, or some of it at least, as they had done.

People in this world should be able, I feel, to do. something useful. If a man goes through his life doing things that are utterly useless, like running about with bits of paper, working in some stupid industry like advertising or even being a meter-reader, he has wasted his life. So I went to a local allotment association and they gave me, for a very small fee, a piece of land. I had not done any really hard work before and the first few weeks were no joke, but I managed to clear it. I sweated on, and still do, and after some time I became quite proficient, I suppose. I live at my own speed.

I could, I suppose, sell the stuff I grow like some of my mates do, but I feel that all business is bad, even small business, so I give away what I have over. My mates don't want to take stuff without giving something back, so we mostly manage to keep supplied with veg all the year, and plants, for if one hasn't got something another usually has.

All the old boys who are my mates know that I go on anti-bomb demos and if I did get put away my plots would be looked after by them. These old people (they are the only people I know) seem to have a more sensible attitude to war than some of the younger folk about. Being ex-workers they are mostly Labour supporters, though one of my best friends is very anti-monarchist and is nearer to a syndicalist position.

When I first came into this movement I was willing to work. I believed in the Cause if you like and wanted to propagate the word. I didn't come in because I wanted to tell everyone what they should do or think, just to help.

I suppose I'm fortunate. I didn't become an anarchist because I was against all authority of all kinds, just because it was there. I've always got on alright with my parents for example. Life's give and take isn't it?

I'm always hearing that people are frustrated. People write in *Freedom* and talk about this lousy world. They sound bitter and fed up with life. I don't have a death wish; I think life's OK. It's not as good as it should be but it's not so bad either, at least for me. I suppose if I poured the whole of my life into demonstrating, never talked or thought of anything but rebellion, I would be bloody frustrated. I don't believe in Permanent Protest because I don't like griping all the time. I want to see a day come when people won't have to go out into the streets and demonstrate, so I'm doing my best to do now what I would do in a free society. I'm not waiting for the workers to make my life worth living, I'm doing something about that myself.

As I type this I'm smiling for I can see the syndicalists reaching for their pens to take up the struggle again, but I'm not interested in starting another argument, just trying to point out what can be had from life.

Anarchism has taught me to think a bit. The trouble with our movement at the moment is, it's full of people who are trying to knock down without trying to build up. They have phrases like workers' control and industrial democracy, but this is only changing economics, it's people that want to change. You must give meaning to youi life in some way or you will become bitter and anarchists are not supposed to be bitter. Anarchism has given me a new purpose in life.' It has given me many good friends of the kind that most men would like but do not have.

I don't enjoy demonstrations but I go on most of them. SOMEONE HAS TO PROTEST! and why shouldn't it be me? Anyway I have to carry the other side of the banner or Peter would drop it wouldn't he?

Since becoming an anarchist I've changed (Mary says so anyway) I think I've changed for the better but it's only a reflection on the people I knock around with anyway.

I've found out that mutual aid works with both anarchists and non-anarchists very, well, for me at least.

John Turner (1864-1934)

John Turner, who from May 1895 to September 1907 lent his name as printer and publisher to *Freedom*, was for a long time one of the best-known members of the Freedom Group.

He was born on August 24th 1864 in a little village near Braintree in Essex, his father being a small farmer. At the age of 14 he came to Woolwich to be apprenticed to a grocer. He attended the 'early closing' meetings of the Early Closing Association of 1878-1880, and joined the Shop Hours League at its inception in 1882; but the League was still a very amateurish and ineffective movement and soon failed (as did a similar effort by Tom Mann and others in 1886 to form a Shop Assistants', Porters' and Packers' Union). So young John Turner was very dissatisfied with the situation, and being "a Socialist before I had a chance of applying my Trade Union ideas", he joined the Socialist League early in 1885, where he received his education as a political agitator and organiser. He could always speak fluently, his difficulty being less in beginning than in coming to an end, and he was soon well known, even popular, among workers. In 1886 he became the League's Financial Secretary, and in 1889 served on its council.

On August 25th 1889 he debated against Herbert Burrows (SDF) at the Patriotic Club, Clerkenwell Green, on 'Anarchy versus Social Democracy' with unexpected and thorough success. Following the Great Dockers' Strike that same autumn, which stimulated trade union activity everywhere in Britain, Turner, A George Maher and 15 others tried their luck again and in October 1889 formed the United Shop Assistants Union, the first permanent trade union for shop assistants in Britain. Turner acted as president, until in autumn 1898 it amalgamated with the National Union Amalgamated Union of Shop Assistants, Warehousemen and Clerks. In these years Turner was also running the Socialist Co-operative Society, and this was the high tide of his anarchist activities, in the Socialist League, the Commonweal Group of 1893-94, and then the Freedom Group. He was later to write that Kropotkin's "personal magnetism exerted an influence upon myself and a group of young fellows who for some time had been 'feeling their way' towards the anarchist view of social and political questions. Much as we were attracted by the *Commonweal* we soon came to look upon *Freedom* ... as our monthly journal", a statement which conflicts with contemporary evidence, for the relationship between the Commonweal Group and the Freedom Group at the time was rather cool. It was not until the spring of 1895, several months after the end of the *Commonweal* in October 1894, that he joined the *Freedom* editorial group on the invitation of the new editor Alfred Marsh. For the next 12 years he was the paper's official publisher.

In March 1896 Turner left England for a first lecture tour to the United States, which seems to have been rather successful. When in 1898 the National Amalgamated Union was formed, Turner became soon a paid official as its first National Organiser: now, according to Max Nettlau, "the United Kingdom was Mr Turner's Parish — his organising area. From Land's End to the Highland Capital, from Yarmouth in the East to Limerick in the West of Ireland, he proclaimed the Gospel, preached salvation by organisation ... He established branches by the score. His recruits were legion". Anarchism and the anarchist movement, however, from now on saw much less if anything of him — except for occasional articles.

In 1900 he was instrumental in setting up the International Federation of Commercial Employees, and in 1903 "he obtained leave of absence" from his employer, the National Amalgamated Union, to do some lecturing in the United States. While he was addressing a meeting in New York he was arrested on October 23rd and imprisoned, being the first prisoner held under the new Act of Congress which provided for the deportation of "persons who disbelieve in organised government". Friends wanting to make a test case of it persuaded him not to return immediately, so he was detained on Ellis Island until the end of April 1904. In contrast to the experience of many others, this did little damage to John Turner, for as a friend later recalled, "when he came here eventually he was as fat as butter, had an American hat and an American accent".

In 1907 he took part in publishing the *Voice of Labour*, though he seems to have done no more than lend his name for the letterhead, and apart from that graciously left all the work to Alfred Marsh and especially Tom Keell. In October 1907 his name was removed from *Freedom*, taking account of the more and more 'strenuous' relationship in the Freedom Group between those who year in and year out did all the donkey work and those who contented themselves by just being venerable "members". As one of Turner's trade union friends was to recall, of a meeting in 1904 where Turner was giving an account of his experiences in the United States, 'the hero of the evening, though he was as entertaining and instructive as he invariably is on the platform, turned out to be as mild and harmless a man as Keir Hardie! So perished one more of my illusions!' Another official of the same Union, though admitting that 'the Executive of that day did not like him being an anarchist', relates that "he never at any time to my knowledge allowed it to show itself during his work for the union".

In 1909 at the Trades Union Congress he seconded a resolution in favour of a Bill for the compulsory closing of shops; when challenged by Tom Keell and asked "if that was consistent with his various articles condemning the Labour and Socialist Parties for their 'middle-class politics'," he said he did not make a fetish of anarchism and was not going to be dictated to by pedants!

The same Tom Keell later had the cheek to remind him that as long as he (Keell) had been in the Freedom Office (since 1903) he "had never known him to help except with an occasional article. Even his 1/6d subscription had to be written for". Turner, who in 1912 became president of his union and later modestly employed the pen-name of 'Excelsus', never rose high enough to forget such mean attacks on his anarchist integrity by a humble compositor. He remained 'president' until 1924, when he retired, then went as a member of the British Trades Union Delegation to Russia (November-December 1924) and did not hesitate to sign its official report which openly applauded the Bolshevik government.

In 1929 he re-appeared on the anarchist scene, joining a new Freedom Group formed by old opponents of Tom Keell who in May 1930 started a new *Freedom*. But Turner could not take part long, due to ill-health. He died in Brighton on August 9th 1934.

John Turner published no books or pamphlets; but he was a prolific journalist and contributed innumerable articles to numerous labour papers, including *Freedom* and the *Voice of Labour* (1907) and especially *The Shop Assistant*; there he published his 'Parting Memoirs' of 40 years in the Shop Assistants' Movement (August-September 1924), and shortly before his death a long series of articles on 'A Changing World' (signed 'Excelsus', May 27th-October 28th 1933). His 'Personal Impressions of the United States' were published from notes taken during several lectures by Turner by Max Nettlau in *Freedom* (March, May 1897). Turner himself published reminiscences on every possible occasion and in articles on the most diverse subjects — for example, 'Labour and Socialism and "Labour Institutions"' in *The Shop Assistant* (April 11th 1908); or on Kropotkin in *Justice* (February 24th 1921).

Articles on and obituaries of him were published in *The Shop Assistant* (October 19th, 1912, when he became general secretary; January 19th, August 30th, and September 13th 1924, when he retired as general secretary; August 18th and 25th 1934); as well as in *Freedom* (September 1934). Further information may be found in the books by E P Thompson on William Morris and by John Quail and Hermia Oliver on English anarchism.

~ *Heiner Becker*

Charlotte Wilson (1854-1944)

Wilson was the main founder and the first editor and publisher of *Freedom*, and the leading figure in the Freedom Group from 1886-1895.

Charlotte Mary Martin was born on May 6th 1854 at Kemerton, a village near Tewkesbury on the Gloucestershire-Worcestershire border. She was the only child of Robert Spencer Martin, a doctor and surgeon from a prominent local family, and of Clementina Susannah Davies, from a prosperous commercial and clerical family.

She received the best education then available to girls, going to Cheltenham Ladies College and then to Cambridge University, where from 1873 to 1874 she attended the new institution at Merton Flail which later became Newnham College. She took the Higher Local Examination (roughly equivalent to the later GCE Advanced Level) at a time when women couldn't take university examinations or degrees at Cambridge.

In 1876 she married Arthur Wilson (a distant cousin who was born in 1847, went to Wadham College, Oxford, and became a stockbroker in 1872), and they lived at first in Hampstead. After a process of political development which remains obscure, she became a socialist and then an anarchist, and at the end of 1885 they adopted the fashionable simple life by moving to a cottage in what was then open country at North End on the edge of Hampstead Heath.

Charlotte Wilson's first known publication was a letter about women workers which appeared in March 1884 in *Justice*, the paper of the Democratic Federation (later the Social Democratic Federation). It isn't known whether she was ever a member of the SDF, but in November-December 1884 *Justice* published a series of articles on anarchism written by her and signed 'An English Anarchist'. This was one of the first English-language expositions of anarchist communism at a time when virtually none of Kropotkin's writings had appeared in English.

In October 1884 she joined the Fabian Society, which had been formed in January 1884 as a group of progressive intellectuals with ambitious ideas but no particular line, and she was the only woman elected to its first executive in December 1884. Her fellow members included such people as Annie Besant, Hubert Bland, Sydney Olivier, Bernard Shaw, Graham Wallas, and Sidney Webb, and she had no difficulty in holding her own with them. In the later memoirs of early Fabians she is remembered as a hostess, like

Edith Nesbit, but she was in fact a leading member of the society for a couple of years.

Also in October 1884 she formed a study group which met at her house to read and discuss the work of Continental socialists such as Marx and Proudhon (which was not then available in English) and the history of the international labour movement, and which provided much of the early philosophical and factual background for the lectures and pamphlets which became the main Fabian contribution to socialist propaganda.

But her particular contribution was to become the leader of an anarchist fraction within the Fabian Society. As Shaw put it with his customary exaggeration in the first of his unreliable histories of the society, when she joined "a sort of influenza of anarchism soon spread through the society" (The Fabian Society: What It Has Done and How It Has Done It, 1892). In fact the fraction didn't have much influence, and it didn't last long, but for a time it was significant. Her own part was summarised in three essays published during 1886 — 'Social Democracy and Anarchism', a paper given to the Fabian Society during 1885 and published in the first issue of Practical Socialist, the short-lived paper of the Fabian Society, in January 1886; "The Principles and Aims of Anarchists', a paper given to the London Dialectical Society in June 1886 and published in one of the last issues of *Present Day*, a short-lived secularist paper, in July 1886; and 'Anarchism'. the second part of a pamphlet called *What Socialism Is*, the fourth Fabian tract, published in 1886.

On September 17th 1886 the Fabian Society organised a meeting at Anderton's Motel in Fleet Street, where the representatives of the various socialist organisations in London debated the question of forming an orthodox political party on the Continental model. A motion to this effect was proposed by Annie Besant and seconded by Hubert Bland. William Morris proposed and Charlotte Wilson seconded the following amendment:

> But whereas the first duty of socialists is to educate people to understand what their present position is and what the future might be, and to keep the principles of socialism steadily before them; and whereas no Parliamentary party can exist without compromise and concession, which would hinder that education and obscure those principles: it would be a false step for Socialists to attempt to take part in the Parliamentary contest.

The parliamentarians defeated the anti-parliamentarians by a two-to-one majority, and the Fabian Society — and the bulk of the British socialist movement — was set on the course which it has followed ever since. Charlotte Wilson resigned from the Fabian executive in April 1887, and took no active part in the society for 20 years, though she maintained her membership.

By that time she had anyway committed herself entirely to the anarchist movement. She was closely involved in the first English-language anarchist paper, Henry Seymour's *The Anarchist*, which appeared from March 1885. She helped to start it, got Bernard Shaw to write for it, contributed money and material to it for more than a year, and became a leading member of the group which was established around it. In January 1886 Kropotkin was released from prison in France, and in March he settled in England, partly as the result of an invitation from Charlotte Wilson's group. For a time the group continued to work with Seymour, and the April and May issues of *The Anarchist* were produced jointly as a journal of anarchist communism. But the experiment failed, producing *Freedom*.

Charlotte Wilson was the organiser of the group, the editor and publisher of *Freedom*, and its main supporter and contributor. She was normally responsible for the editorial article in each issue and most of the political and international notes, but she contributed few signed articles, signing herself austerely as C M W or C M Wilson. The most important of these was a series of "The Revolt of the English Workers in the XIX Century" (June-September 1889). For a few years she was also active as a lecturer and speaker at various kinds of meetings all over the country.

In January 1889 *Freedom* was temporarily suspended because of her illness, and when it was resumed in March 1889 it was edited by James Blackwell with the help of a committee of workmen'. She took over again in February 1891 when Blackwell left, but in January 1895 the paper was temporarily suspended again because of illness in her family. This time she resigned permanently as both editor and publisher of *Freedom*, and she ceased to take an active part in the group, though she kept in touch and continued to contribute money and material until 1901. As well as *Freedom* itself, she helped to produce a series of Freedom Pamphlets from 1889 onwards, editing and translating some and also writing Anarchism and Outrage (a reprint of the *Freedom* editorial of December 1893).

Charlotte Wilson was not involved in left-wing politics during the next decade, during which both her parents died (her father in

1896 and her mother in 1903), and when she did resume political activity she returned not to the anarchists but to the Fabians. In 1906 she became involved in the society again, and in 1908, at the time of the rise of the militant campaign for women's suffrage, she was the main founder of the Fabian Women's Group, which met at her home in St John's Wood, and she was its first secretary and most active member until she resigned because of illness in 1916. She was again a member of the Fabian executive from 1911 until 1914. She also joined the Independent Labour Party and several other parliamentarian organisations.

Charlotte Wilson took no further part on politics after the First World War. Arthur Wilson died in 1932, and she was looked after until her death by Gerald Hankin, a distant cousin of theirs. They went to the United States, and she died in an old people's home at Irvington-on- Hudson on April 28th 1944, a few days before her 90th birthday.

For a decade Charlotte Wilson was the best-known native anarchist in Britain. Her work as a writer and speaker was distinguished by reticence, reliability and respectability; she always remained very much an intellectual, and very much in the background. She steered her way between militants and moderates in the anarchist movement, but she was definitely a communist rather than an individualist, and she later moved towards parliamentary socialism. Her particular contribution to the work of the Freedom Press was to set it up and to set it on its way as a serious publishing organisation with a solid basis, providing a model which it has followed ever since.

Anarchism and Outrage was reprinted in 1909, at the time of the judicial murder of Francisco Ferrer in Spain. Fabian Tract Four was never reprinted by the Fabian Society, but Charlotte Wilson's contribution was reprinted as the first Free Commune pamphlet in 1900 and has occasionally been reprinted by the anarchist press since then. All three 1886 essays were reprinted as Three Essays on Anarchism (Cienfuegos Press 1979, Drowned Rat 1985) with an introduction by Nicolas Walter.

References to Charlotte Wilson appear in letters, missives or biographies of Peter Kropotkin, William Morris, Edith Nesbit, Sydney Olivier, Henry Seymour. Bernard Shaw, and Sidney Webb; in accounts of the Fabian Society by Edward Pease, Anne Fremantle. Margaret Cole, A M McBriar. Willard Wolfe, and Norman and Jean McKenzie; and in accounts of Bntish anarchism by Max Nettlau, George Woodcock, John Quail, and Hermia Oliver.

~ *Nicolas Walter*

Lilian Wolfe (1875-1974)

Lilian Gertrude Woolf (later Wolfe) was involved first in the suffrage and then in the anarchist and anti-war movements. This feature article by Sheila Rowbotham was conducted for Wildcat no. 6 in March 1975.

I met Lilian Wolfe for the first time on September 9th, 1973 at the Rudolf Rocker Centenary Celebration at Toynbee Hall, Whitechapel. The name of the East End anarchist who organised the Jewish clothing workers had become well known to me through my friendship with William Fishman, anarchist historian and the principal of Tower Hamlets College of Education, where I had taught during the 1960s. By 1973 I had also met the anarchist writer Nicolas Walter.

I went to interview her a few weeks later at the War Resisters' International in Kings Cross where she was busy stuffing copies of Peace News into envelopes. She explained her very impressive filing system to me and fed me on vegetarian food from the Cotswold community, Whiteway, near Stroud, Gloucesteshire while we talked.

Lilian Wolfe's father Albert Lewis Woolf was a Jewish jeweller and politically conservative; her mother Lucy Helen Jones, had been an actress who left the family when Lilian was thirteen to join a touring opera company, leaving Lilian and her three brothers and two sisters, "to think and do as we liked".

Her eldest brother paid for her to train as a telegraphist at the Regent Street Polytechnic and Lilian went to work as a telegraphist at the Central Office (GPO) in London and "hated every minute of it". She had already drifted towards socialism without remembering quite how – "I found myself thinking that way". Her younger brother was also interested in socialism and so was one of her friends, Mabel Hope, who was also at the GPO Central Office and the Telegraph Department of the Civil Service. Through her work Lilian joined the Civil Service Socialist Society.

She was initially shocked when she first heard of the suffragettes' militant tactics, "I thought it was terrible the way they were acting". Then her supervisor in the Civil Service took her to a meeting and they explained they used tactics like burning letter-boxes in order to make it impossible to ignore them. But she found the leaders, Emmeline and Christabel Pankhurst too arbitrary and authoritarian and joined the Women's Freedom League, a breakaway from the Pankhursts' Women's Social and Political Union. Formed in 1907, the Women's Freedom League adopted non-violent direct action. There was considerable hostility to supporters of women's suffrage regardless of their tactics. Once while speaking on women's suffrage with a friend in Salisbury market place Lilian remembered how they were pelted with cabbages by hostile onlookers.

There was a strong current within the left before World War One which rejected working for reforms through Parliament and believed in direct action. The suffragettes were in a curious half-way position. They were using militant direct action to influence Parliament. Lilian began to feel increasingly that all the effort to persuade politicians to change their minds was misplaced, and along with Mabel Hope, she began to move towards anarchism and direct action ideas.

In 1913 she and Mabel Hope joined the Anarchist Educational League. This had been started by Fred Dunn, who worked for the Post Office in a sorting office and whose father had been a founding member of the Social Democratic Federation. When they thought of restarting an anarchist paper directed at workers, *Voice of Labour*, it seems to have been Mabel Hope who introduced them to Tom Keell, the compositor and editor of the anarchist paper *Freedom*,.

Lilian recalled her first encounter with him. "When we were going to start the *Voice of Labour* we held a meeting to know how we should go about it. We had no experience". Tom Keell came along with what Lilian described as "a watching brief". After they had talked in circles for some time he stood up and explained clearly how they could get started. Lilian was indignant at his silence and the time wasted and demanded, "Why couldn't that man have spoken before?"

"That man" was to become her companion for many years. An extremely skilled compositor, Tom was renowned for his ability to set type at the same time as having a spirited debate. Lilian remembered him with affection and pride. "We got friendly and eventually fixed up together. He was the nicest man I ever met. The sort of man you could discuss anything with". She said the years they spent together were the happiest in her life.

The *Voice of Labour* reappeared in 1914, edited by Fred Dunn, helped by Lilian's organisational efficiency. "I did the hack work", she told me. It was a weekly, becoming a monthly when the First World War began. It strongly opposed the war.

Tom Keell as editor of *Freedom* was confronted by a dilemma, for Peter Kropotkin, who had been associated with *Freedom* since the nineteenth century and was a loved and revered figure in the anarchist movement, argued that they should side with the allies. Tom Keell himself was opposed to this and published a reply by the anarchist thinker Errico Malatesta contesting Kropotkin's position. The painful split became bitter but Tom Keell was supported by the *Voice of Labour* group Lilian, Fred Dunn, Mabel Hope and her friend

Elizabeth Archer. In March 1915 *Freedom* published a passionate anti-war statement, the *International Anarchist Manifesto on the War*, which appeared later in several anarchist publications in Europe and the US. Among the signatories, which included Malatesta, Alexander Berkman, Emma Goldman and the Christian pacifist F. Domela Nieuwenhuis were Fred Dunn, Tom Keell and Lilian G. Woolf.

Lilian told me how early in 1915 an anarchist community was started at 1 Mecklenburgh Street, off Bloomsbury Road, London. Domestic work was divided by the people who lived there who included Lilian and Tom. They held meetings and socials every Saturday night to raise money for *Freedom* and the *Voice of Labour*. They had a piano and Lilian described how youngsters from Rudolf Rocker's anarchist group in the East End used to come and dance. Imagining wild ragtime, I enquired what kind of dances? Lilian replied that it was waltzes mainly, adding "The older ones used to come and talk and talk".

When I asked Lilian about anarchist groups in this period, she did not remember any actual groups apart from the East Enders and one group in Stockport. She recalled individual people just being around rather than specific groupings. I have often puzzled away at this and wished I had questioned her more deeply.

East End anarchists of course had a long tradition and strong international links. The Stockport group she mentions met at the Communist Club in Park Street, Hazel Grove. They were not isolated for they had been in contact with sympathisers in the locality who helped them to establish the Club. They also had links with other Workers' Freedom Groups which inclined to anarchist communism and existed elsewhere (including in Bristol). Anarchists held conferences at the Stockport Communist Club's premises and Fred Dunn uses the term 'The Movement' to describe the congress which gathered at the Club in April 1915 to oppose the war. This was probably how Lilian knew of the Stockport group.

Alongside the conferences, publications and manifestos, networks among anarchists were also formed through friendships and personal love affairs. These could be profoundly important. I think this might be why Lilian recalled individuals being just around. For example, there is a 1915 photograph of Lilian at the anarchist holiday camp at Harlech with Fred Dunn, Emily Wilkinson who taught Morse code in the Post Office, her brother George Wilkinson and Bert Wells.

Ken Weller in his 1985 book of *Don't be a Soldier* traces how rebel networks formed among those who were opposing the war in North London in which anarchists, socialists and pacifists combined. Amid the repressive circumstances of the war personal friendship networks also overlapped, connecting anarchists, pacifists and socialists. Several

Stockport anarchists who were imprisoned with Fenner Brockway for opposing the war joined him in resisting the prison regime.

The intelligence agents, many of whom were recruited from the armed forces and accustomed to rigid command structures, struggled to establish leaders amongst those they were pursuing and tied themselves in knots trying to work out links between opponents of the war. Subsequently historians too have faced problems detecting interactions and groupings in informal organisational networks, especially of course those that were necessarily operating in secret. Buried beneath the No Conscription Fellowship, there were shadowy networks helping men to escape to the US. But numbers and names are obviously difficult to trace.

But despite flexibility and fluidity in how the movement against the war can be construed, there were also differences in emphases and tactics. Lilian helped to start the uncompromising anarchist No Conscription League which called on workers to refuse call-up.

After the Military Service Act in January 1916 such absolute resistance was extremely dangerous. When Fred Dunn defied being drafted, he was arrested, put in a military prison and sent to a regiment, but managed to flee to the Scottish Highlands. On the run along with George Wilkinson and Bert Wells, he contributed an article called "Defying the Act" by 'one of those outlawed to the Scottish hills' to the April 1916 issue of *Voice of Labour*. Nevertheless, no doubt through the anti-war networks, he managed to flee to the United States where he taught at the libertarian Modern School which adopted the educational ideas of Francisco Ferrer.

By May, however, most of the other men in hiding in the Highlands had been arrested. Tom Keell printed 10,000 copies of the article as a leaflet and Lilian with her customary efficiency distributed them, even though when the article was being written she had urged restraint. Copies, including one to Malatesta, were intercepted by the police, the Freedom Press offices were searched and she and Tom were arrested and tried in June under the Defence of the Realm Act (DORA) for "conduct prejudicial to recruiting and discipline". Tom pleaded not guilty and Lilian guilty. He was fined £100 and she was fined £25. When they refused to pay, Tom got three months for printing the leaflet and Lilian was sentenced to two months. Mabel Hope took over editing *The Voice of Labour* but had to stop in August 1916. She and Elizabeth Archer later went to America.

Lilian was pregnant in the summer of 1916 so she spent her sentence in Holloway prison hospital, to the bewilderment of the prison doctor who appeared never to have "had to deal with a pregnant woman before. He seemed very confused". Her vegetarianism caused more confusion; she begged to be given the "water the cabbages were boiled in" because she was afraid that the prison diet would be harmful to the baby she was carrying. She was allowed one precious apple a day, saving it until the evening as a treat.

Psychologically the prison affected her very badly though she was not physically ill-treated. "I thought I was going mad. My head was going round and round. But the only person nasty to me was the clergyman – he shouted at me that I was German. So I lived for some months in terror that they would repatriate me".

She paid her fine two weeks before she was to be released because she was afraid for her child's safety. She had already resigned from the Civil Service and from the work she had always hated before being imprisoned. "I wasn't going to wait until they chucked me out". She applied to go into Queen Charlotte's Hospital to have her baby, but they refused her, not because she wasn't married but because she was an unrepentant sinner who intended to live with the baby's father afterwards. "I certainly was one of the first single women to have a baby deliberately". Her son was born when she was 41 years old and she called him Tom after his father.

Although free unions were being discussed by people on the left, it took considerable courage to act on your principles. This was particularly difficult for women because the double sexual standard meant they were always more vulnerable to moral censure than men. Lilian said the decision to have a child came from her anarchist rejection of the authority of the state rather than from feminism. When I asked her about feminism she said she had not really been interested in it though her friend Mabel Hope was. (Mabel Hope had campaigned for women's rights at work and spoken at both Labour Party and Social Democratic Federation meetings before writing for *Freedom* and editing *Voice of Labour*.)

After becoming a mother Lilian did not become economically dependent on Tom. Indeed, quite the reverse; she worked to keep Tom, young Tom and *Freedom* going by running health food stores in London and then in Gloucestershire. Friends like Emily Wilkinson were at the Whiteway Colony and Lilian and the two Toms lived there in the 1920s and 30s.

Whiteway, a self-governing community formed upon Tolstoyan principles, adopted the Quaker custom of decision-making by general agreement until conflict between anarchists and Marxists made voting necessary. Sylvia Pankhurst came to stay for a short time and Lilian got to like and admire her while retaining her old animosity to Emmeline and Christabel who had moved to the right.

Tom died in 1938. Lilian continued to run a health food shop in Stroud through the Second World War, despite queues and ration cards. After *Freedom* folded in the 1930s a new group of anarchists emerged including Vernon Richards and Marie Louise Berneri. In 1943 Lilian went to London to work with them on *War Commentary*. Once again the intelligence service were keeping tabs on them. A raid in December 1944 was followed by arrests in 1945 amidst protests from, among others, Fenner Brockway.

Lilian's political activism continued in the Campaign for Nuclear Disarmament, (CND) and she went on the Aldermaston march from 1958 onwards. The non-violent direct action of Committee of 100 brought socialists, pacifists and anarchists together once more and contributed to a critical approach to the state which influenced the new left. Between 1961 and 1964 Lilian sat down with Committee of 100 and was arrested and fined yet again.

This was the period in which I became aware of new left ideas as a student and, through friends active in CND and Committee of 100, read Kropotkin as well as Marx. I discovered Colin Ward's magazine *Anarchy* published by Freedom Press before meeting William Fishman in East London and winding my way down the Whitechapel alley to the revived version of *Freedom*. I was unaware then that *Freedom* had sent a truly extraordinary anarchist woman off for a holiday in America to celebrate her 90th birthday. Lilian experienced her first ever aeroplane flight and reconnected with many old friends.

By the time I met Lilian Wolfe she was in her late 90s. This great encourager and helper had carried on working without expecting any recognition, saving money from her pension to give to anarchist papers, political prisoners and other radical causes. She still remained open to new movements and ideas. Though she did not agree with 1970s feminism, she was pleased when Sandy Martin's article appeared in the Stratford Women's Liberation group issue of *Shrew* and she was quoted in my *Hidden from History* (1973). She did not seem to mind that I was not an anarchist, but was distressed to find I was not a vegetarian and shook her head when I said I didn't like cheese.

Feminist or not, I certainly detected more than a twinkle when she described how she did the 'hack work' on *Voice of Labour* and I responded by commenting on how a lot of women on the left who went into women's liberation when it started had found themselves in the same position. I felt a very close affinity with her brave commitment to living her politics because that was what many of us who were socialist feminists in the early 1970s were also struggling to do. But that's another story.

BIBLIOGRAPHY

Books and Monographs
Memoirs of a Revolutionist, by Peter Kropotkin (1899)
A Girl Among The Anarchists, by Olivia Rossetti (1903)
Dogmas Discarded by Guy Aldred (1913)
Wars and Capitalism, by Peter Kropotkin (1914)
A Short History of Anarchism by Max Nettlau (1932)
Personal Recollections of the Anarchist Past, George Cores (1940)
Owning Up: The Trilogy, by George Melly (1965)
Anarchism Today, David E. Apter, James Joll (1971)
Children's Strikes in 1911, Dave Marson (1973)
The Slow Burning Fuse, by John Quail, (1976)
The Anarchists in London 1935-1955, Albert Meltzer (1976)
The International Anarchist Movement in Late Victorian London, by Hermia Oliver (1983)
The Angry Brigade: Documents and Chronology, 1967–1984, Various authors (1985)
Freedom / a Hundred Years Heiner Becker, Nicolas Walter, Philip Sansom, and Vernon Richards (1986)
Tom Brown's Syndicalism (1990)
What is Anarchism? An Introduction, edited by Donald Rooum (1992)
Fabianism, Permeation and Independent Labour by Mark Bevir (1996)
I Couldn't Paint Golden Angels, by Albert Meltzer (1996)
Paths To Utopia, by Matthew J Thomas (1998)
Italian Anarchists in London 1870-1914 (2004) by P Di Paola
Granny Made Me an Anarchist by Stuart Christie (2004 ed)
A Short History of British Anarcho-Syndicalism by Solidarity Federation (2006)
Nicolas Walter: The anarchist past and other essays, edited by David Goodway, (2007)
Before The Storm: Anarchist thought through the pages of 'Freedom' by Selva Varengo (2010)
A British Anarchist Tradition, by Carissa Honeywell (2011)
Anarchist Seeds Beneath The Snow, by David Goodway (2011)
The French Anarchists in London, 1880-1914, by Constance Bantman (2013)
The Albert Memorial by Phil Ruff (2016)
The Texture of Politics: London's Anarchist Clubs, 1884–1914 by Jonathan Moses (2016)
Wildcat Anarchist Comics, by Donald Rooum (2016)

Periodicals, TV and web essays

Articles culled from *Freedom* itself are numerous enough that I have tried to point at them within the main text rather than necessitate too much jumping around — many of these can be found in the Freedom online archive of digitised papers at freedomnews.org.uk/ archive. With references from other publications I have specified editions and article names.

Old and New London Vol 5, Cassell, Petter & Galpin (1878)
Freedom (1886-1927)
Mother Earth (1906-17)
Freedom Bulletin (1928-1932)
Freedom (New Series) (1929-1936)
Spain and the World (1936-39)
Revolt! (1939)
War Commentary (1939-45)
Freedom (1945-present)
World Labour News Vol 3 No. 1 'Pages of Labour History', Tom Brown (1962)
Direct Action (SWF) (August 1964)
Anarchy Series 2 no.12 'What's Wrong With Freedom?' (1973)
Wildcat Inside Story No. 1 'Witness for the Prosecution', by Colin Ward (1974)
Wildcat no.6 'Lilian Wolfe: She Lived Her Politics', by Sheila Rowbotham (March 1975)
The Raven 1 'Notes on Freedom and the Freedom Press 1886-1928' by Heiner Becker, (1986)
Black Flag Supplement no. 3 'Liars and Liberals', Albert Meltzer (1986)
New Anarchist Review No 13 'The Freedom Press Centenary Series: A Progress Report (April 1989)
The Raven 21 (1993)
World in Action, Combat 18 investigation interview with Charles Crute (1995)
The Guardian 'Anarchy among the Anarchists' by Richard Boston (November 16th 1996)
The Guardian 'Obituary: Vernon Richards' by Colin Ward (February 2nd 2002)
New Statesman 'The NS Essay — How My Father Spied For Peace' by Natasha Walter (May 20th 2002)
Black Flag 'The UK anarchist movement — Looking back and

forward' by Nick Heath (2006)
Ethical Record, 'British anarchism and Freedom Press' by Donald Rooum (June 2008)
Information for Social Change Number 27, 'A Short History of Freedom Press' by Donald Rooum (Oct 2008)
The Institute of Social History 'Anarchists in court, England, April 1945' by Huub Sanders (April 2010)
History Workshop 'Freedom, an Obituary', by David Goodway (2014)
International Review of Social History 'Anarchism and the British Warfare State: The Prosecution of the War Commentary anarchists, 1945' by Carissa Honeywell (August 2015)
Bristol Radical History Network, 'The Torch of Anarchy 1891-1896' (retrieved 2018)

Freedom's frequency

An approximation of how well or badly Freedom was doing at any one time can be seen from how it was being produced, as good times tended to see frequency rise, crises would usually mean fewer issues, at least until the internet upended publishing in the 1990s.

1886-1932: Various, mostly monthly (457 issues including *Bulletin*)
1936-8: *Spain & The World* (47)
1939: *Revolt* (6)
1939-45: Monthly/fortnightly as *War Commentary* (118)
1945-51: Fortnightly (113)
1951-61: Weekly (675)
1961-71: 40 per year (400) + monthly *Anarchy* (118)
1971-75: Weekly (200)
1975-82: Fortnightly (154)
1982-90: Monthly (96)
1990-2011: Fortnightly (504)
2011-14: Monthly: (36)
2014-present: Infrequent/biannual (8)

Totalling 2,814 (minus any missed/compound issues, more if including Cores' *New Series*).

ALSO FROM FREEDOM...

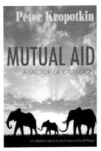

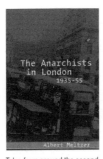

DIRECT SALES AND ENQUIRIES

Freedom Press
Angel Alley,
84b Whitechapel
High Street, Londo
E1 7QX

Telephone
(07952) 157-742

Email
admin@
freedompress.org.u

Web
freedompress.org.u

Social media
@freedom_paper
facebook.com/
freedombookshop

Trade orders may
be placed via
Central Books:

50 Freshwater Roa
Chadwell Heath,
London RM8 1RX

Tel 44 (0)20 8525
8800
Fax 44 (0)20 8525
8879
contactus@centra
books.com

centralbooks.com